how to raise happy and successful children

Esther Wojcicki is a leading American educator, journalist and mother. A leader in blended learning and the integration of technology into education, she is the founder of the Media Arts programs at Palo Alto High School. Wojcicki serves as Vice Chair of Creative Commons and was instrumental in the launch of the Google Teachers Academy. She blogs regularly for *Huffington Post* and is co-author of *Moonshots in Education*.

how to raise happy and successful children

esther wojcicki

arrow books

1 3 5 7 9 10 8 6 4 2

Arrow Books
20 Vauxhall Bridge Road
London SW1V 2SA

Arrow Books is part of the Penguin Random House group
of companies whose addresses can be found at global.
penguinrandomhouse.com

Penguin
Random House
UK

First published in the USA by Houghton Mifflin Harcourt in 2019
First published in the United Kingdom by Hutchinson in 2019
First published by Arrow Books in 2020

www.penguin.co.uk

A CIP catalogue record for this book is available from the
British Library.

ISBN 9781787462168

Typeset in 9.4/15.76 pt Miller Text
by Integra Software Services Pvt. Ltd, Pondicherry

Printed and bound in Great Britain by Clays Ltd, Elcograf S.p.A.

To my husband, Stan, my three daughters, Susan, Janet, and Anne,
my ten grandchildren, and all other members of my family,
a wish for TRICK in their lives and in the world.

Contents

Contents

KINDNESS

how to raise happy
and successful children

Foreword

AS THE THREE "WOJ" offspring, we thought it was only fitting that her children do the foreword on what it was truly like to be raised the Woj Way. Woj, of course, is the affectionate nickname coined by our mother's students decades ago — it stuck — and her method focuses on trust, respect, independence, collaboration, and kindness (TRICK), the universal values she explores in the coming pages.

Life has brought all kinds of surprises, from our careers at Google, YouTube, 23andMe, and the UCSF Medical Center, to the challenges of parenting our own children, a total of nine among the three of us. As we have ridden the ups and downs that come with any life, we owe much of our ability to thrive to the way our parents raised us.

When our mother told us she was writing this book, we dug up stashes of our journals from grade school through college. Our mother, forever the journalist, thought it was a great idea for us to keep journals for every trip, especially when we moved to France in 1980. While there are many fun stories of fights and bad behavior, there are also some key themes: independence, financial responsibility, actionability, open-mindedness, fearlessness, and an appreciation for life.

One of our greatest joys today is the feeling of independence. Our parents taught us to believe in ourselves and our ability to make decisions. They trusted us and gave us responsibility at an early age. We had the freedom to walk to school on our own, bike around the neighborhood, and hang out with our friends. We gained confidence that our parents reinforced by being respectful of our opinions and ideas. We don't remember ever having our ideas or thoughts dismissed because we were children. At every age, our parents listened and acted like it was a two-way street for learning. We learned to advocate for ourselves, to listen, and to realize when we might be wrong.

In tenth grade, Anne had an eye-opening discussion at our temple about relationships between parents and children. The parent she was partnered with talked about how it was the child's job to listen. She explained that in our family we argued, but that our parents always listened to us; they never just said, "No, because I'm the parent." She later wrote in her journal how grateful she was to have parents who didn't rule because of authority. We rarely fought. We argued, but we didn't fight. As a result, we are extraordinarily grateful to them for the early independence we experienced.

Hand in hand with independence is financial freedom. Financial freedom does not mean being rich; it means being careful with money and planning for those items or aspects in life deemed essential. Our parents are fiercely disciplined with spending and saving. Both grew up as children of immigrants and reminded us often of how people waste money on unnecessary items and then suffer by not being able to afford what they need. The importance of this came as daily lessons. We would go out to dinner but never ordered drinks or appetizers. Before we went grocery shopping, we always cut our coupons and went through the newspaper ads. Once, our mother brought home the extra airplane food from her recent trip and served it to Anne as dinner — her childhood friends have never forgotten!

When we were in grade school, our mother showed us a compound interest chart, and we became determined to save at least a couple thousand dollars every year. We got credit cards and checkbooks before we could drive because our mom wanted to teach us the discipline of paying off our credit card monthly and balancing our checkbooks. We were also encouraged to start our own little businesses as kids. We sold so many lemons from our neighbor's abundant tree for years that the neighbors called us the "lemon girls." Susan had a business selling "spice ropes" (spices on a braid to hang in a kitchen) and made hundreds of dollars as a sixth-grader. It was her idea, but our mom bought the supplies and supported her going out to sell them. We sold hundreds of Girl Scout cookies door to door. And when we were really bored, we would package up our old toys and try to sell them to the neighbors, who actually bought them — sometimes.

As a family, travel and education were our top priorities, and everything else got minimal financial resources. (Note: Our father has been wearing the same pair of sandals for sixty years.) When we traveled, we stayed in the cheapest hotel, and always with a coupon. Spending money was all about making intentional choices. We were never wealthy, but our spending decisions allowed us the financial freedom to have the experiences we wanted in life.

Our mother is a master at never procrastinating or whining. If something can get done today, she's getting it done! She taught us all how to do the laundry, clean the house, vacuum, make phone calls, and exercise — all at the same time and in under an hour. We have never met anyone as efficient as our mother. She taught us how painless it is to just get something done versus procrastinating, how much better the weekend can be when homework is finished on Friday versus having it hang over your head all weekend and then finally doing it on Sunday.

While most of our mom's philosophy was about building skills, she would occasionally resort to bribery. One example Susan remembers years later is her bad habit of biting her nails. Our mom promised her a bunny if she stopped. After six weeks of Susan not biting (Mom said this was the period of time necessary to break a bad habit), Mom bought her a pet rat since the storekeeper convinced her that a rat was a better pet than a bunny. In fact, she bought three pet rats: Snowball, Midnight, and Twinkle.

Our mom is a people person. She truly enjoys being around all different types of people and gives off a very warm, approachable air because she is open-minded about learning new things at all times. She is a natural entrepreneur, constantly open to change and innovation. It was not a coincidence or "good luck" that she was successfully able to incorporate technology into her lesson plans and classrooms as Silicon Valley was burgeoning; she loves to innovate. She is constantly learning from her students, and this is, in part, why they trust and respect her — because she believes (and thrives herself) in their visions for change. Adults can be reluctant to change routines, making it difficult for them to engage with teenagers. But our mom — herself a "senior citizen"! — is completely the opposite, and that's why students flock to her. They know she will respect them and encourage their ideas, no matter how crazy. Sometimes it appears that she prefers the crazier ideas! We are often astounded that our mom, who is in her seventies is energized (yes, not tired!) after a late night (almost midnight) with teenagers working on the school newspaper.

One of her best traits in being a teacher and parent is trying to really understand the student as a person and working within the student's interests to be self-motivated rather than forcing them to do something. If one of us would come home and say we didn't like a subject, she would ask why. She would try to understand what was happening: Did we need the help of a tutor? Or did we have an issue with a teacher or other students? She would then try to come up with a solution that fit our needs and would help us solve the problem. Similarly, she worked to understand our passions over the years. She supported Anne's interest in ice-skating, Janet's focus in African studies, and Susan's efforts with art projects. She inspired us with books, interesting articles, talks, and classes. She always let her students pick the topics for their newspaper and argue their own points of view. When we talk about parenting, she reminds us that we can't force a child to do something: we need to motivate them to want to do it themselves.

We would also like to emphasize our mom's fearlessness, particularly in the pursuit of justice. She is the first person in the room to call out the emperor who is wearing no clothes. She is not afraid to state her mind, defend the underdog, or challenge the status quo. This is a natural fit in the context of journalism and freedom of the press. Janet remembers being in line at a store where the clerk was trying to sell us something below par, and of course we had to ask for the manager or invoke the threat of "reporting them to the California Bureau of Consumer Affairs." Our mother's mantra was always "If you don't speak up, speak out, or complain, then the exact same thing is going to happen to someone else." Another of Janet's memories: our mom challenging the pediatrician who wanted to prescribe antibiotics. "Does she really need them?" our mom would ask. "Can I look at her ear too?" Convention, authority, and power were not to be feared. On the flip side, it was not always fun to have a mother who would freely speak her mind to teachers, parents of friends, boyfriends, etc. After all these years of having her as a parent, it's impossible to think of a situation in which our mom would feel uncomfortable or be unwilling to state her honest opinion. She is not even shy about giving the secretary of education her candid appraisal of the education system. This type of approach to the world fosters an environment in which young people gain the strength and endurance to follow dreams and passions, without giving up or being intimidated. We believe that a large part of our drive and determination comes from an early modeling of our mother's unwillingness to give up or give in.

Lastly, and most memorably, our mother taught us to love life. She is silly. She makes jokes. She has few formalities and breaks stereotypes. She absolutely loves to have a good time. She first ran into our father (literally) when she was sliding down some stairs in a cardboard box in her dorm at Berkeley. She has gotten us kicked out of restaurants for her (not her kids') bad behavior! At the age of seventy-five, she discovered Forever 21 and decided it was the best clothing store ever for herself. Ten years ago she called Anne from NYC with a dozen of her high school journalism students in tow, saying, "Anne! We found a bargain on stretch limos, and we are riding around NYC with our heads out the sunroof! What club should we go to? We want to dance!" Our mother celebrates adventure and exploration. Her students love her because she balances her ability to execute and be serious with her openness and creativity. She is serious about teaching journalism but she has no problem with her students riding exercise bicycles during class while they listen. As we were writing this, we just saw our mother post pictures of herself dressed like a hot dog at Target. We may not wear Forever 21, but we certainly have learned how to have a positive attitude and find happiness every day because of her.

We three sisters are the original output of our mom's philosophy, but after us came many thousands of students in her journalism program. All around the world we meet people who stop us to say, "You know, your mom really changed my life. She believed in me." She doesn't just influence people while they are in her class. She influences them for life.

As proud daughters, we just want to say, Thank you, Mom, for raising us the Woj Way!

— *Susan, Janet, and Anne Wojcicki*

Introduction

THERE ARE NO NOBEL Prizes for parenting or education, but there should be. They are the two most important things we do in our society. How we raise and educate our children determines not only the people they become but the society we create.

Every parent has hopes and dreams for their children. They want them to be healthy, happy, successful. They also have universal fears: Will their child be safe? Will she find purpose and fulfillment? Will he make his way in a world that feels increasingly driven, competitive, and even at times hostile? I remember how all of those unspoken and largely unconscious worries crowded into the small birthing room as I held my first daughter.

I lay in the hospital bed cradling Susan on my chest. The nurse had wrapped her in a pink blanket and put a tiny yellow knit hat on her head. Stan, my husband, sat by my side. We were both exhausted but elated, and in that moment, everything was clear: I loved my daughter from the second I saw her, and I felt a primal desire to protect her, to give her the best life possible, to do whatever it took to help her succeed.

But soon the questions and doubts started to creep in. I couldn't figure out how to hold Susan, and I didn't know how to change a diaper. I'd stopped teaching only three weeks earlier, which didn't give me much time to prepare. And I never really understood exactly *how* I was supposed to prepare in the first place. The ob-gyn told me to take it easy for at least six weeks after the birth. My friends and colleagues gave me all kinds of conflicting advice. They told me labor was going to be long and hard, that nursing was too difficult and restrictive, that bottles and Similac were better. I read a few books on nutrition for adults (there weren't any titles specific to children at that time), and I bought a crib, some clothing, and a small plastic bathtub. And then suddenly Susan was there in my arms, with her big blue eyes and peach-fuzz hair, staring up at me as if I knew exactly what to do.

I was just on the verge of being discharged when I really started to worry. This was 1968. Back then you got three days in American hospitals after your baby was born. Now most hospitals discharge you after two days. I don't know how mothers today do it.

"Can I stay for another day?" I pleaded with the nurse, half embarrassed, half desperate. "I have no idea how to take care of my baby."

The next morning the nurse gave me a crash course in infant care, including, thankfully, how to change a diaper. This was the era of cloth diapers and safety pins. I was warned by the nurse to make sure that the pins were closed properly or they could stick the baby. Whenever Susan cried, the first thing I did was check the pins.

Even though it wasn't popular at the time, I was determined to breastfeed, so the nurse showed me how to position the baby's head and use my forearm for support. The baby had to "latch on" and only then could I be sure that she was getting milk. It was not as simple as I had hoped, and sometimes poor Susan got sprayed. The plan was that she should keep to a four-hour schedule and I agreed to follow that as best I could.

"Make sure you hug your baby" was the last piece of advice the nurse gave me. Then Stan and I were on our own.

Like all parents, I saw my daughter as hope — hope for a better life, hope for the future, hope that she might change the world for the better. We all want children who are happy, empowered, and passionate. We all want to raise kids who lead successful and meaningful lives. That's what I felt the moment Susan was born, and later on when we welcomed our other two daughters, Janet and Anne. It's this same wish that unites people from all different countries and cultures. Thanks to my long and somewhat unusual teaching career, I now attend conferences around the world. Whether I'm meeting with the secretary of education in Argentina, thought leaders from China, or concerned parents from India, what everyone wants to know is how to help our children live good lives — to be both happy and successful, to use their talents to make the world a better place.

No one seems to have a definitive answer. Parenting experts focus on important aspects of child-rearing like sleeping, eating, bonding, or discipline, but the advice they offer is mostly narrow and pre-scriptive. What we really need isn't just limited information about the care and feeding of children, as important as that may be. What we most need to know is how to give our kids the values and skills to succeed as adults. We also have to face the massive cultural shifts over the past few years — especially technological changes and how those changes impact our parenting. How will our children succeed in the age of robots and artificial intelligence? How will they thrive in the tech revolution? These anxieties are familiar to parents the world over. All of us are overwhelmed by the pace of change and the desire for our children to keep up. We know that our families and schools need to adapt to these changes, but we don't know how, and we don't know how we hold on to the values that are most important to us and to raising children who thrive.

As a young mother, I felt the same way — some of the challenges may have been different, but they were just as daunting. I took what little guidance and advice I could find, but for the most part I decided to trust myself. It may have been my training as an investigative journalist or my distrust of authority that had come from my childhood, but I was determined to find out the truth on my own. I had my own ideas about what kids needed, and I stuck to them, no matter what other people thought. The result was — to many people's eyes — idiosyncratic at best, or just plain odd. I spoke to my daughters as if they were adults from day one. Most mothers naturally turn to baby talk — a higher-pitched voice, simpler words. Not me. I trusted them and they trusted me. I never put them in danger but I also never stood in the way of them experiencing life or taking calculated risks. When we lived in Geneva, I sent Susan and Janet to the store next door to buy bread, on their own, when they were ages five and four. I respected their individuality from the beginning. My theory was that the most important years were zero to five and I was going to teach them as much as I could early on. What I wanted more than anything was to make them first into independent children and then into empowered, independent adults. I figured that if they could think on their own and make sound decisions, they could face any challenges that came their way. I had no idea at the time that research would validate the choices I had made. I was following my gut and my values, and what I saw worked in the classroom as a teacher.

It's rather strange to be a "famous" parent and to have your family profiled on the cover of magazines. I certainly don't claim all the credit for their successes as adults, but all three have turned out to be accomplished, caring, capable people. Susan is the CEO of YouTube, Janet is a professor of pediatrics at the University of California–San Francisco, and Anne is the co-founder and CEO of 23andMe. They rose to the top of ultracompetitive, male-dominated professions, and they did so by following their passions and thinking for themselves. Watching my daughters navigate the world with grit and integrity has been one of the greatest rewards of my life. I'm especially impressed by how they compete and cooperate, focusing not on being the only woman in the room, but on finding solutions to the problems we face.

Meanwhile, as a journalism teacher to high school students for more than thirty-six years, I have been doing something similar. Every semester, I have approximately sixty-five students, ranging from sophomores to seniors, and from day one I treat them like professional journalists. They work in groups and write on deadline. I provide support and guidance when students need it, but I've found that project-based, collaborative learning is the best way to prepare them for the challenges they'll face as journalists and as adults. I've watched thousands of students excel through my teaching methods, and Facebook helps me stay in touch with them — even my students from the 1980s. They have had amazing successes and become incredible people. I've had the privilege of teaching so many young people, including my first editor in chief of the student newspaper, Craig Vaughan, now a child psychologist with the Stanford Children's Hospital; Gady Epstein, the media editor at the *Economist*; Jeremy Lin, a Harvard graduate and point guard for the Atlanta

Hawks; Jennifer Linden, a professor of neuroscience at University College London; Marc Berman, a California State Assemblyman from the district that includes Palo Alto; and James Franco, the award-winning actor, writer, and director. I have had hundreds of students tell me that my belief in them and the values I taught them in my classroom made a profound difference in how they saw themselves and who they would become.

As my daughters rose to prominence in the tech and health sectors, and as my journalism program gained national and international recognition, people started to notice that I was doing something different. They saw how my parenting approach and educational method could offer solutions to the problems we face in the twenty-first century, and they wanted to know more. Parents constantly ask me for advice — okay, sometimes beg for the strategies I used with my daughters that they might apply to their own parenting. Teachers do the same, wondering how I escaped being a disciplinarian and instead found a way to guide students who are genuinely passionate about the work they're doing. Without really intending to, I found I'd started a debate about how we should be raising our kids and how to make education both relevant and useful. What I'm offering, and what has struck a chord with so many people across the world, is an antidote to our parenting and teaching problems, a way to fight against the anxiety, discipline problems, power struggles, peer pressure, and fear of technology that cloud our judgment and harm our children.

One of the biggest mistakes we make as parents is to assume personal responsibility for our children's emotions. As Dr. Janesta Noland, a respected pediatrician in Silicon Valley, argues, "Parents are so compelled to hold their child's happiness . . . they feel like they are responsible for it, and that they control it." We'll do anything to prevent our children from struggling or suffering, which means that they never have to deal with hardships or adversity. As a result, they lack independence and grit, and they're fearful of the world around them instead of empowered to innovate and create. Another big mistake: We teach them to focus almost exclusively on themselves and their own performance — because they must have a perfect grade point average, must be selected by a top-tier college, must find an impressive job. They are so busy focusing on themselves that they rarely have time to consider how they might help and serve others. Kindness and gratitude are often overlooked, even though these are the qualities that research shows will make us most happy in life.

There is also dysfunction in the classroom. Schools and universities are still teaching in the style of the twentieth century, essentially preparing students to follow instructions for a world that no longer exists. The lecture model, based on the assumption that the teacher knows everything and that the role of the student is to listen quietly, take notes, and take a test, is still dominant worldwide, despite the fact that technology now allows us to find information on our own — in an instant, with the library we all have in our pockets, the cell phone. Students learn *about* required subjects instead of learning *through* interest-based learning or experience. Curriculums are geared toward statewide exams and assessments rather than project-based learning that teaches real-world skills and allows students to find their passion. And tests and exams are the last things that promote passion and engagement, which research shows are the foundation of effective education and happiness in life. Above all, this outmoded system teaches us to obey — not to innovate or think independently. When it's time to graduate, we celebrate the end of learning! We should be celebrating the mastery of skills that will allow us all to continue to educate ourselves throughout life.

Is it any wonder, given how we're teaching and parenting, that kids end up depressed and anxious, completely unprepared to face the normal challenges of life? According to the National Institute of Mental Health, an estimated 31.9 percent of thirteen- to eighteen-year-olds in the United States suffer from anxiety disorders, and when researchers looked at mental health problems that occurred during 2016, they found that roughly two million teenagers experienced at least one major depressive episode. A 2016 study from Brazil reported that almost 40 percent of adolescent girls and more than 20 percent of adolescent boys suffered from common mental disorders such as anxiety and depression. In India, a study showed that one-third of high school students displayed clinical symptoms of anxiety. A survey conducted by the Norwegian Institute of Public Health found that among participants between the ages of fourteen and fifteen, more than 50 percent reported regularly feeling "sad or unhappy," and almost half reported feeling "restless." This epidemic is universal, and it should be a call to action for us all.[1]

There is a better way. We've made parenting into an incredibly complicated, unintuitive endeavor, filled with fear and self-doubt. We're stressed out because we've become slaves to our children's happiness. We're worried that they won't make it in this highly competitive world that we live in. We get upset when they don't get into a prestigious preschool, or when they don't yet know the alphabet but all the other kids their age seem to know it. We are the ones who are creating this frantic, overly competitive world for our kids. In truth, parenting is really quite simple — as long as we rediscover the basic principles that allow children to thrive in homes, in schools, and in life. Through my decades of experience as a mother, grandmother, and educator, I've identified five fundamental values that help us all become capable, successful people. To make it easy to remember in all walks of life, I call these values "TRICK":

TRUST, RESPECT, INDEPENDENCE,
COLLABORATION, AND KINDNESS

TRUST: We are in a crisis of trust the world over. Parents are afraid, and that makes our children afraid — to be who they are, to take risks, to stand up against injustice. Trust has to start with us. When we're confident in the choices we make as parents, we can then trust our children to take important and necessary steps toward empowerment and independence.

RESPECT: The most fundamental respect we can show our children is toward their autonomy and individuality. Every child has a gift, and is a gift to the world, and it's our responsibility as parents to nurture that gift, whatever it may be. This is the exact opposite of telling kids who to be, what profession to pursue, what their life should look like: it's supporting them as they identify and pursue their own goals.

INDEPENDENCE: Independence relies upon a strong foundation of trust and respect. Children who learn self-control and responsibility early in life are much better equipped to face the challenges of adulthood, and also have the skills to innovate and think creatively. Truly independent kids are capable of coping with adversity, setbacks, and boredom, all unavoidable aspects of life. They feel in control even when things around them are in chaos.

COLLABORATION: Collaboration means working together as a family, in a classroom, or at a workplace. For parents, it means encouraging children to contribute to discussions, decisions, and even discipline. In the twentieth century, when rule-following was one of the most important skills, parents were in total control. In the twenty-first century, dictating no longer works. We shouldn't be telling our children what to do, but asking for their ideas and working together to find solutions.

KINDNESS: It is strange but true that we tend to treat those who are closest to us without the kindness and consideration that we extend to strangers. Parents love their children, but they are so familiar with them, they often take basic kindness for granted. And they don't always model kindness as a behavior for the world as a whole. Real kindness involves gratitude and forgiveness, service toward others, and an awareness of the world outside yourself. It's important to show our kids that the most exciting and rewarding thing you can do is to make someone else's life better.

TRICK is essential to functional families, and it's also the solution to the challenges we face in education. The most effective classrooms are founded on trust and respect, encourage independent thought, and include project-based collaborative learning that mimics work in the real world. Educational leaders are finally starting to realize that rote memorization and lecturing are completely inappropriate for teaching the skills of the twenty-first century. I've spent over three decades perfecting my own "blended learning" model, a style of teaching that gives kids some control over their education and emphasizes the responsible use of technology. Teachers across the country are now emulating my methods, and I routinely travel throughout Europe, Asia, and Latin America, speaking to educational leaders and helping to implement new governmental policies based on the core values of TRICK.

Businesses, too, are recognizing the power of TRICK and starting to adopt these values in their company culture. TRICK is not just how we raise happy and successful children; it is also how we bring out the best in people at any age. Companies seek employees with grit, creativity, independent thinking skills, and the ability to collaborate and adapt to a constantly changing world. When the Educational Testing Service conducted an analysis of the Occupational Information Network, a large employment database maintained by the U.S. Department of Labor, they found that today's jobs require five key skills that stem from the TRICK values: problem-solving, fluid intelligence, teamwork, achievement/innovation, and communication. Flexible thinking, problem-solving, and innovation all arise from a strong sense of independence, which itself is built upon trust and respect. Teamwork and communication aren't possible without the kindness and collaborative spirit required to consider other people's opinions and ideas. This is why a global hotel chain is now using TRICK to train and empower their employees. This is why the founders of the Gap, the worldwide clothing retailer, recently met with my daughter Anne and me, hoping to learn how to create more successful business leaders like her. And this is why so many major companies — like the top global consulting firm Deloitte; Mercado

Libre, Latin America's most popular e-commerce platform; Panera Bread, the bakery and café chain; and even Walmart and McDonald's — are now embracing TRICK-like philosophies and encouraging independence, collaboration, and innovation among their workers.

When I spoke at the Conscious Capitalism conference in 2017 to a room packed with business leaders, the audience was so excited by TRICK that no one wanted to leave. I talked with CEOs such as John Mackey of Whole Foods and Daniel Bane of Trader Joe's, both of whom lead successful grocery chains known for employee empowerment. Amit Hooda, the CEO of Heavenly Organics, an environmentally friendly food manufacturer, Jeffrey Westphal of Vertex, the tax software provider, and many others told me they wanted to help spread my philosophy across the world. TRICK values permeated every discussion at this conference, because we need to empower the people we work with, and collaborate to make a real difference. The leaders I met with talked about training their employees for the twenty-first century through hands-on, project-based learning, just like what I've been doing in my classroom at Palo Alto High School.

The ultimate goal of TRICK is creating self-responsible people in a self-responsible world. This is what we're doing as parents, teachers, and employers — not just raising children or managing classrooms and boardrooms, but building the foundation of the future of humankind. We're evolving human consciousness, and we're doing it faster than ever before.

This book is about how to raise successful people. It doesn't offer yet another parenting fad or a precise recipe for putting your child to bed — it shows parents how to use a universal philosophy of human behavior to confront the problems we face today and prepare our children for the many unknown challenges that lie ahead. It doesn't offer a new curriculum for the classroom, but rather a new way to teach the curriculum, a new approach to teaching (in school and at home) that leads to empowerment and independence and always builds from a foundation of trust and respect. In the chapters that follow, I present the core principles that will help you to create a home (or classroom) that will allow you and your children to thrive.

What I did as a parent is no different than what parents have done throughout human history when they were forced to trust themselves, value their children's independence, and approach parenting as a community collaboration. The ultimate proof is that my methods have been scientifically validated to work across the world, and also by parents' own powerful, collective experience. They have been used in my classes for the past thirty-six years and with my own children starting fifty years ago. TRICK really does work for everyone, no matter the age, culture, or circumstances. And it's never too late to start. You can correct early parenting mistakes and missteps, improving both your life and the life of your child. Best of all, embracing TRICK will make you the kind of parent you want to be, and will help you raise the kind of child you want to be around — a child who also wants to be around you. The kind of child that others want, need, and value, and the kind of child who will confront the challenges we face as communities, as countries, and as a world.

It is a joy and a privilege to share stories and principles that arise from TRICK with you in the pages ahead. I hope they will guide you back to a deep trust in yourself and in your child, and be memorable so you can use them to guide yourself. You are the parent your child needs, and with your trust and respect, your child will become exactly the person they are meant to be.

1

The Childhood You Wish You'd Had

WE ALL TEND TO PARENT the way we were parented, but when I became a mother, the one thing I knew for sure was that I didn't want to repeat the mistakes of my parents. Every one of us has trauma and challenges from childhood that influence the way we relate to our children, and if we don't understand that trauma, if we don't carefully assess what went wrong, we're destined to repeat it. Failing to examine our unconscious patterns and programming undermines our best efforts to raise a family based on TRICK. As you'll see from my story, I wasn't raised with these fundamental values. I had to learn them the hard way. By sharing my experiences as a child and my parents' approach to parenting, I hope I'll inspire you to explore your own story, so you can understand the role model you witnessed and how it was or was not based on TRICK.

The story of the parent I became begins in a tenement building on New York's Lower East Side. I lived there in a small one-bedroom apartment with my parents, Russian Jewish immigrants who came to this country with nothing. My mother, Rebecca, was from Krasnoyarsk, Siberia, a place that seemed impossibly cold and remote to me as a young girl. She told me it snowed so much there that her entire house would be buried. They had to dig tunnels to get out. She was strikingly beautiful — people tell me that whenever they see her pictures — and she had an accent no one could place, some combination of Yiddish and Russian that I picked up but lost when I started school. My father, Philip, was an artist who specialized in watercolor and charcoal drawings, and was even awarded a scholarship at Rensselaer Polytechnic Institute. Sadly, he couldn't accept it because he had to support my mother and me. He and his family had fled the pogroms in the Chernivtsi region of the Ukraine, walking all the way to Vienna, where they could apply for papers to the United States. For years, I disbelieved the story of them walking so far. He used to tell me how they put all their possessions in a wooden cart and pulled it until their hands bled. It seemed an absurd exaggeration — until I read about the Syrian refugee crisis and how those people walked for hundreds of miles to escape the war. I still regret that I never thanked my father for what he did.

We were always on the verge of financial ruin. Beyond art, my father had few skills — we weren't exactly living the American Dream. So when he ran out of the odd jobs that kept us afloat, he heard the "Go west, young man" call of the day and decided to seek his fortune in California. It seemed like the land of sun, fun, and opportunity. It seemed like we could make a whole new life there. Unfortunately, it didn't turn out as he'd planned.

I still don't know why my parents picked Sunland-Tujunga, an agricultural community at the northeastern corner of the San Fernando Valley. The San Gabriels towered in the distance, and the streets were wide and made of dirt. A few years later, my brother and I started a business by freeing cars that got stuck in the sand. It happened often, and I was thrilled to earn a dollar each time. Grapevines were everywhere, as were gray stones that came tumbling from the foothills. We lived in a small house built of those same stones, and just behind us was the Tujunga Canyon Wash, a tributary of the Los Angeles River, where rattlesnakes hid between the giant boulders along the bank.

My father tried a variety of commercial art jobs in California, and even attempted to work in the entertainment industry, without success. Finally, he was forced to take a job as a gravestone cutter, one he kept for the rest of his life. You can still see hundreds of the gravestones he made in cemeteries all over Los Angeles — the only artistic legacy he ever had. The work was grueling and the pay low, and at night he would come home, slam the door, and proceed to stomp around the small house, saying nothing. It always scared me. I learned to stay away from him. If I didn't, I'd be caught in the middle of a firestorm. "Spare the rod, spoil the child" is something he said to me often, and he meant it. My mother did her best to protect me from his outbursts, and sometimes even bought me my favorite foods — green Jell-O and canned apricots — rare treats that became our little secret. At night I'd sit in my room and listen to them fight. Always, always about money.

The most difficult part of my life was dealing with the Orthodox tradition that deemed men the most important members of the family. And not only the family: men were the most important members of society. The whole community was focused on men. Kaddish, the prayer for the dead, can only be read by men; the Torah, our sacred books of the Bible, can only be held and read by men. Essentially, if you want to talk to God, you have to be a man. I guess that's why Orthodox men awake every morning and thank God they weren't born women.

I spent my Saturdays in a small synagogue where I sat upstairs with the women and children. It was always warm, yet the women wore long sleeves and hair coverings as the religion required — conservative, definitely not comfortable. I liked it there because I got to whisper to the other kids while the men prayed beneath us. They seemed to exist in a different world, one I knew I could never enter.

Women in the Orthodox Jewish tradition have one clearly defined role: mother of the family. That means women don't need an education. They only need to know how to take care of the children and their husband, and how to maintain a household. As I grew up, I realized that all the women around me were in subservient positions. My mother always had to listen to my father. The women at the synagogue dutifully obeyed their husbands. My grandfather on my father's side, Benjamin, who had been a rabbi, controlled the whole family. The goal for me was to marry a rich Jewish man when I was eighteen and have lots of children. The fact that I had different goals caused a rift in my relationship with my grandfather that lasted until his death.

The importance of men was dramatically illustrated to me when my brother Lee was born on May 23, 1945, three days before my fifth birthday. My parents brought him home on my birthday, and I could hardly contain my excitement when my father opened the door and led my mother inside. He was holding a basket, and inside was my new little brother. I thought of him as my own special gift. I ran forward, wanting to see him up close, but my father caught me by the shoulder and pushed me back. "Don't get too close to the baby," he scolded. "You could make him sick." I stopped in my tracks, more confused than hurt. My mother stood there, silent. Then my father told me something that still shocks me to this day. "Your brother Lee is a boy," he said plainly, "and in our family boys are more important." He delivered this news as if he had no understanding of how it might affect me. Even now, it's hard for me to imagine someone saying that to a young child. At first I didn't really understand what he meant — that now I would be second in line — but I knew it wouldn't be good. Prior to Lee's birth, I had been the darling of the family, the only child and the center of attention, even if that attention was sometimes negative. But I quickly learned how this would play out. Lee's needs were prioritized over mine. He got dozens of toys when I got none. He got new clothing instead of hand-me-downs from our cousins in New York. He could eat all he wanted at dinner, while I was reprimanded for taking too much food.

Looking back, I realize I wasn't bothered as much as you might expect. Part of what helped me cope was the constant love of my mother; she was patient, never critical, and she made me feel important despite what my father had said. I also genuinely liked Lee. He was a very cute baby and it was fun to play with him. He was like a life-sized doll for me, and I enjoyed helping my mother and feeling like a useful member of the family. As I got older, I was expected to do almost everything on my own because resources were limited and all the attention was focused on Lee. But even this was a blessing in disguise, because I became unintentionally empowered from so much independence. I learned how to do the laundry, wash the dishes, clean the house, cook meals for Lee, run errands, make the beds, and sweep the floors and carpets (we didn't have a vacuum). I grew up thinking I could do anything. Meanwhile, Lee grew up thinking he always needed help and support. He was pampered to the point of paralysis, an unintentional consequence of all that devotion.

My independence wasn't appreciated at school, however. There learning happened through force and strict obedience. I'd always been somewhat of a contrary student, and was sometimes even paddled by the principal. Corporal punishment is still lawful in public schools in nineteen U.S. states, and in all private schools except those in New Jersey and Iowa (people don't know this, but they should) — I was just one of many kids who suffered because of this inhumane policy. Often, the teachers didn't seem to have any idea what to do with me. When I was in second grade, my teacher threw me under her desk when she found me helping other students instead of staring into space once I'd finished my assignment. She got even angrier when I waved to my classmates from under the desk. I was given an "Unsatisfactory" in "Deportment," the only grade my father cared about. As you can probably guess, he wasn't happy with me.

The public library was my sanctuary. I loved to put on my roller skates, zoom over to the tiny Sunland-Tujunga library branch, and sit down with a tall stack of books. Reading helped me to think for myself, and it offered me glimpses into other worlds, those that were very different from my own. One summer I even won a prize for reading more books than any other student in the city. I also sold more Girl Scout cookies than any other girl in Sunland-Tujunga. I had no lessons, afterschool classes, or special performances, but the public school loaned me a violin and I dutifully practiced every night in my bedroom. Music was and still is a great passion for me. By fifth grade, I was good enough to be in the school orchestra, and I was fortunate to play all four years of high school. Even back then I seemed to understand that music makes it easier to be poor.

In 1948 my parents had another son, David, which put even more financial stress on the family. He was a beautiful baby, with bright blond hair and translucent blue eyes. I remember him being very curious, and that he cried a lot. My mother was overwhelmed by taking care of three children and couldn't always meet David's needs. I did my best to help her. I played with him, and carried him around the house and backyard. I showed him my favorite pepper tree near the creek and told him in a few years I'd teach him how to climb it.

One day, when David was sixteen months old, he was playing on the kitchen floor and came across a bottle of aspirin. He thought it was a toy and started shaking it. Out came dozens of pills (back then Bayer did not have safety caps), and he swallowed all of them before my mother realized what had happened. She called the doctor's office and was told by the nurse to put David to bed and check on him in a few hours (we had only one car, which was with my dad at work). I suspect this nurse didn't offer a better answer because we couldn't pay full rate at the clinic. My mother did just as she was told. A few hours later David woke up vomiting.

We then took him to the county hospital, where they pumped his stomach and released him. He got worse. We took him back. They told us there were "no beds available" (code for "no proof of payment"). So we took him to Huntington Memorial, where they also claimed they had no beds, and then to another hospital, St. Luke's, at which point he was in such bad shape that the doctors agreed to treat him. But it was too late: David died there that night. When I think of my childhood, the most powerful emotion I have is the pain of this loss, how it covered our house like a black cloud, how my parents never really recovered, especially my mother. David's death affected me like no other event in my childhood. Except one.

A few months after David's death, my brother, Lee, who was five at the time, fainted and collapsed on the living room floor. My mother picked him up and shook him, but he didn't wake up. Within minutes, I started to feel faint too. At that point my mother was smart enough to run out of the house, but she told me to stay put. "Lie down on the bed and I'll come and get you," she said, rushing Lee outside. I was woozy and disoriented, but I refused to listen to her. Already my skepticism was taking over. I held on to the walls for support, and once I was out of the house I lay down on the gravel in our front yard and started to come to. I saw my mother sitting with Lee on the concrete strip of our driveway. He had also woken up. But we still had no idea what was happening. My mother called a neighbor, and after a few more hours it was determined that our faulty wall heater had filled the building with carbon monoxide. Lee was the smallest and most vulnerable, so he fainted first. I would have been next, and had I stayed there on the bed like I'd been told, I wouldn't have survived.

That incident, together with the tragedy of David's death, set me on a course that deeply influenced the rest of my life. It solidified my decision to think for myself no matter what. I would always ask what was sensible, even if it sounded wrong, even if I had to challenge my parents or my teachers. I felt I needed to do it. If I didn't, I could be injured or even killed — that's how serious it was to me. I didn't blame my mother for being obedient. It wasn't her fault that David died, or that she didn't think to get us all out of the house in a moment of clear danger. Yet in a way it was her fault, or at least that's how I saw it as a child. She was a victim of poverty, and she was an immigrant with little education. She'd never been taught how to think things through, and she blindly trusted authority because of the tradition she was brought up in, just like many people at that time. But listening and obeying and not thinking critically led to the greatest loss a parent can endure. I decided I wanted to live a different kind of life. I wanted a life where girls and boys were treated equally. I wanted a life in which I could make smart decisions and didn't always have to worry about money. I wanted out of the world I'd been born into, and I resolved to do it by thinking for myself.

I did get out, eight years later. I won a full scholarship to UC Berkeley — I wouldn't have been able to afford college otherwise, as my father had cut me off financially. I was supposed to get married to a wealthy Jewish man, not go to school. In August of 1959 I got on a Greyhound bus to Berkeley with my two suitcases and never looked back. During my sophomore year, I met my future husband, Stan, an experimental physicist. I was sliding down a flight of stairs in a giant cardboard box — just another Monday night in the Sherman Hall co-op — and happened to land on his feet. We fell in love. I realized he also had a certain skepticism toward the world. He grew up in Krakow during World War II, right next to the train tracks that transported Jews to Auschwitz. The Nazis occupied part of his family's apartment, forcing them into two small rooms. He and his brother and mother survived only because they were Catholic. His father worked in the Polish government in exile in London. After the war, Stan escaped to Sweden, along with his mother and brother, by hiding under the coal storage bins of a cargo ship. In a tragic turn of events, his father was told there was not enough room on the ship and to come on the next one. There was no next one. He was arrested on the dock by the newly established Communist authorities. He was kept as a political prisoner until 1955 when Stalin died. Not surprisingly, Stan had a strong distrust of authority and government, and he was also deeply skeptical of historical documents, something I hadn't even considered. He knew from experience how governments change history to reflect the views of the winners. It makes sense that he dedicated his life to studying neutrinos, the smallest of the elementary particles, and challenging Einstein's theories. He was seeking the origins of the universe, trying, somehow, to make sense of the world.

After we got married, Stan received a National Science Foundation Fellowship and we spent a few years living in Geneva and Paris. I first enrolled at the University of Geneva in the School of International Relations and then at the Sorbonne in Paris. I loved living in Geneva and Paris and loved learning and speaking French. Then we moved back to Berkeley, and a year later to Palo Alto when Stan was offered an assistant professorship in physics at Stanford. We didn't expect to stay long because it was a non-tenured job, but in 1967 he was offered a tenure track position. We were thrilled. In 1968, we became parents. Neither of us really knew what we were in for. It was incredible to become a mother, of course, but it was so much harder than I thought. Stan focused on being the provider and giving the family stability and structure. His work as a Stanford professor was extremely demanding. He was always under pressure to "publish or perish," and he worked constantly. He also traveled all over the world for academic conferences and presentations. His passion was high-energy particle physics, which meant visiting research laboratories in Brookhaven, New York, the Fermi Lab in Chicago, and CERN (European Organization for Nuclear Research) in Geneva. We still have a world map on the wall in our family room that has a pushpin for every place Stan has visited. There are hundreds of pushpins. When he was home, he was a good father — but he was rarely home. Though I was frustrated, and sometimes I wished I had more support, I learned to accept it.

It was up to me to raise our three daughters. I got a lot of medical help from my doctors at Kaiser in Redwood City, California, but they didn't offer parenting advice. The advice from my friends didn't really meet my needs. None of the books I read made any sense until I found Dr. Spock, the parenting guru of the 1960s, and his iconic book, *Dr. Spock's Baby and Child Care*. His message resonated with me from the start. He told me and thousands of other new mothers: "You know more than you think you do . . . You want to be the best parent you can be, but it is not always clear what is best. Everywhere you turn there are experts telling you what to do. The problem is, they don't often agree with each other. The world is different from how it was twenty years ago, and the old answers may not work anymore." I read that passage and felt as if he was speaking directly to me. The old answers didn't work for me. The religion and culture I grew up in didn't value me as a human being. Experts and authority figures didn't have my best interests at heart. I was the only one who knew what was right for my daughters, what was right for me.

Many mothers read Dr. Spock, but few of them raised their children the way I raised mine. I found my own path, mainly by rebelling against my own childhood. I was scared of falling into patterns from the past. I knew that if I wasn't careful, I could expose my daughters to the behaviors and values that caused me so much suffering as a child. I did want to recreate the strong emotional and physical attachment to my children that I had with my mother, but that's where the similarities ended. Somehow I realized that if I wanted to do things differently, I would have to consciously address my own childhood. I didn't read about it. Dr. Spock didn't teach me that, nor did anyone else. It just seemed to make sense. In order to change, I couldn't be on autopilot, parenting the way I'd been shown. I would need to be reflective instead of reactive. I would need a lot of patience, and a lot of resolve.

It turns out that my intuitive understanding is explained by the field of attachment research. Attachment was first described by John Bowlby, a British scientist whose research from the 1950s forged a new understanding of human relationships. Bowlby's theory of attachment suggests that the way we interacted with our parents when we were young will help determine our interpersonal relationships as adults, dramatically influencing the way we relate to other people, and most importantly to our partner and our own children.

In the 1970s, L. Alan Sroufe, a psychologist and researcher at the University of Minnesota, began collecting data for the Minnesota Longitudinal Study of Parents and Children. Sroufe was inspired by Bowlby's work and wanted to know if early attachment patterns could predict behavior in adult life. The results of this ongoing study suggest that early attachment does indeed influence our behavior as adults, especially in the categories of self-reliance, emotional regulation, and social competence. Sroufe and colleagues found that "attachment experiences provide certain core attitudinal, motivational, and emotional components that are a platform for entering the world of peers and coping with the challenges that arise."[2] In other words, your early experiences with attachment give you a sort of compass for navigating your life. Take self-reliance, for instance. Sroufe's study showed that nursery school children with anxious and avoidant attachment patterns were more dependent on their teachers. Another analysis of the same longitudinal study found that securely attached children were rated more sociable by their grade school teachers, had more friends at age sixteen, and were better able to resolve conflicts in their romantic relationships as adults.[3]

These findings affirm what we all know is true: Childhood experiences deeply affect us as adults. But here's where it gets really interesting. Another psychological researcher, Mary Main, wondered whether these patterns could change over the course of our lives, and if so, how. In order to find out, she and her colleagues developed a questionnaire called the "Adult Attachment Interview." During this research interview, an adult subject would discuss his or her childhood experiences with a researcher, answering questions like "Which parent did you feel closer to and why?" "When you were upset as a child, what did you do, and what would happen?" and "How do you think your overall early experiences have affected your adult personality?" The results of these surveys were groundbreaking. Main found that adults are actually able to change and revise their attachment patterns throughout life. We can move from insecure to secure attachment. But how? Positive relationships with people other than our parents (which introduce us to other forms of attachment) were found to be helpful, but equally important was conscious reflection on one's childhood. Main's analysis showed that those participants who had coherent narratives about what had happened to them as children, who spoke thoughtfully about their parents and what they themselves struggled with, were associated with secure attachment — regardless of whether they'd experienced difficulty, trauma, or loss as children. Those subjects whose narratives were less coherent, dismissive, or contradictory were associated with anxious or insecure attachment that had persisted into adulthood.

I think all of us know this instinctively. We tend to parent the same way we were parented, primarily because this is the one model we have. The family values we learn as children can influence us so deeply that we may not always be able to feel or understand the extent of that influence. We often find ourselves saying things or doing things that our parents did and wondering how our parents got into our head or under our skin. In some families there are cycles of violence and intergenerational abuse, with people seemingly trapped within the same dysfunctional patterns for generations. One study found that one third of abused children went on to be neglectful or abusive parents themselves.

The first thing every parent should do, then, is reflect on their experiences. It sounds simple, but we often fail to do it. As the psychiatrist and UCLA researcher Daniel J. Siegel writes in *Mindsight*, "The best predictor of a child's security of attachment is not what happened to his parents as children, but rather how his parents made sense of those childhood experiences." Siegel, Main, and others have discussed how this experience of making sense of your life results in "earned secure attachment." We all have the ability to "earn" security through conscious self-reflection, which we can then pass on to our children.

I wish I would have known all this earlier. I wish someone would have told me *how* to reflect, what questions to ask, what answers I should be looking for. Somehow I figured it out on my own. For one thing, I had the laboratory of experience. Whatever I was doing was working: my girls were happy, thriving, capable. But there were so many challenges I couldn't have predicted.

What I realized, through a lot of conscious effort, is that parenting gives us perhaps the most profound opportunity to grow as human beings. As Dr. Siegel cautions in *Parenting from the Inside Out*:

"When parents don't take responsibility for their own unfinished business, they miss an opportunity not only to become better parents but also to continue their own development." In other words, if you don't act as your own therapist, and interrogate your own childhood, you won't be the best parent you can be. A parental perspective allows you to understand the challenges your parents faced that you might not have recognized as a child. A child's perspective is myopic, and it's impossible for us as children to understand all the factors that influence our parents' behavior.

Our childhood memories can also be distorted. As an adult I went back to that stone house in Sunland. In my memory it was a big house with a backyard that stretched all the way to the foothills. But when I saw it again, I was shocked by how small it was. I couldn't believe that all five of us lived there. The backyard was a narrow lot that stretched only to the next row of small one-story houses. The tragic events that happened there were so profoundly important to my life and my understanding of myself that I'd made a massive house in my mind, when in reality there stood only a modest stone home for a family of modest means. Seeing the house helped me to recognize how much my parents must have struggled. I saw my father as partly a victim of his circumstances, like so many other imperfect parents. He had a life of physical labor combined with anger at a world that never supported him. He gave up his dreams of being an artist for us. He came from a culture that shaped his authoritarian behavior. Understanding all of this allowed me to forgive him. I had succeeded in spite of the ideas he had for my life, and deep down I knew forgiving him would allow me to move on.

Parenting is how culture gets transmitted to the next generation.

It's your chance to pass on your core principles and values, and to use all of your wisdom and insight in order to improve someone else's life. It's also your chance to affect eternity. I'm reminded of one of my favorite quotes about the art of teaching: "Teachers affect eternity; they can never tell where their influence stops." The same is true for parenting. You never know how your parenting will impact future generations.

I think the most important question we need to ask ourselves is whether the principles and values we're handing down to our children are ethical, and whether they're beliefs we want to perpetuate in society. We are all part of a community, part of a country, part of the earth. Are you teaching your children the things you want to see them teach their own children? Will this improve their lives, the culture, the world?

Even after I left the Orthodox tradition, I still experienced gender discrimination — as a reporter, I couldn't get into the San Francisco Press Club because they only accepted men. I couldn't get a credit card in my name in the 1970s. It was easy for me to want a different path for my daughters, a path where they could be who they wanted to be, a path where they were not subservient to their husbands, where they had a voice and a passion in life. I wanted my daughters to have some control early on, and I was determined to develop their decision-making skills. I was always asking, "Do you want grapes or an apple?" "Do you want to do an art project or play outside?" I helped them become skillful decision-makers from a very young age, and now, some forty years later, I'm in awe as I watch them make some of the most complicated and important decisions in health-care and media. So how does this relate to you, the reader? The primary goal of this book is helping you understand, think about, and implement effective parenting strategies that will positively affect you, your children, your family, our society, and future generations.

I knew it wasn't going to be easy to get there — family culture can be hard to change or revise — but I wanted to try. One empowered, purpose-driven child positively affects you, your family, your community, and the whole world. It's a powerful ripple effect, and it starts in the home.

TRICK QUESTIONNAIRE

I may have figured out a lot on my own, but I'm the first to admit that parenting would have been much easier with some guidance. So that's what I'd like to offer you here — guidance. Below you'll find a set of questions to help you think about your own experiences and how they align with the values that lead to lifelong success. You'll also look at your partner's values, and the values held by your community, both of which deeply influence the way you parent. This kind of reflection can help you at any stage of parenting, whether you're expecting your first child, confronting problems with a rebellious teenager, or working to repair a relationship with an adult child. It can also help if you are a teacher, grandparent, or other caregiver responsible for the well-being of children. We all need Trust, Respect, Independence, Collaboration, and Kindness, and we all need to be conscious of these important values in order to practice them.

Please use these questions as you make your way through the coming chapters. My hope is that in answering them, you'll discover which aspects of your childhood to keep, and which to leave behind. You may wish to reflect on these, write them down in a journal, or discuss them with your partner or a trusted friend.

1. YOUR FAMILY. How were the TRICK values either encouraged or discouraged in your family? What could be improved or revised?

    TRUST — Was your home a trusting environment? Did you trust your parents as a child? Did they trust you? How was trust shown or demonstrated in your family? Was there ever a breach of trust? If so, how was it resolved? How could you improve upon what you learned about trust as a child? What kind of a trusting environment do you want to create for your child? What are some little things you can do to help develop trust with your children? Make a list.

    RESPECT — Did you feel respected as a child? Were your ideas and opinions taken into consideration? Did you feel like an important member of the family? Did you ever feel disrespected? If so, were you able to regain respect? How? How could you improve upon what you learned about respect as a child? What are some small things you can do to help show your children you respect them? It can be as simple as letting them wear whatever they want to a special occasion or letting them help create the menu for a dinner party. Make a list for yourself.

    INDEPENDENCE — Did you feel a strong sense of independence as a child, or were you dependent on your parents for daily activities like meals, cleaning, and homework? What steps did your parents take to encourage your independence? How could you improve upon what you learned about independence as a child? What can you do to help promote your child's independence?

    COLLABORATION — Was there a collaborative environment in your household? How did your parents encourage collaboration? Did you feel as if your family functioned as a team, or that there was usually one person in control? How could you improve upon what you learned about collaboration as a child? What are some small things you can do to encourage collaboration? What about having your children work on a communal project of their choice?

KINDNESS — How was kindness shown in your household? Were you taught to appreciate and be grateful for what you had? Were you raised with a sense of service toward others in your community? How could you improve upon what you learned about kindness as a child?

2. YOUR CULTURE

Your community, culture, and religion also have a deep impact on the way you raise your child.

What are the assumptions about child-rearing in your community and religion (if applicable)?

What do you agree with? What don't you agree with?

Which practices are evolving or in need of challenging? For example, so-called snowplow parenting means you eliminate all obstacles for your child, never exposing them to any kind of risk. How could you introduce experiences that teach kids independence and grit? What about your culture might be holding them back?

Which beliefs and practices align with the TRICK values? Which ones don't?

3. YOUR PARTNER'S FAMILY AND CULTURE

If you're parenting with a partner, you should answer these questions together to determine how you will function as a parenting team. I suggest you have a discussion (not an argument) about the pros and cons of different approaches to parenting — and you should do this earlier rather than later. What are the best aspects of how you were raised? What ideas and practices from your partner might help your child succeed? Can you come up with a philosophy that combines the strengths of each approach? Stan and I had no idea what kind of parents we would become. It turns out that we had very different parenting styles, which isn't surprising given that he grew up in a very different culture, with his father in exile in London. He and his mother and brother were in the countryside in Poland, hoping to avoid the bombing. So when we started to parent, Stan had somewhat strict Polish ideas of how to make our daughters behave. Spanking was considered okay in Polish culture. But I, having experienced hitting as a child, did not think it was acceptable or helpful. I know it is hard to resist hitting or spanking, because even with my positive attitude, I sometimes had problems resisting the urge. But I wanted to have an emotional connection with the kids. I wanted to treat them kindly. (I won the debate partly because Stan was away so often — victory by default.) Differences in parenting styles is one of the main contributors to relationship stress and can even result in divorce. Seek to understand one another's values and their grounding in each other's childhood and culture. TRICK is not a culturally specific approach to parenting. These are universal values that exist in all cultures and increasingly are being seen as the basis for health, happiness, and success in the world of today — and tomorrow.

A FINAL WORD: ACCEPT YOURSELF—
NO ONE CAN BE PERFECT

Parents are human: despite all your thinking and planning, you *will* make mistakes. I made tons of them. I punished the wrong child for something the other one did, or I got mad for no reason, or I used the wrong shampoo and it got in their eyes. On a cross-country campervan trip from Palo Alto to Chicago, Anne had what looked like bites all over her legs and body and I kept spraying her with Off, thinking she'd been bit by mosquitoes. I did this for days before I realized she had chicken pox!

We moved our family to Geneva, Switzerland, when my daughter Anne was an infant and Janet was only three. Janet had a really hard time adjusting to her new sister—she used to ask me if we were going to take Anne back to the hospital. "I am done playing with her, Mommy," she would tell me. She was also confronted with a new culture (Swiss) and a new language (French). What she needed most at that time was security, and yet her world had changed in an instant. I underestimated how much of a challenge this would be for her, and for all of us. Yet, like all families, we made the best choice we could at the time, and who's to say this experience didn't help her build grit and independence?

My grown daughters still joke about what Stan and I did wrong as parents. Anne should have had more tennis lessons, Susan should have had more art classes, and Janet should have had more piano lessons. They always tell me we should have gotten them another dog. (Okay, these are the jokes of happy, successful adults. I made more serious mistakes too, believe me.)

Our goal is not to create a stress-free and hardship-free environment for our children. The painful and difficult experiences are often how we grow. Our goal is not to take these challenges and the growth that results from them away from our children — the fatal flaw of helicopter parenting — but to help our children face these challenges and learn from them. We don't need to be perfect, but we do need to make sure our children can use the TRICK values to persist even in the face of difficulty.

There is no perfect parent, spouse, or child. We all try our best. What you want to do is use the TRICK values consistently and not give up. Don't beat yourself up when you make mistakes. The first person you need to forgive is yourself. Life can be complicated and difficult. If you do something counterproductive as a parent, recognize it and try to avoid it in the future. You may make the same mistake again. And again. It takes time to learn as parents as much as it takes time for our children to learn. Focus on creating intimate relationships with your children, and raising them with the values of TRICK so that you'll be proud of the people they become. We all want to raise good humans.

We each have a story. We all have experienced trauma and in many cases tragedy. I resolved to do the best I could to not recreate my childhood, but I also understood that my children would face difficulties no matter what I did. It wasn't my job to be perfect or make their lives perfect, but to do my own reflection and spare them any unnecessary suffering. As we explore the values in this book, I encourage you to keep questioning and examining your own experiences. Think about what could be improved, and how. And then be willing to change: for yourself, your children, and the world.

TRUST

2

Trust Yourself, Trust Your Child

BEING A PARENT IS HARD. Being a grandparent is no joke either.

It was early morning in San Francisco, and the traffic was fierce. I was on grandparenting duty for the week while my daughter Janet was working on children's nutrition in Rwanda and Kenya. My first task was to drive my grandkids to school, which sounds simple enough, except for the Bay Area traffic. And the fact that they went to schools on opposite sides of the city. And the fact that I'd no sooner dropped off one child before I found out that I had to drive back to my grandson's school to deliver homework he'd accidentally left in his room.

By ten a.m., I was done with driving, but then it was time to walk the dog, administer antibiotics to the two family cats, who'd come down with some kind of infection right before Janet left, and then clean up from breakfast. I wondered again how Janet managed to juggle this on a daily basis. The traffic alone was enough to unravel me. This is why most people in the Bay Area meditate — we would all be facing road rage charges without it.

My kids used to walk to school by themselves, but times have changed.

The next day, Saturday, was more chaos, but of a different kind. I was helping my daughter Susan in addition to taking care of Janet's kids. Susan asked me to take her daughters to Target for school supplies. Janet's son needed a haircut.

It was about time. He looked like a shaggy dog.

The traffic was a little better in suburban Los Altos, but with all the errands in front of us, I decided that this particular Saturday would be a great opportunity to transform a day of chauffeuring into a day of learning.

Why not show the kids I trusted them? Less driving. More trust. More fun for the kids. It would be a win-win.

I brought my grandson (age twelve) to the hair salon and let him handle the appointment on his own. He knew exactly what kind of haircut he wanted, and he'd been going to the same salon on and off for a year. Then I drove my other two granddaughters (both age eight) to Target. On the way, we went over the list of school supplies they needed, which they saved on their phones. The plan was for them to meet by the registers in an hour and contact me. I would come in and pay with my credit card, but it was up to them to make sure they gathered everything on the list. If they needed me, they could call. But I was sure my granddaughters would be fine. I'd been shopping with them dozens of times. I'd taught them how to conduct themselves in stores, use a shopping cart, stay together, and find what they needed. I'd taught my own daughters the same skills. They'd learned how to shop early on at Patterson's Dime Store on California Avenue, about a mile from our house in Palo Alto. They'd bike there on their own and agonize — for hours — over which tiny toy or piece of candy to buy with their allowance. They had to make sure their purchases were under a dollar, which involved careful math and difficult decisions. They would come home so proud of themselves, beaming and carrying their little paper bags filled with goodies. Maybe I'm just a teacher at heart, but I always saw shopping as an opportunity to empower kids, and also to have some fun. Why not help them learn the skills for life as early as possible? And why get stressed about the errands you have to run when you can make each trip into a little adventure?

I watched my granddaughters pass through Target's sliding-glass doors, feeling as proud as I did of my own daughters years ago. I drove back to the hair salon. My grandson was waiting for me, as planned, with his long hair transformed from an unkempt mess into a short cut that made him look like a dashing young man. Back on the road, we listened to Beyoncé on the radio, and in the back of my mind, I was thinking about what we were all going to have for dinner. We'd just about reached Target when my cell phone rang.

It was Susan. I told her about my grandson's fancy new haircut, and she asked where the girls were.

"They're shopping at Target," I said.

"You left them alone? How could you have done that?"

I was surprised by her alarm. She was talking about Target as if it were a dangerous place where kids should never be left unsupervised.

"It's Target," I said. "It's a well-run store."

"But, Mom—"

"And the girls know how to shop by themselves. They're going to text me when they're done."

Susan was polite—*controlled* might be a better word—but she was mad. I pulled into the parking lot and saw my granddaughters waiting inside. Turning off the engine, I told Susan that they were fine.

"You shouldn't have left them there," she said. "It isn't safe."

"Well," I said, walking toward the entrance with my grandson, "they seem pretty safe to me."

In the end, it all worked out. Susan was stressed for a few minutes — really stressed — but I called her while we were at the checkout to confirm that the kids were safe and had done a great job selecting their school supplies. My granddaughters loved it, by the way. They'd had a lot of fun shopping on their own and felt empowered. Susan had a bit of a breakthrough too: Kids were more capable than she realized.

I'm not suggesting that everyone immediately drop their children off unsupervised at stores around the world — but the question of where our children are safe, and where they aren't, is an important one. As is just how much we can trust them to handle on their own. Those back-to-school shopping lists (the source of stress to parents everywhere) are a great place to start.

THE CRISIS OF TRUST

All parents need to understand this: The digital age and the ease of transmitting information has resulted in a crisis of trust, and it's affecting the way we live and the way we parent. We don't trust ourselves and our own instincts, we have a hard time trusting our partners and our children, and many of us live in fear of our neighbors and fellow citizens. But living without trust is miserable. It makes us dysfunctional. We become so fearful and anxious — and what do we do? We pass this fear and anxiety on to our children. They grow up nervous and afraid, just like us, and we wonder why more and more kids are incapable of transitioning to adult life. If you think this is an issue that only affects families, you're wrong. The global erosion of trust is bad for mental health, relationships, business, and foreign relations, and it's especially bad for democracy.

Distrust has seeped into every sphere of our lives. The 2018 Edelman "Trust Barometer," a measure of the general public's average trust in institutions, found that the United States dropped nine points in the Global Trust Scale, the steepest decline in trust ever measured in this country. Italy dropped by five points, and Ireland, South Africa, Japan, and Russia were ranked last in terms of public trust. The same thing is happening in our neighborhoods. A recent Pew Research report found that just 52 percent of Americans agree that they trust all or most of their neighbors. Even more disturbing, only 19 percent of millennials agree that most people can be trusted — a lower percentage than all other segments of the population.

Here in Palo Alto — arguably one of America's safer communities — I rarely see kids playing in the street or walking to school. Back when my daughters were young, there were kids everywhere. We had a street sign that read SLOW — CHILDREN AT PLAY to alert drivers. Those signs are gone now. Kids stay in their backyards or, more often, inside in front of their phones. When it comes to children, we don't trust our neighbors, and we definitely don't trust daycare centers. That's why parenting blogs are filled with posts like "Can You Trust Your Babysitter?" and "Ten Things Your Daycare Center Doesn't Want You to Know." We have to install cameras in order to monitor the situation. We even do the same with dog daycare!

The effects in schools are just as troubling. Teachers are not allowed to be in a room alone with a student. We're told never to hug students. I almost got into trouble at Palo Alto High School for giving a ride to a student — until I proved that the kid in question was my grandson who had come to visit my class for the day. We don't trust teachers to do their jobs. That's why we burden them with statewide exams. No one seems to have faith that teachers are teaching what they're supposed to, so when a child does poorly on an exam, the assumption is that the teacher is at fault, not the outdated curriculum or lack of resources. Parents don't feel they can trust anyone at the school — administrators, teachers, or even other students and their parents. Almost 50 percent of teachers leave the profession after five years. They cite lack of trust and respect as the main reasons for leaving. In many states we have a major teacher shortage, which only appears to be getting worse.

Now, I'm exposed to the twenty-four/seven news cycle like everyone else. I hear stories that frighten me all the time, and I understand why parents are frightened too. It's normal to be afraid, especially in a world with so much distrust, so much uncertainty. Just the other day, I ran into a former student with her two-month-old baby, and as we were talking, she mentioned how concerned she was about having a child in this unsafe world. This was in Palo Alto, for heaven's sake. We are all extrapolating from what we read online. We're reading too many scary things, watching too many scary news clips. Having lived in France and Switzerland, and because I travel all over the world to give talks, I sense that Americans are more fearful than most people. So it's important for us to really look at the statistics and challenge our assumptions about just how dangerous our lives are. In Steven Pinker's eye-opening book *Enlightenment Now: The Case for Reason, Science, Humanism, and Progress,* he tackles these assumptions head-on. Of our fears that the world is getting less safe, less predictable, less hospitable, he claims:

> Contrary to the impression that you might get from the newspapers — that we're living in a time of epidemics and war and crime — the curves show that humanity has been getting better, that we're living longer, we are fighting fewer wars, and fewer people are being killed in the wars. Our rate of homicide is down. Violence against women is down. More children are going to school, girls included. More of the world is literate. We have more leisure time than our ancestors did. Diseases are being decimated. Famines are becoming rarer, so virtually anything that you could measure that you'd want to call human well-being has improved over the last two centuries, but also over the last couple of decades.[4]

Our own institutions reflect this too. Data from the FBI and the Bureau of Justice Statistics shows that violent and property crimes have fallen since 1990, though most Americans — six in ten — believe that crime rates are increasing each year. The Office of Juvenile Justice and Delinquency Prevention states that between 1999 and 2013, both the rate of missing children and the number of missing children reported to the police have decreased. The National Crime Information Center's Missing Person and Unidentified Person reports show that the number of missing children under the age of eighteen fell from 33,706 in 2016 to 32,121 in 2017. Furthermore, the National Center for Missing and Exploited Children confirms that family abductions and runaway cases are much more common than stranger abductions, the most feared kind.

What Steven Pinker argues over hundreds of pages, and what all the data shows, is that there is a clear downtrend in violence over time. Yes, I know we're saturated with school shootings and the trials of serial child molesters and myriad news stories that can terrify you as a parent. In the media business, bad news sells better than good news, and every shooting can become a huge story in the echo chamber of social media. It can be really hard to accept that the world's safer than ever when we hear anecdote after scary anecdote. But it's the truth. We all need to take a collective deep breath. Here are some simple statements that you should read and repeat to yourself:

The majority of people are trustworthy.

The last thing you want to teach your child is that people, in general, can't be trusted, or to overprotect them to the point where they lack the independence necessary to thrive on their own. And don't we want our children to have an open-minded attitude toward the world, not to be closed off to life's possibilities?

We have to start somewhere. We have to combat all this fear and reestablish trust in ourselves and the world around us. The solution starts in the home, and that means it starts with you.

TRUST YOURSELF

A culture of trust in your family paves the way for all the subsequent values we're going to explore. As I've said, we might not all be able to trust our parental conditioning — that is, we might not want to repeat everything about the way we were parented. But if you (and your partner) do the work of sorting through your past, and if you honor the core human values represented by TRICK, you can trust your instincts when it comes to parenting.

And you must. Why? Because you're the one who truly knows what works for your family. You might find, as I did, that the parenting philosophy in your culture isn't a good fit. Nor is what your pediatrician tells you to do, or what everyone in your neighborhood is doing. You are the foremost expert on your family, which means that *you* know better than any other parenting experts, including me. I'm writing a parenting book, but I don't know you, and I don't know your children. Only you can determine how best to apply these universal principles. My goal here is to give you guidelines — not prescriptive advice — and permission to trust your own expertise, because if you don't trust yourself, you won't be able to instill trust in your children.

Still, I know how hard all of this is. Socially, it can be challenging if you don't follow the rules and do what everyone around you is doing, even when your kids don't fit in with those rules. Even when problems arise. We're afraid our children might fail, and their failures will be our fault. We're racked with anxiety about not knowing what we're doing, but we're certain that whatever we choose, we'll screw everything up.

The culture has trained us to think we need to consult a specialist for every problem or challenge. When it comes to kids, there are ADD and ADHD specialists, autism specialists, psychologists, psychiatrists, and multiple types of doctors. Some families have tutors for each child, each grade level, each subject. All of this specialization and expertise undermines our ability to think for ourselves as parents and to make the best choices for our children. Somehow we're convinced that all of these other people know better than we do.

But that's not true.

You have to trust that you know what's best for your child and your family.

WALK THE TALK

My grandson Ethan still wasn't talking at two and a half years old. He walked and slept through the night and knew his favorite foods, but he didn't want to talk. It can be nerve-racking for parents when a child lags behind the normal developmental curve, and it's important to investigate and ask questions. And yet it's a simple fact that some children acquire skills later than others. Some of us adults do as well. In most cases it means nothing about our intelligence or abilities — it's just the way it is. That's how my daughter Janet thought about it — at least at first. But as time went on, we wondered when Ethan would start talking, and we got a little worried. So Janet took him to the pediatrician, who recommended a specialist, saying it was nothing to worry about, that lots of kids need speech therapy. And that's what we did. Ethan cooperated, sort of, but he still wasn't talking after several sessions.

His parents took matters into their own hands. They read him books every night, every weekend, after every nap. They bought him a tape recorder, a pair of big headphones, and some children's books on tape (and even recorded a number of stories themselves). Ethan absolutely loved those stories. He'd sit in the family room with his headphones, just listening at first. He loved riding in the car and taking walks — always wearing his headphones. We reassured ourselves that there's no timetable for development except in parenting books — and kids don't read those books.

I learned that Albert Einstein didn't talk until he was three.

Ethan was in good company.

It was more than three months of therapy before Ethan finally started talking, and when he did, instead of speaking in single words, he spoke in complete sentences. He had always been obsessed with elevators, and one of the first things he said to me was "I want to ride in the elevator." He listened to his taped stories for years after, and still loves audiobooks. Now he's a voracious reader, a leader in his class, and on the debate team.

Sometimes you question your abilities because your child is not developing as you'd like. One thing I failed to do was teach proper table manners when my children were little. I kept postponing the lesson. When was the right time to teach manners? I didn't have a clue. Well, it turns out they learn good manners (or bad manners) from the start. There is no such thing as "baby manners" or "kid manners," and if you allow them to behave poorly at the beginning, they will think that is the way to behave at the table. Breaking a bad habit is more difficult than establishing good ones at the beginning. I wish I'd known how important it is to teach basic manners early on — it took me a long time to correct this mistake.

Our dinners back in the seventies were complete chaos and constant whining — enough to drive me crazy! Restaurants were the worst, especially when we lived in Switzerland and France. I'd look at the other tables and the perfectly well-behaved kids and think, *What have I done?* The Swiss and French didn't take any crap from their children. Those kids sat patiently waiting between courses. They certainly didn't seem to be struggling as I was. A few years later, at an Italian restaurant in Mountain View, my daughters started flinging peas at each other. One pea shot off Stan's forehead, and I made the mistake of laughing — because it was hilarious — and we were promptly kicked out. We've avoided that restaurant for years. My girls did learn their manners eventually, and I came to realize that their behavior wasn't a reason not to trust myself as a parent. It was a sign that there were still lessons to be learned.

Here's another challenge: How many of us grew up in an environment full of trust? Not many. I sure didn't. As I said, my father was in total control of the family, and my mother and I lived in fear of crossing him. A lot of us have a hard time building trust, and can be more susceptible to anger, frustration, and depression. It sometimes seems like it's impossible to trust ourselves, let alone our children.

If this sounds familiar, I suggest that you write down all the negative things your parents said, all the breaches of trust you experienced, all the pain and anger. Then analyze each one. It's not going to be easy, but it's going to help you. Ask yourself: Was what your parent said actually true, or was it a comment that came from a lot of anger that had nothing to do with you? Were you at fault for the mistakes in your childhood, or were you simply part of a dysfunctional family system, through no fault of your own? Why did breaches of trust happen? Is it because your parents were raised in an environment short on trust? As adults, we have the ability to look back and see how flawed some of our parents' statements were and to perceive how we got caught up in the emotional shortcomings of other people. Just doing this work of unpacking painful memories helps you to see the past more clearly and to have faith in yourself as a parent.

It helps to make a list of things you do well. It sounds simple, but writing this down can quickly increase your confidence. Everyone does something great — absolutely everyone. I use this exercise with my students at the start of the semester. They interview each other and are tasked with finding out something special about the other person, something at which they excel. At first the kids are shy — both the subjects and the interviewers. Some of them are convinced they don't do anything well, which is a pretty tragic reflection of the experiences they've had at school and at home. But if the interviewers persist, and if they get creative with their questions, they can uncover all kinds of special talents: juggling, dog walking, being a good sister, listening.

These conversations build trust in our classroom and help students feel good about themselves and their ability to succeed. It can be so helpful for parents to find people who trust in their abilities, just as my students trust in each other. Who supports you and understands that you're doing the best for your family? Surround yourself with people who will build your confidence, even when things go wrong, as they inevitably will.

No matter what challenges we face as parents, we can all see the evidence before our eyes. Look at your children. Observe them. Talk to them. Are they happy? Are they thriving? We are subjected to so many influences — especially other people's opinions — that we forget to simply look at our families and see what's working and what's not. If something isn't working, you can change it. Assess the situation honestly without blaming yourself or becoming insecure. All parents struggle. But struggle doesn't mean we should lose faith: It means we need to believe in ourselves even more.

BUILD TRUST IN YOUR CHILD

All you need is one person, just one person who trusts and believes in you, and then you feel you can do anything. Unfortunately, a lot of children don't have even one person. Michael Wang, a former student of mine, was one of these kids. He was an editor in chief of the *Campanile*, Palo Alto High's newspaper, in 2013, and his struggles represent those of so many of my students at Paly, and students across the country and world. For Michael, the pressures and expectations started early.

"I had very strict parents," Michael says. "They would tell me if I didn't do well in school, I'd be homeless."

His elementary school teachers weren't very supportive either. Michael now knows he gave off the impression of being tired and upset, but it was extremely difficult for him to wake up at seven a.m., and he always felt like his brain didn't work. He would stare at a piece of paper, knowing he couldn't read it, couldn't discern what it meant, and he resigned himself to failure. People misinterpreting his behavior and motivations was a common theme in his life.

"I would get admonished," he says, "by peers and educators telling me if I followed the rules and paid attention, of course I'd do better. It was almost part of my core being, to be this thing that was trodden on; everything I did turned into some kind of moral shortcoming."

By the time he made it to my class, Michael described himself as "completely burned out like a pile of ash." The school newspaper was the only thing he derived any meaning from, and still he could barely muster the will to show up. But he did. I got to know him as a really bright but disconnected kid: he'd come into class and have no idea what he wanted to do, no idea what he wanted to write about. He was six feet tall, a big kid, and you stick out when you're that tall and unsure of yourself.

I've seen so many students like this. They're afraid but also rebellious. They're not cooperative. They're difficult, even aggressive, and that's because every single one of them feels bad about himself. They have such low self-esteem that they fight back, but that's from trying to prove to themselves that they're better than everyone thinks.

During one of our production nights for the school newspaper, Michael was struggling with his music theory homework. "I was exhausted, trying to figure out this assignment," he says, "and I was half-assing it. A few sanctimonious peers took it upon themselves to share some wisdom I'd obviously never heard before: Suck it up, study harder."

Other students teased him for struggling, and he thought to himself, as he often did, *That's right, I can't do it.*

I saw what was happening, walked up to these kids, and said, "He's taking longer because he's smart." Michael was a talented writer — he just needed more time to focus on his work. And I knew deep down he wanted to get it right, not just rush through it.

That was the first time an adult had said that his abilities and intelligence were seen and respected. "To hear outside confirmation that someone believed in me," Michael says, "even in the presence of other students who didn't — it was awesome. It helped me not to crumble."

That day was a turning point for Michael. In truth, he was smart — he just had an attitude problem. For the first time, he started to trust himself, and he called upon this newfound confidence throughout his undergraduate years whenever he encountered obstacles or someone who told him he'd never make it. He went on to earn his degree in neuroscience at Johns Hopkins, where he's now a neuro-psychiatric researcher. He'd found his one person to believe in him by accident, and that made all the difference.

Parents and teachers have to know that one word, sentence, or phrase can build a kid up, can save his life — or shatter his confidence. We forget how important we are in the lives of our children, how much control we have in shaping their confidence and self-image. And it all starts with trust, with believing your child is capable, even through setbacks and surprises and all the complications that come with growing up.

Trusting is empowering in the classroom and in the world at large — and this process starts earlier than you think. Infants who are securely attached to their parents — that is, infants who feel they can trust and depend on their parents — avoid many of the behavioral, social, and psychological problems that can arise later. Your child's fundamental sense of security in the world is based on you being a trusting caregiver.

This is why children are so highly attuned to their environments. They're wired to figure out whom they can trust, to identify the person who will respond to them and meet their needs. Studies show that four-year-olds can accurately identify trustworthy adults and later seek them out. I see this in my four-year-old granddaughter, Ava, all the time. When I walk in the door, she smiles at me, but sometimes she runs away and hides. She knows me, but she's constantly sizing me up to see whether I can be trusted.

Remember, trust is mutual. The degree to which your children can trust you will be reflected in their own ability to trust. When children don't have a sense of trust and security in the world, they experience all kinds of difficulties. Studies show that children rated as less trustworthy by their teachers exhibit higher levels of aggression and lower levels of "prosocial behavior" such as collaborating and sharing. Distrust in children has also been associated with their social withdrawal and loneliness.

If we don't feel trusted when we're kids, or if there isn't anyone close to us we can trust, we don't get over that. We grow up thinking we're not trustworthy, and we accept that as a character trait. Our relationships are turned upside down. We become what we think we are, and we suffer for it.

So how do we go about building trust in our children? We think of trust as handing our teenager the car keys, or letting our twelve-year-old stay home alone for the first time. But we underestimate the power of children — especially infants. Trust needs to start when they're born. We usually don't think of building trust in babies, but we should. They're smarter and much more perceptive than we think. Your child is watching you from day one.

Trust me on this. Your baby is observing your every move. They're learning how to get what they need from you. They know exactly what they're doing. Every time you fumble with a diaper, they see it. They know how to make you smile. They know how to make you cry. They may be dependent on us for everything, but they're a lot more intelligent than we give them credit for. You do need to respond to their needs, especially early on, so that they feel you and their environment are trustworthy, but this is also a fantastic time to start teaching your child some of the most important lessons in life.

So, let's talk about sleep.

And trust.

And how as parents you can use trust to solve those ever-persistent sleep problems.

Sleeping was really important for my girls when they were infants, and it was important to my husband and me — we knew we wouldn't survive years of not sleeping. We're not vampires! It is important for all parents and it has become an international problem. There are entire books devoted to getting your child to sleep. I saw sleeping as fundamentally about trust, and I saw it as a teachable skill. From day one, babies are learning about the world, their circadian rhythms are adjusting, and, though my daughters seemed to have their clocks set for the wrong continent, they needed to learn their most important infant skill: how to put themselves to sleep. It never occurred to me that they would have trouble sleeping beyond the first six weeks. Why wouldn't they be able to sleep? It's one of the three things they could do from birth: eat, poop, and sleep. They grow when they sleep; their brains develop when they sleep. Sleep is a natural state for babies and toddlers. I trusted they innately knew how, and if they needed some reassurance, I was there to help.

We didn't have a lot of money when the girls were young. Susan had a crib and a small bed that I created out of a wicker laundry basket with a nice little mattress (Susan still uses the same basket today, though not for sleeping). The point was to keep them safe and nearby. They slept in their own cribs and in their own rooms from the beginning (except when we were in our small apartment in Geneva and there weren't enough rooms — then Anne slept near us in a little box fitted with blankets). We were fortunate not to have to deal with colic or illness — these parents do have to be more responsive than usual to keep their child safe. Still, I think what I did will work in the majority of cases. I simply placed them on their stomachs, patted their backs, sat with them a few minutes, and let them fall asleep on their own. If they were restless and started to whimper or cry, I'd make sure they weren't hungry or didn't need to be changed, and then I reassured them with a soft pat on the back and they went back to sleep. Of course, now we know that the safest sleeping position for infants is on their back, in which case parents can pat the child's stomach. Babies have short sleep cycles and tend to wake up and cry or whimper, but they can often put themselves back to sleep. I was always there to comfort my daughters, but it wasn't always necessary to pick them up. I trusted they could get to sleep on their own, and they did. By the time they were three months old, they were sleeping most of the night. And as toddlers, they slept for twelve hours, from seven p.m. to seven a.m. Their sleep habits were such a gift to Stan and me. All parents need some time to be together.

I intuitively knew to trust my daughters, but I realize it can be hard for parents to project a strong sense of trust that then empowers their children. What they often project is fear. They think their child will be afraid to sleep by himself, that he needs his parents, that he can't do it on his own. How do you think a child learns to become afraid of sleeping? From exactly this kind of thinking on the parents' part.

I'm not out to blame anyone. I just want to explain how our ideas affect our children. Many parents are operating from their own insecurities or doubts: Doesn't their child need them? And if he doesn't, what kind of parents are they? You'll hear this message loud and clear from me throughout this book: You want your child to *want* to be with you, not to *need* to be with you. The first place this tension arises is with sleep. Your children can and will sleep on their own if you believe they can do it, and if you teach them how. Their beds can be a sanctuary instead of a scary place. Kids learn to self-soothe — when given the opportunity — by sucking their thumb or using pacifiers, or playing with toys. My daughters always had stuffed animals in their beds. Sometimes I'd wake up and find Susan talking to her teddy bear. Janet used to sing in bed. They all felt comfortable. We'd built a relationship of trust, and they learned that they could entertain themselves and meet a lot of their own needs — which meant that Stan and I got to sleep! A win-win.

As kids grow, they can be given more and more opportunities to build their own trustworthiness. Remember, the choices you make with your child will dictate the culture of your family. You always want to ask whether you're actively building trust or shutting your child down. For young children, each little achievement builds their trust and belief in themselves. They tie their own shoes, and it works! They put on their own clothes, and it works! They walk to school, and that works too! They can see the tangible results of their efforts. You can't trust a small child to make intelligent choices, but you can guide him in considering options and picking the best one. If I gave my nine-year-old grandson a lollipop and told him not to eat it, I know he still would. But if I explained why he shouldn't eat it, that sugar isn't healthy — that it might even give him cavities — and that eating before dinner will spoil his appetite, he'd be able to learn how to make better choices. Okay, he might still eat the lollipop, but if we worked on these kinds of decisions over time, he'd eventually build the skills for living a healthy life. And then I could trust him to take care of himself.

Each age brings its own instances of trust. Feeding is another opportunity. I gave my daughters as much finger food as possible, as soon as they were ready for solid food. It allowed them to learn to feed themselves. I still remember how they would "clean up" when they were done eating, which meant throwing the food they didn't want on the floor. The floor was a mess, but my daughters were also capable of feeding themselves and determining when they were full. A little later on, when they were around five years old, I could ask whether they were hungry, and I believed their answer. I did bring all kinds of snacks with me in case they misjudged their hunger. I was famous for carrying little yogurts whenever we left the house. When the girls were hungry, even little warm yogurts were welcome. And if we were on a long car ride and they didn't want to eat, I'd explain that we wouldn't stop at another restaurant for several hours and then let them determine what to do. I trusted them with their food decisions.

For teenagers, parents can build trust in a series of steps. For instance, here's how I would build trust with shopping, one of my favorite educational activities: 1) the parent does everything (selecting and buying the items needed); 2) trust your child to go with you to the store and make most of the purchasing decisions (giving kids a specific budget is a wonderful way to teach financial responsibility); 3) now your child is capable of gathering the items on her own, and you can meet afterward at the registers — on time — and make the final purchases together; 4) once you've built a foundation of trust and you've taught your child how to be responsible with money, give them your credit card and let them shop on their own (many major credit cards allow you to add a minor as an authorized user). Of course, make sure to check the charges and teach them to verify the credit card statement at the end of the month as well.

You can also gauge your teenager's trustworthiness by testing whether they make good on their word. They said they'd be home by eight p.m. Were they? If they were late, did they call? If they prove themselves trustworthy, keep increasing their freedoms and responsibilities. If they still need to learn to come home on time, have a conversation about what went wrong and troubleshoot together for the next time. Some kids just have a hard time being on time. Don't give up. Give them more opportunities to learn. Time management is a skill that many adults lack. That's why we have so many self-help books on time management. It's one of the most important skills for success in life.

If children aren't empowered with trust, if they don't feel trustworthy, they'll have a very difficult time becoming independent. The main problem is that they don't learn to trust and respect themselves. When we are fearful and hover over our children, they become afraid too. Yet children need to take risks. Kids really do copy what we model for them. I'm afraid of heights, but I wanted to make sure my kids weren't, so I was careful not to show my fear to them. I let them climb all kinds of playground equipment — but I stayed back. My daughters, though, were completely fearless.

Here is another simple mantra for you: Children need to take risks. You might need to repeat this to yourself on multiple occasions. Too many parents instinctually resist the idea.

TRUST IN ACTION

You'll be surprised what's possible. For sixteen years, I brought groups of fifty-two students on field trips to New York. The point was to visit editors at the nation's top publications and learn more about journalism in the real world. We met with staff at the *New York Times*, the *Wall Street Journal*, *Vanity Fair*, and *Sports Illustrated*, as well as with David Remnick, editor of *The New Yorker*, and other leading journalists such as Anderson Cooper. Every year was different, and every year was amazing. The kids loved it; I loved it, and it became legendary in Palo Alto. Everyone wanted to go on the New York trip. One of my motivations was to give students some freedom, to allow them to discover New York City, one of our country's most amazing cities, and to convince them that they were capable of a lot more than they thought. This was the most valuable lesson I could teach before they finished high school and left for college — belief in themselves to navigate a big city. I also wanted them to enjoy themselves, and I don't think anyone on any of those trips ever complained about not having enough fun.

In the mornings, we'd visit the publications and speak with editors, and the kids would navigate the subways with me — when I wasn't lost myself. I didn't know where I was going half the time, and it was empowering for the kids to lead me. They were much better at reading maps (in the 1990s) and using their phones (from 2000 on) than I was. They also saw me get lost and figure my way out of that. Getting lost is not a problem, provided you don't get stressed. I never did, even one day when I got on the train with half of my kids and watched the other half of the group zipping by in the opposite direction. There were a few frustrating minutes, but they used their cell phones and made their way to our destination despite the unintended detour. In all those years I never lost a kid. I did lose one chaperone who almost missed her flight back to San Francisco, but not a single child.

In the afternoons, they were free to explore the city in groups of four. I figured I'd taught them how to navigate and they'd be fine on their own. I was right. I also gave my students some control when it came to planning our excursions. They could decide what we would do in the evenings. Sadly, most high schools today do not allow any field trips that include even a little unchaperoned travel — kids may need to learn how to navigate a big city, but they won't learn that through school.

BROKEN TRUST

Whatever you do as a parent, your child will end up violating your trust at some point. That's part of life and part of the learning process. One student told me he was helping a friend who "had a bad day." At first I thought, *Oh, that's nice of him.* Then I found out that he was at the shopping center across from the high school and had spent his afternoon not helping a friend, and not participating in my class, but eating cookies!

Well, I had to confront him. When he came back the next day, I told him I knew he'd been at the store. I also told him that the first thing he had to do was buy me a cookie! I use humor for many situations like this, whenever the infraction is not deeply serious. It was important to call him out, however, and important to give him even a lighthearted assignment. Kids should take an active step to repair the trust they've broken. It helps them to understand the impact of what they've done. But I'm not mean about it. Having a sense of humor keeps me from rupturing a relationship. Yes, I do get upset, and there is a penalty — trusting doesn't mean not holding kids accountable — but the punishment isn't to revoke trust. It's to enforce trust *even more*.

I always say that lack of trust and respect causes the problem, and these values are also the solution. Use trust to get trust. Instead of getting mad and cutting off a relationship when trust is broken, repair it. Look at those marriages that could be saved if people talked to each other. Students want my trust — even when they've screwed up. My actions told this particular student that he was important to me, though I was disappointed in his recent behavior. I gave him the chance to rectify things so I could continue believing in him. And something amazing happened: He never screwed up again.

This goes for more serious infractions, too. I once discovered that several of my students were storing their beer in the darkroom and drinking it on school property. They would spend hours in there — I thought they were developing photos. But one day I overheard a conversation and then realized what was really going on. After observing the situation for a few days, I called them all into my office. It was a pretty tense discussion. I could tell they were scared.

I didn't yell at them, but I told them in no uncertain terms how disappointed I was in them, how they had violated my trust, and how they'd put the entire newspaper at risk. Unfortunately, if there is a serious violation like alcohol or drug consumption on campus, bullying, or any kind of sexual harassment, then it is out of my hands. I'm required to report it to the administration. That is true in most schools in the country. So I turned the kids in, and they were suspended from school for a week (the suspension was also noted on their transcripts). I didn't publish any of their stories in that week's edition of the paper.

Fortunately, none of them ever did it again. They were regretful and upset by what they'd done. And they understood why I had to turn them in, because we'd talked about it, and I'd explained my side of the situation. Like so many things when it comes to teenagers, it was just poor judgment on their behalf. I forgave them, they learned their lesson, and we were all able to restore the trust that is so important in my classroom.

Another inevitable truth of parenting is that at some point, despite your best efforts, your children might lose their trust in you. This happened to me — briefly — and has become one of our most famous family stories. The problem was that we had three teenage daughters who wanted to drive at the same time. Not easy for a family on a budget. Susan inherited our 1963 Volvo — with stick shift on the floor! — that we'd bought while living in Europe and shipped to California. I figured Volvos were the safest cars on the road and perfect for the beginning drivers in our family: anyone in an accident with a Volvo would lose. They're built like tanks — all steel, no plastic. By the time we gifted that car to Susan, it had more than 300,000 miles on it but was still going strong. When she took her driver's test, the DMV employee looked terrified! She passed with flying colors, probably because he wanted to get out of that ancient Volvo.

Susan was taken care of, but I still had to figure out what to do about Janet and Anne. We couldn't afford two more cars. But then I stumbled on a bargain: another trusty Volvo, this one a four-door sedan in that muted shade of brown that screams the 1970s. I love bargains, and I love Volvos. So I bought it and came up with a creative solution that I laugh about to this day. First, I gave the car to

Janet, who was a freshman at Stanford. She wanted to keep it with her at school, but I wisely said that there were parking problems on campus and it was expensive, and so she should leave the car at home. She agreed. But since the car was often sitting there, I decided to also "give it" to Anne, who was still in high school. Both girls thought it was "their car." A little white lie.

I know it sounds kind of crazy, but it worked for over a year. And then one day they found out that they'd each been "given" the car. As you can probably guess, they weren't happy with me. Actually, that's an understatement. They were furious. I apologized profusely and tried to explain myself. Eventually they listened. I told them I understood that they felt betrayed, and explained that my motivation had been to give them both the gift they wanted. In the end, they forgave me, partly because I agreed to buy another old car, but also because I listened to them. Listening makes such a huge difference. Plus, we could all laugh about it. Eventually. Even today they bring up this story. At least now they acknowledge my creativity: I'm never beyond being creative. Whenever I give Anne a gift, she always asks if it's really for her or if I've given it to Janet too!

By the time your kids get out into the work world, their ability to trust themselves, their ideas, and their coworkers will be a huge asset. Fearless kids have the best chance of succeeding — especially if they're innovators. I remember the early days of Google when Larry Page and Sergey Brin, the company's co-founders, agreed to rent the ground floor and garage of Susan's house as their first office space. They were two young computer scientists with a great idea, and they needed somewhere to work. Susan needed help paying her mortgage. It seemed like a perfect arrangement, and Larry and Sergey were obviously up to something super interesting, but Susan had no clue that they'd be there *all the time,* hunched over dozens of computers in the garage. Cables ran up and down the hallway, which I tripped on every time I visited. There was even a computer perched on the bathroom sink!

Having them in the house was exciting, but it also had some drawbacks. One was that they were hungry at night (not surprising because they never stopped working), and the closest food was in Susan's refrigerator — not part of their rental. When you're starving at two a.m., you just "borrow" the food and then plan to replenish it the next day. But when Susan came down in the morning for breakfast, her food was gone. Eventually she gave them her refrigerator when she bought herself a new one. That solved the problem — as long as they remembered to keep it stocked. Now there's food available twenty-four/seven for Google's employees, and that may be inspired by all those all-nighters at Susan's house.

Larry and Sergey were smart enough to understand that they had to focus on their product — Google — and that was more than a full-time job. Once they started hiring people, they were incredibly selective, and then were willing to delegate and give their workers massive responsibilities. This is how startups work: Employees have multiple jobs because there aren't enough people to fill each role. It's exhilarating but also exhausting. Their business model was about hiring the smartest and best people they could find and then trusting them to do the job. Of course that process was often chaotic, full of mistakes and missteps, and required that they have faith in their team. They were creating something new — these were uncharted waters. They completely rejected the idea that success was about perfection and tidiness and certainty, and that mind-set made all the difference.

When Larry and Sergey first moved in, Susan was working at Intel. She took a chance and joined Google as its sixteenth employee, and was immediately given large responsibilities, including marketing Google and creating several key consumer products such as Google Images and Google Books. Larry and Sergey were focused on the search engine and making the world's information searchable and useful to all of us. Their goal was not to make money; it was to make the best search engine, which was no small task. Susan was accustomed to having faith in herself and taking on big challenges, and she loved the atmosphere of freedom and trust, despite all the chaos. This company ethos powered some of Google's most renowned policies, including the 20 percent time policy, which was based on trust and respect for an employee's interests. Employees were given 20 percent of their time to work on individual projects that in some way related to Google's goals. They could choose anything they were passionate about. Gmail, for example, came out of a 20 percent project, as did a lot of other innovative programs and concepts. It was a perfect example of the role of trust in innovation. Google is consistently voted the number one place to work. And the company continues to show us that work can be a place to trust and respect each other in the process.

Don't we want to extend this same kind of trust to our children? Of course we want to train our children to work in an environment where they are trusted and respected, not monitored all the time. If we do, if our children have the trust and confidence to thrive on the cutting edge, they'll be the ones that companies like Google seek out. And they'll be the ones to have the next big breakthrough.

In 1998, I flew halfway around the world to Johannesburg, South Africa, to visit my daughter Janet. At that time Johannesburg was considered one of the most dangerous cities in the world outside of any active war zone due to the high crime rate. Janet had arrived there a year earlier and was teaching social anthropology at the University of Witwatersrand. She did not seem to be bothered by that statistic, but I was. Typical mother behavior. What kind of parent would want her child to willingly live in a high-risk, dangerous environment? I certainly didn't. Honestly, I was terrified. Before Janet left California, I tried to be logical. "Why Johannesburg? Why now? Isn't there somewhere else you could go, somewhere a little safer?" But I knew I couldn't stop her. And if I did try to fight her decision, I was sure I would lose.

On my second day there, she asked if I wanted to stay at home or go to work with her. Never one to turn down an adventure, I agreed to accompany her to the clinic in Soweto, or South Western Township, part of Johannesburg (1.8 million people) that was created during the apartheid years to separate and house the African population. Janet, true to form, failed to tell me much about Soweto, an area that both Nelson Mandela and Desmond Tutu had once called home.

We made our way in Janet's red Volkswagen through the streets of Johannesburg, onto the highway, and then into Soweto. Soweto is a heterogeneous area comprised of middle-class neighborhoods with larger homes and informal settlements with homes made out of corrugated iron that do not have running water or electricity. Janet explained to me that the population she was serving were sex workers and HIV-infected women. Poverty was rampant in certain parts of Soweto, and some women were forced by the lack of employment opportunities to exchange sex for money, which had contributed to the ongoing HIV epidemic. Janet had been brought in to study the epidemic and to do something about it. That sounded noble to me, of course, but it also sounded dangerous. I kept thinking: *What has Janet gotten herself into?*

Janet had always been passionate about African culture. At Stanford, she participated in a semester abroad program in Kenya, and she went on to receive a master's in African studies at UCLA. And then she went to Johannesburg to teach at the University of Witwatersrand. She'd found her calling, a way to use her unique talents and passions, and as scared as I was for her safety, I didn't want to stand in her way.

We parked in front of the clinic. For a second I hesitated. But Janet motioned to me and started toward the door. She looked so confident, so capable, in this place so very different from where she'd grown up. She was in her element. I still didn't quite understand it, but I wanted to support her, and I wanted to know more.

Inside the clinic was a big waiting room filled with women, some in traditional African dress — brightly patterned skirts and wraps — sitting on chairs and on the floor. Dozens of children were there too. In the center was a big table made out of a door propped on cinder blocks. Janet greeted the women in English and Zulu and introduced me, the new guest, as her mother. The women sprang to their feet, started talking excitedly, and many of them hugged me. They were so kind, so enthusiastic. We later learned that bringing your mother to meet your friends is the very highest honor in the culture. And it was worth celebrating. Many of the women rushed back to their houses and prepared dishes with what little food they had. Soon the repurposed table in the clinic was filled with traditional South African food — vegetable stews, roasted squash, beans, and yellow rice. The food was delicious, and I was overwhelmed by how much these women had celebrated my daughter and me. The experience was more powerful than any Mother's Day I'd ever had. And while we were enjoying our meal inside the clinic, the men were outside, washing Janet's car. Again, to honor me, her mother!

I came away with a tremendous appreciation for the people of Soweto, and also such respect and pride for my daughter. I'd taught her to be fearless and to live with purpose, and there she was, contributing to the world, making it better each day.

Now, I'm not saying that Janet's work didn't make me nervous. It did, and it still does, but who am I to tell her what to do? My anxiety has to do with my fear, not hers. And I've learned over the years that I can't and shouldn't project my fear onto my daughters, despite how they always seem to be testing my resolve. When Susan lived in India after college, she got extremely ill and was fortunate enough to have taken Septra, a powerful antibiotic, with her. Thankfully it did the trick. She didn't tell me until she got home, but just hearing about it gave me nightmares. People can die from the kind of gastrointestinal infection that she had. Later, Janet was bitten on the butt by a rabid dog in Kenya (on her first trip to Africa)! Again, she didn't tell me. She couldn't. She was in a remote region and there were no cell phones. I found out only later that she'd done the whole rabies protocol on her own, and I was impressed that she'd known how to take care of herself. Similarly, my daughter Anne once told me she was taking "a tour" through Russia from Istanbul on the Trans-Siberian Express. Later I found out she was on a tour of one — that is, she did it all by herself. At one point I hadn't heard from her in months, and I got desperate. I knew she was visiting Krasnoyarsk, my mother's hometown in Siberia, so I decided to track her down. I hadn't spoken Russian in years, but you'd be surprised what you're capable of when you think your child might be in danger. I called every single hotel in Krasnoyarsk — and I found her.

When she answered the phone she was shocked and she said, "Mom! How did you find me?" I told her, "It wasn't easy, but I persisted." She wasn't very happy to hear from me, and of course she was fine. My daughters' travels were really a test of my trusting them to be independent and follow their dreams, and it had worked — even if it was hard on me. When their lives were different from the ones I'd imagined for them, I couldn't stop them. I gave up trying to ever control them: we weren't connected by some magic string. I could only support them in what they wanted to do. Sure, I was nervous a lot of the time. But I believed in them and we all got through it.

As parents we have to take ourselves in hand and trust that we taught our children to make good decisions. We have to trust the basic goodness of people and the basic goodness of the world. And sometimes, our children can be our greatest teachers.

RESPECT

3

Your Child Is Not Your Clone

LET THEM LEAD

My first grandson, Jacob, didn't want to walk. When he was eighteen months old, the whole family would watch in anticipation as he scooted around the living room on his butt, waiting, just waiting for him to prop himself up and take that first step. It was cute but concerned us. Susan, his mother, was really worried. So was I. But the doctor assured us there was nothing wrong with Jacob's legs. He was a healthy, normal toddler — except for the walking part. He seemed satisfied, scooting on the carpet to grab his toy truck or a stray Lego. It was as if he'd decided he would skip walking altogether. He couldn't understand what all the fuss was about.

Jacob's greatest love at that time was basketball. I used to visit him several times a week, and the main thing he wanted me to do was hold him up so he could throw a basketball into the hoop at the nearby park or into any hoop in anyone's driveway that he spotted from his stroller. I helped Jacob make baskets for hours on end. So did his parents. He would squeal in delight as the ball wound around the rim and then dropped through the basket. To him, it was the greatest thing on earth. So one day I took him to Gymboree, a gym for children, so he could crawl around and play — and be around a lot of basketballs.

The second we walked through the door, Jacob spotted a group of kids playing basketball. He lit up watching every move as they dribbled the ball and darted from side to side. One kid scored a three-point shot. After a brief celebration, the game was over. The basketball sat at center court. I swear to you Jacob got up and *ran* to the ball. He didn't walk: he ran! I watched him bend over and hoist the ball to his chest, triumphant. He'd known how to walk and stand the whole time. He just hadn't found a good reason to do it.

When we got back to Susan's house, I said, "Guess what? Jacob walks."

"What?" she said, turning off the tap and looking at me as if I were crazy.

"He walks and he runs," I told her.

Well, it wasn't exactly a magical transformation. The minute he got home, he was back to scooting on his butt. It took a few more days for him to realize that walking was a faster way to get to a basketball hoop. It also meant he could hold the ball at the same time — a very important skill. But once he understood the clear advantage of walking, he was completely hooked. And the rest of us relaxed.

I'm going to say this more than once: Parents need to calm down. Your kids will walk. They will talk. They will learn to use the bathroom. They'll do it in their own time. No one asks how old you were when you were toilet trained. Or when you gave up your pacifier. This is never cocktail conversation. My grandson was adhering to his own schedule, and he's turned out to be incredibly smart.

Respect is a complicated topic. First, there is respect for your child as an autonomous person. Respecting the timeline of a child's development isn't only about walking and talking. Patience — sometimes lots of it — is needed there. Development is also about turning into the person we're meant to be. And this process requires a deeper layer of respect: accepting a child for who he is and letting his life unfold accordingly. Kids need to be allowed to take the lead. That means *you* follow *them*. Children know who they are. Your job is to honor and respect that.

It pays to start early. Letting kids take the lead when they're young is important training for parents. It gives us the skills we need to deal with more, should I say, *advanced* tasks once they're older. Finding out who you are can be a messy and inefficient process. When kids are leading, they take all kinds of detours. Few find their passion right away. Honestly, most kids go through a period where they don't know what the heck they're doing — but I promise you eventually they'll figure it out.

Anne was the daughter who showed me the value of patience in parenting. She got her degree in biology from Yale, came back home to Palo Alto, and decided to become a professional babysitter. Yep, that's right: a babysitter. "Really?" I said. "After you worked so hard at college? What about biology?" The next thing I knew, she'd posted a handwritten advertisement at our local swim and tennis club, and shortly after that she was working for two families she adored. A month went by, then two. I was trying to give her time to figure out what she really wanted. Recent college graduates need to decompress and get their bearings. I wasn't one of those parents who had been forcing my daughter to interview for jobs during her entire senior year. Her college education was *her* experience. Still, I realized this might be a time when she could use a little advice.

One morning I said, "Anne, there's a job fair in Santa Clara. Don't you think you should go?" I figured it might show her what else was out there. Well, she went, but only as a favor to me. She came back and said the whole thing had been boring.

"You didn't meet anyone interesting?" I asked. It turns out she *had* met someone interesting, an investor who wanted to bring her to New York for an interview. What Anne was excited about, however, wasn't so much the prospect of her first major job out of college but the free trip to New York. Of course, I wanted her to go. The company put her up in the Helmsley Hotel on Forty-Second Street, and on the first night she called me from what sounded like the middle of a terrible rainstorm. "There's a phone in the shower!" she said, and proceeded to describe the hotel's amenities.

Her interview went well, and after a week the company offered her a job in their biotech investment fund. Stan and I were thrilled. What a great opportunity for Anne. It seemed like the perfect start to a fascinating career. For a moment I thought my work was finished.

"I don't know," Anne kept saying. "I like these families I'm babysitting for." At this point I was about ready to have a heart attack. I thought to myself: *There's no way this brilliant girl is going to be a babysitter for the next thirty years.* But I forced myself to say nothing. I knew I had to be patient, and to respect her choices, even if I disagreed with them.

Anne thought about her decision for a couple days, and then turned the offer down.

Okay, at this point I wanted an explanation. She kept saying she loved the kids she was babysitting, but I kept pointing out that she'd been offered a dream job. I wished *I* could have taken that job. But it wasn't what she wanted. So I had to calm down. And I did. I bought her a T-shirt that said BEST BABYSITTER, which she was. At least she was doing something productive.

After a few weeks, and likely after picking up on some ideas from her friends and from Stan and me, Anne started wondering if she'd made the wrong choice. "It might be fun to live in New York," I said. "It sounds like a good job."

Two weeks later, she called them back.

"We've been waiting for you," they told her — but they needed her to do one final interview, this time in Palo Alto. Always the California girl, Anne wore shorts and flip-flops. Imagine going to an interview in shorts and flip-flops not even knowing who'd be interviewing you! This was pre-Google, and she hadn't done her research. But we had to let her make her own decisions (and mistakes). How else would she learn?

The person who came to meet her was none other than Marcus Wallenberg himself, the prominent Swedish investor. It turned out to be a great interview despite Anne's choice of wardrobe, and that's how she started working in the Investor AB biotech fund for the Wallenberg family, an experience she loved and that led her to a career on Wall Street.

It all worked out well for Anne, but some children need a bit more guidance. Nowadays, many college graduates have no idea what they want to do, so they come home and sit there. Not a good plan. How do you know when to let them find their way and when to intervene? Here's my policy: They have to be doing *something*. Not doing anything is the problem. And "something" does not mean playing video games, unless your child is serious about becoming a gaming programmer. What we want is for our children to contribute to society in some way. They should earn a paycheck, or have an internship.

And there should be a limit on free rent. You want to give them time to land on their feet, but after six months or so, they should be paying to live in your home, even if it's at an insider's price. This is also a part of respect: holding your children to standards. Respectful parenting is supportive *and* demanding.

As a student at Berkeley, I had the unglamorous job of cleaning houses. It paid well, and it provided a good service to my customers. I also had the glamorous job of being a runway model for Roos Atkins, an upscale department store in San Francisco, and a catalogue model. That paid very well. In addition, I worked as a playground supervisor at the local Berkeley public schools. In some way, each of those jobs contributed to the world we live in. I wasn't sitting around waiting for a handout. I was a responsible member of society, and I was learning how to be an adult.

Susan had a temporary summer job filing and answering the phone at Palo Alto Sanitation, where she was in close communication with all the garbage trucks in Palo Alto. It was her responsibility to make sure they followed the route and got washed after they were finished each morning. Not a high-prestige job, but very useful and important. And it came with perks. I remember one day she called me excitedly to tell me that the workers had picked up a really nice red couch, and did I want it for the school. Of course I did. It was promptly delivered and became the most popular lounging spot in the media center. That red couch helped a lot of students write a lot of articles.

Beyond temporary jobs, seeing the world is the best education kids can have. It gives them great ideas. They can travel with a friend, volunteer in a foreign country, spend a few months learning another language, or work with a foundation they believe in. I serve as an advisor on Roadtrip Nation, where kids can travel around the United States and meet people from all walks of life. I'm also on the advisory board of Global Citizen Year, a gap-year program that helps connect kids with their passion. I always say to my students, "Take your pick, but do something!" And I have the same advice for parents: Be open-minded and let your child lead the way.

SEEING OURSELVES IN OUR CHILDREN

Sixteen-year-old Greg was a genius in graphic design. I first saw his drawings in the 1990s, when he was a student in my journalism program, and I knew he was something special. He'd draw the most beautiful landscapes and complex architectural designs, and he loved making page layouts for the school newspaper. At that time graphic design was still being done on paper, but I had a hunch that computer-based design would be big in the future, so I suggested Greg use a computer to draw. Why not add technology to his art? He loved the idea and ran with it.

The problem was that Greg's father was a physician and his mother was a medical researcher. The very last thing they wanted their son to become was some creative type, let alone a graphic designer. He was supposed to be a doctor, a lawyer, or — best of all — a scientist. His parents demanded he take an overwhelming load of AP science courses, so he spent most of his time studying and fighting for a little time to practice the art he loved. Greg did well academically because he was very smart — but he was miserable. Everyone could see it. By the time he got to his senior year, he was really depressed.

One day, about halfway through the fall semester, Greg's mother called me to discuss his grades. I invited both parents to talk after school. I was concerned about Greg and wanted to help. The parents told me that science was very important to them, and I respected their accomplishments. I could see why they wanted their son to follow in their footsteps. Here's the thing: The vision that parents have for their child's life is important. They sacrifice a lot for their children. I gave up my career for a decade to raise my daughters, and Stan worked day and night to support us (and because he was so passionate about physics). Our opinions and ideas matter. But sometimes a child has a different dream, a different path to follow.

Greg's parents and I brainstormed different strategies for using journalism to inspire him when it came to science. "How about having him write some articles about research at Stanford?" his mother suggested. They were laser-focused on making him "interested" in science. "I'll see what I can do," I told them, but at the same time I knew Greg already had different interests. Ones his parents refused to acknowledge.

I did suggest that Greg write some articles about scientific topics, which he did without much enthusiasm, but he kept drawing . . . all the time. He had notebooks and notebooks full. Drawing was inborn, part of his DNA. I was reminded of my father and what a great artist he was, but also how poor we were. Greg's parents were right to be concerned about what his life would be like if he chose a creative path. But their child simply didn't want to be a scientist.

I've seen this situation so often in my thirty-six years of teaching. Parents tend to define their goals for their children solely in terms of their own interests and experience — and they do this because they desperately want their children to succeed. I get it. It's coming from a good place. Parents also tend to project their fears and anxieties onto their children, especially when it comes to less familiar career and life choices. Better to do something safe, they think, than forge a new path. I see parents of elementary school kids who program their children into afterschool activities that the parent wants, not the child. What the child wants is to come home, hang out with friends, and play outside. In other words, to be a child. Later on, parents of high school kids are upset because their kids are "distant." Well, they're distant because they don't want to be told what to do all the time. They want to follow their passions and live their own lives. And instead they feel disrespected and misunderstood.

None of this got me anywhere with Greg's parents. The mother started calling me every week to "check in." She kept saying, "See what you can do to change his mind." Then his parents decided he needed a therapist. Greg went to the sessions, but nothing changed. He kept rebelling in his own polite way. He did his schoolwork for those science classes, but at the same time he dedicated himself to graphic design. He refused to fight with his parents, but he also refused to do what they told him. His whole existence was fixated on not becoming a physicist.

My policy is always to support students while also meeting the needs of the parents. It is tough. I told Greg, "I know we have to deal with your parents. Don't worry, I'll help you." And I did. I told him the only thing he had to worry about in my class was becoming who he wanted to be. In all of my years as a teacher, I've learned it's usually the parents who have a fit when they don't get what they want — not the kids.

My class became his passion, the antidote to the drudgery of his AP science classes. He spent hours creating graphic designs for the newspaper; he created an exceptional graphic for the back of our T-shirts; he helped redesign the pages so they looked professional.

He was always checking out magazines for new ideas. I subscribe to about twenty magazines and when I am done, they all end up in my classroom — even today.

Some twenty years later, Greg is a well-known graphic artist and web designer who runs a successful company in Los Angeles. He took a few physics classes in college to appease his parents but ultimately pursued his dream.

Another student, Lisa, wasn't as lucky. She was a beautiful girl, outgoing and social, a student body president and a born leader in my journalism program. Her dream was to be a teacher, but her parents wanted something more prestigious for her: medicine. And because she was a good daughter who wanted to please her mom and dad, she did what they asked. She completed pre-med studies at an Ivy League college and got into a prestigious medical school. She did well, graduated, and got married, in that order. Everyone expected her to go into pediatrics because she loved kids, but she decided to "postpone" practicing. That postponement has lasted twenty years. She never went into medicine. She decided she didn't want to be a doctor, no matter what — and she quit.

Lisa is now in her fifties. She took up valuable space in medical school, spent years studying something she never wanted to study, and did it all only to please her parents. What she ultimately wanted was to be a stay-at-home mother, and that's what she is today. She's happy. Finally.

The lesson in all of this: Children will listen to you — they want your approval and love — but if they want to be happy, they're going to have to listen to themselves.

Another one of my students was in constant war with her father about having to wear a headscarf at school. The family had moved to Palo Alto from Cairo, and though they were looking for a new life, the father was convinced that his daughter should conform to their religious norms. Most immigrant parents want their children to maintain the culture of the country of origin, for understandable reasons. Tradition is important. It's what sustains and defines us. But at the same time, these parents want their children to "become American." For a child, this is pretty confusing.

The parents are also confused. They make great sacrifices to give their child a better life, but they can also have a hard time respecting the culture of the new world. I remember my grandparents struggled with seeing me growing up as an American. They lived next door to us in Sunland-Tujunga and expected me to be like a religious Jewish girl from Chernivtsi, Ukraine. There was always tension about what I was doing and saying when I was a teenager. I definitely didn't act like I'd been raised in Ukraine. There were two things that shocked them: one was my height. I am five-ten and come from a family where the women were about five-two and the men were five-seven. Sunday family conversation always included someone asking, "Has Esther grown this week again?" much to my horror as a self-conscious teen. I always worried that they had picked up the wrong baby in the hospital until my brother, Lee, grew to be six-two. My wanting to be a journalist was just as shocking. Girls were never journalists. "That's a career reserved for smart men," they told me, and at that time the journalistic world would have agreed with them. In so many cultures, children are assumed to be some mirror of the parent or grandparent, reflecting all the same values and choices — even physical characteristics, and when this doesn't happen, relationships break down.

My student from Cairo didn't come to me right away, but when I found her crying in the computer lab, I suggested she talk to her father honestly about her struggles. She tried that. It worked for a few weeks, but then her father told her she had to wear the headscarf. They continued to fight. Her father said that unless she conformed, she'd be thrown out of the house.

She was so desperate that she went to look at homeless shelters and asked her friends if she could live with them. Can you imagine a sixteen-year-old girl moving into a homeless shelter — on her own? She did end up moving in with a friend. And while she was out of the house, things got a little better. Thank goodness for the friend who took her in. But the problem was that she missed her family and they missed her. She was a teenager. She needed them. After a few months, the father said she could come back home, but only if she wore the headscarf, so she agreed. What an ordeal for all of them. This student was put in a position of having to choose between following what she thought was right and being part of her family. And her father, who wanted the best for her, failed to realize that sometimes moving to a different country means adapting to a different culture. Here's the hardest lesson for parents: You can't win a battle like this. You might say, "Until you are eighteen, you have to do it my way!" But your child knows she will turn eighteen, and she has every right to her opinions. Don't win a battle while losing a war.

We tend to see our child as an extension of ourselves. This is one of the primary reasons that we have kids — to live out our goals and dreams forever, to create replicas of ourselves so that all the wisdom we've gained won't be lost. Isn't that one of the first things you hear about a baby, that little Johnny looks just like his dad? Parents are always looking for signs of how their child is similar to them in looks and in personality, or like someone else in the family. It certainly doesn't help when a child looks exactly like her parent or behaves in the exact same way. It can be really confusing. Some people even think that a deceased relative has been reborn in the body of the new child. Sometimes it feels like our fates are sealed the day we're born. I recently met a man who told me that there were ten generations of doctors in his family, back several centuries. He was proud of this lineage, and he should be, but I wonder about the children who didn't want to follow that path.

Psychologists might call this the "ego" in parenting. "*I'm* the mother. This is *my* daughter." Naming kids after their parents or grandparents is a common symptom of parental ego: We think of that child as a replacement. Sometimes we try to measure our self-worth according to what our children achieve, the type of car they drive, or how much money they make. I call this the pet show — parading a child around to boost your own ego. "Look at what my kid can do, and he's only two years old!" I've seen videos of kids who can translate up to five languages by the time they are five, or kids who have memorized the times tables by age six. Who is happy about this? Clearly, it's the super-proud parent. I'm not so sure about the child. And have you ever wondered why some parents have trouble teaching their own children? It's because they see themselves — and all their insecurities and imperfections — in their children. When the child doesn't understand something right away, or god forbid fails, the parent is instantly angry and frustrated, the exact opposite of a good teacher.

If you think about it, this assumption that our children will follow in our footsteps is pretty problematic in the twenty-first century. It's so much harder to prepare for a career — because we don't know what the jobs will be. Ten years ago, who would have thought we'd have synthetic biology or 3D printing? Even seemingly stable professions like medicine are changing. Doctors now use electronic records, or they rely on robotics for surgery, and they take notes with Google Glass during consultations. In the near future, your x-rays might be more accurately read by robots. So maybe it isn't wise to encourage your child to become an accountant, even if it's been a great profession for you. Maybe accounting is a dying field. As Thomas Friedman says, this is the century of self-learning and passion. I think it's time we define "success" as "passion." And we all know kids don't develop passion through force.

Attempting to clone your kids in your own image, the failure to see and respect your children for who they are, can be a serious problem. As a teacher, I can see that kids are getting more depressed and desperate every year. According to the Department of Health and Human Services, roughly three million teens between the ages twelve and seventeen had at least one major depressive episode in 2016. There are a lot of reasons for this, ranging from the insecurity that comes from social media to an unmanageable load of high school classes to the pressure to get into the school of their dreams — or is it the school of their parents' dreams?

When the stress is too much to handle, kids can even be pushed to suicide. The CDC found that in 2016, suicide was the second leading cause of death for both ten- to fourteen-year-olds and fifteen-to twenty-four-year-olds. The overall trend is disturbing: Between 1999 and 2016, total suicides increased by 28 percent. Here in Palo Alto, we've had a string of teen suicides that shook our community to the core. Both local high schools, Gunn and Palo Alto, have taken serious steps to reduce the pressure on students. The former Palo Alto High principal Kim Diorio started a successful program with the help of Denise Pope, a Stanford education professor. The objective is to take the parental and societal pressure off kids so they can be themselves, focus on what is important to them, and realize that getting a B is not the end of the world. But how many other schools in the United States and across the world have adopted similar programs? How many kids are stressed and depressed? How many feel overwhelmed and misunderstood? The answer: lots.

Depression and suicide are complicated topics, I know. There are all kinds of risk factors. But at their core, aren't they really about kids feeling trapped, feeling forced into lives that aren't their own? And in some cases seeing no way out? When a researcher at Yale surveyed adolescents in affluent communities like Palo Alto, trying to discern the kinds of pressures they were under that might lead to suicide in extreme cases, she found two main causes of distress. The first was "pressure to succeed at multiple academic and extracurricular pursuits." This we know. But the second cause was isolation from parents. That's what happens when kids are not respected for their ideas, passions, or preferences. They learn to fear or resent their parents, which shuts down all communication. They are pushed away when they most need support.

Being respected for who we are is so fundamental that if someone — anyone — can show kids a little respect, they can be rescued, even when all seems lost. When I think about how important it is to find and nurture a kid's passion, to really understand him, I think of Caleb, a tall, handsome African American student in my freshman

English class. He smiled a lot, but there was a sadness in his eyes. This particular class had fifteen boys and three girls, all of whom were the lowest-performing English students in the school (below two or more grade levels in reading). I'd volunteered to teach the class. There weren't a lot of other teachers chomping at the bit to take on this challenge. But I wanted to help. I also wanted to know if my methods would work with non-performing kids. These students were struggling with all sorts of personal problems, and the traditional education system had done next to nothing to empower or encourage them.

As a teacher, I expect to have a few difficult students each semester, and Caleb was one of them. He didn't want to work. I could see he was depressed, even though he didn't display the common signs of depression. He had spent the first eight years of his schooling getting into trouble, and he figured this year would be no different. He had no goals. Well, he did have one goal: to disrupt the class. He got attention that way. A few weeks after school started, it became clear that Caleb was lost and unmotivated.

One day I stopped him after class. "Caleb, it looks like you'd prefer being somewhere else other than school," I said. "Is that true?"

"Yeah," he said. "I hate school."

"Really? Hate it?"

"Yeah. I really hate it."

We kept talking, and it came out that he lived in a small two-room apartment in East Palo Alto. His mom and sister were in the living room, and he was in the bedroom. It was hard for him to be in school with kids who had parents with so much money. His mom worked as a housecleaner, and the family struggled to pay the bills. "It isn't fun to hear what everyone is doing on the weekend, how much money they have," he said, looking pretty downtrodden. You can tell when a kid is depressed. Just look at their eyes. There's a dullness there, a lack of light. Caleb figured his chances of living past twenty-five were nil. He told me, "Black boys die early."

"Not all black boys die early," I said, "and you are going to be one who survives."

I decided to find out what he was interested in — everyone is interested in something. Turns out he was interested in shoes, of all things. Why? Shoes had status in his community, and they were something he could afford. People with certain kinds of shoes were considered "cool."

My next step was to encourage him to become an expert on shoes and how to buy them. I asked him to search for the kinds of shoes he wanted and compare the prices. Which shoes were the best and why? Which site offered the best price? I had him share his information with his friends. He liked that, too. Whenever kids can be experts in something, they feel good about themselves. They can be experts in Minecraft or in insects or whatever they want. It doesn't matter. They just need to be experts.

It sounds so simple, and hardly life-changing. But two things had happened: He now had a subject that he "owned," and he had one teacher who believed in him. Caleb started showing up on time, because he wanted to. His face changed. He smiled and wanted to talk to me all the time. And he did his work.

Caleb and I are still in touch. I take him to lunch sometimes. He's a sophomore now at a nearby community college with plans to be an electrician with his own company. What happened with Caleb can happen with all kids: we can rescue kids, through kindness and caring, through finding out about their passions and through having some trust and respect. Every student has potential, every student is worth rescuing.

WHEN RESPECT IS A CHALLENGE

Parenting presents so many challenges to the simple mandate to respect your kids. Take birth order, for instance. Raising one child is hard, but two is harder. And three or more means managing a daily circus. You only have two hands, and if there are three kids, what does the third kid hold on to? Every child is special and wants something different. Every child needs to differentiate themselves from their siblings, and every child needs to challenge their parents, especially as they grow older.

Birth order plays a major role in kids' development and how they choose to challenge you. With my daughters, I dealt with three individuals at three stages of development who all wanted different things. The firstborn child has the distinction of being the first, and the youngest child is the baby. But what about the middle child? If they're a different sex, he or she has that distinction, but if not, well, it isn't easy, but it's possible.

All of my daughters wanted to be held, have my attention, and, most important, be my "favorite." I remember one of their best-loved questions, always at inopportune times, such as at six thirty a.m.: "Mommy, am I your favorite?" You don't want that question at six thirty a.m. My answer was always this: Half asleep, I would hold up my hand and ask them, "Okay, which finger is my favorite? If I have to cut one off, which one should I cut off today?" That would do it. They would stop asking. Until the next week.

That explanation didn't stop Janet, the middle child, from wanting to be number one all the time. Younger siblings have two choices to attract attention: compete with their siblings, or rebel and be as different as possible. Janet chose the first. She always wanted to beat Susan, the firstborn, and she almost always did. She wanted to swim faster, run faster, read faster, talk faster, get more hugs, and be snuggled more. She did math early and started kindergarten at age four. It was amazing to see. She kept trying to be taller than Susan, though to her chagrin that didn't work. When Anne came along, Janet not only wanted to be as good as or better than Susan, but she also wanted to be as cute as Anne. She did a pretty good job, but it was hard to compete with Anne, who distinguished herself by being the ultimate charmer. You could see that in her even when she was only one year old. Smart kid. Being cute was the way to get what she wanted.

Birthday parties were tricky. I solved the problem by giving Janet birthday presents on Susan's birthday and doing the same thing for Susan on Janet's birthday. They agreed it was a great idea. Everyone got presents once Anne joined the family. A great boon for all.

Thousands of studies have looked at the effects of birth order, and most of them confirm what we know instinctively. People say that firstborns are more likely to conform. It's partly because they are outnumbered by two parents. But it's also because they have advantages over their younger siblings, so they can win parents' attention the easy way: just do what Mom and Dad want. According to Dr. Kevin Leman, a psychologist and author of *The Birth Order Book* and *The Firstborn Advantage,* firstborns are also held to higher standards. Well, you can see that didn't work in my family. Janet held herself up to the highest standards, and she succeeded. Leman says the middle child tends to be the "family peace-keeper" and is usually more agreeable and loyal. Maybe for some families. But I would never call Janet a peacekeeper. She was always up for something exciting and fun. If anything, she was the challenger, the inspirer, the creative spark. And in general, younger siblings are more likely "born to rebel," as the title of Frank Sulloway's book on the subject puts it.

What's buried in the research but rarely explicitly stated are the expectations we have for our children. If firstborns tend to be first at everything, that's probably because parents *expect* the first child to be first at everything. In our family, I expected *both* Susan and Janet to be good at what they wanted to do, and if they weren't good at it, they tried again. It was okay to make mistakes and start over. In fact, it was encouraged. After all, that's how children learn. And kids rise to your expectations. I had high standards for Susan, but I didn't exclude Janet from those standards. I expected both of them to meet my expectations, and when Anne was born, I had the same high expectations for her.

It bears repeating: Respect includes setting high standards. You don't respect your children's abilities if you coddle them. But you also don't respect your children if you force them to excel in activities that have no personal meaning for them. Enforcing high standards only works when kids can bring some passion to what they're doing. You want them to be successful in whatever *they* pick, not what *you* pick. That's one of the main problems: the parents are picking. Of course you can guide your children, but you should never force them. Otherwise there's a good chance they'll end up depressed and resentful. I watch Susan guide her five children; it isn't easy, because they have very different interests, but she respects that and encourages excellence in whatever they choose. Jacob loves music, so Susan supported his passion for the piano; Amelia is a gifted athlete, so Susan supported her joining the soccer team. Each child has the ability to choose, but the expectation is that they'll all perform at the highest possible level.

Sometimes your child might lose respect for you — but it can be repaired. It's harder when they're older, but it's still possible. One of the hardest things to do as a parent is to respect your child's privacy. And all kids need privacy — even infants. I asked my daughter Janet numerous times to clean her room when she was thirteen. She didn't listen, so one day I got fed up and decided I'd do it myself. Guess what I found underneath the bed? Her diary. I'm sorry to confess that I gave in to temptation and read it. It was fascinating to learn what she was doing and thinking, but I immediately knew that I'd violated her privacy. I felt horrible.

Some parents would probably have replaced the diary exactly as they found it and kept the incident a secret. But that didn't feel right to me. The only thing I could do was turn myself in. When Janet came home from school the next day, I confessed. I sheepishly gave the journal back to her. She screamed at me. She slammed her door and wouldn't let me anywhere near her room, but I kept apologizing. I explained to her that I'd lost my patience and done something I knew was wrong. I told her I was ashamed. Sometimes you have to help your children understand both sides of the story and the emotions you yourself are experiencing. I promised Janet I would never disrespect her privacy again. And she was kind enough to forgive me. Your children will see you make mistakes. They will learn more from how you respond to your own mistakes than from the mistake itself.

I can remember another time when my daughters did not want

me to come to a party where there were other parents. "You'll talk too much, Mom, and dominate," they said. My feelings were hurt, of course. But I thought to myself, *I don't want to invade their space if they don't want me there.* And they were probably right: I would dominate the conversation. So I didn't go and didn't hold a grudge. It was fine. I respected them, and it seemed as though we'd turned a corner. The next time there was a party, I was invited. I tried my best not to talk too much (a bit hard for me). What I think happened is that they wanted to feel in control, and when I agreed not to go, even just once, I reassured them that they were in control of their social lives. Saying it is not enough. Actions speak louder than words. That one party opened the door to my inclusion the next time, and I like to think I learned something they'd been trying to teach me.

I confess I had some learning to do when it came to my own grandchildren. I assumed that grandparents were like parents — a mistake a lot of people make — and that I could have as much control as I did with my daughters. Wrong. I was one of the worst about buying toys, clothes, candy. Just a relentless stream of gifts for my grandchildren, because I loved them. It turns out these gifts weren't always welcome. Susan looks at me suspiciously when I enter with a box or bag full of toys for the kids. "They don't need any more stuff, Mom," she tells me. "Okay," I say, "how about letting them play with the toys for an hour?" And I try to cut back, I really do. But I struggle.

I got into a habit of buying my granddaughter Sophie special sugar cookies that came not in a regular box but inside a plastic teddy bear. If you pushed a lever, a cookie came out. They were simple cookies but the packaging made them irresistible. What could I do? I kept buying them. But one morning Anne complained that Sophie had cried through the night: "She wanted *you*," she told me.

She was crying for me, but not because she wanted me. She wanted those cookies. Lesson learned. I was an overly enthusiastic grandmother who needed to be toned down. My daughters took care of that! *They* are the parents. I have to respect their ideas and wishes. They have their own families now.

TEACHING RESPECT MEANS LIVING IT

Sure, you should respect your child, and it would be great if that child also respects you. But have you ever thought about how you live in the world, how you show respect to the people around you, and what you're really modeling for your children? Everything — and I mean everything — is a learning opportunity. Kids don't miss a beat. They see (and feel) the respect that you show your spouse, other family members, neighbors, and friends. They hear how you talk about your boss and colleagues at work. They see how you respect yourself. And they pattern their own behavior and values from every single one of these.

Teaching respect means living it. Every day. It means respecting all the people in your life. If you model it, your kids will follow. Most of the time. They might need a little coaching. Whenever my girls misbehaved, I'd have them write me an apology and reflect on how they could improve (I guess I'm in good company, because Ruth Bader Ginsburg reportedly assigned essays when her children misbehaved). I'd have them apologize for anything they had done that was problematic. It could be fighting with their sister, being late for something, failing to do a job around the house. Writing is thinking, and thinking prompts change.

I've spent the past thirty-six years running my classroom as if it were the staff of a professional newspaper. That's how my program works. I don't give my students exercises that simulate a newspaper — they're tasked with all the real-world responsibilities, and they experience the real-world consequences. The student publications are self-supporting. That means the students go out and sell advertising to pay the publication costs. At the beginning of the semester, the whole class goes to downtown Palo Alto with contracts in hand and a copy of the newspaper to get advertising for the year. The students come up with the story ideas — not me. Some of those ideas are questionable, to say the least. But during our story idea session, led by the kids, the terrible ideas disappear on their own. The students always figure it out themselves. It happens naturally in the process of thinking it through and hearing other people's feedback.

Next, the editors make critical decisions about which students write which stories, and some of those stories are very sensitive. In the past we have written about poor teacher performance, student depression, students' attitudes toward sex, and irregularities on the school board, just to name a few. The most recent topics were about gun control and the Parkland, Florida, shooting as well as the resignation of our school principal.

What I've found over the years is that to meet deadlines and work under pressure, we have to have an atmosphere of respect. Journalism requires a lot of criticism and a lot of revision. I push the students to go far. Not only that, they push themselves and each other. They know I have their backs, so I don't mince words. When it comes to an editorial or feature article, I'll flat out say, "This ending needs some work. Do you want me to help you, or do you want to think about it yourself?" and we'll discuss how to make it better. You want to be sensitive to people who've worked hard. You want to respect them and their efforts. But I don't believe in everybody getting first place, and my students know it. I'll share which stories I think are the best for each issue and explain why. They do the same, and their opinion actually matters more. It is their newspaper or magazine, not mine. I am only the advisor. All of my students understand that I'm trying to make them more effective. I'm preparing them for the workplace, where they'll get criticism whether they want it or not. When they have a job and someone critiques their work, they'll be able to say, "Yes, I've experienced this before. I know what I need to improve, and I know I can improve."

Or it's the students who do the critiquing. My student editors are responsible for leading discussions about their fellow students' work. They have to manage a class of sixty kids, all of whom are reading and critiquing one another's articles. Imagine what amazing lessons they are learning, the most important of which is how to treat others with respect. My admonition at the beginning of the school year is "Be respectful if you expect the class to respect you. Never say mean things to anyone, and don't embarrass anyone in front of the class." I remind them that if they lose the respect of the class, getting it back is almost impossible. I don't let the editors yell at the class or say things like "Shut up." It's counterproductive. It shows lack of respect and creates a negative working environment. The kids get it right away. I don't have to belabor the point. They are all working toward the common goal: an outstanding newspaper. Have you ever seen groups of teens beg to stay at school late at night? That's what happens when they own the product and are obsessed with perfection. They realize the power of passion in life's work.

In 2016, we had an important election for new school board members. The *Campanile,* Palo Alto High School's newspaper, always makes recommendations about which candidates to vote for, and those recommendations are taken very seriously by the local community. In talking with my students, I realized we completely disagreed about which candidates to support. We all made our cases, arguing for what experience and expertise these people would bring to the school board. I respected their opinion, and they respected mine — but it's their newspaper. In the end, they won. The paper came out with the students' recommendations, and that article influenced the election.

Student teachers taught me another lesson about respect. For decades, I was a mentor for teachers earning their degrees at Stanford and the College of Notre Dame. I could usually size them up within the first two weeks as to whether they'd have a hard time learning to be an effective teacher. The main thing I looked for was their ability to connect with and respect the kids, to like the kids, and to laugh at themselves. If they strove for perfection through grades and punitive measures, it was going to be tough. Strict teachers expended a lot of energy getting angry at the kids for not following instructions, while they followed to a T their own guidebook on how to maintain control in the classroom. A former marine sergeant who couldn't communicate very well had a difficult time. While he had a lot to offer and was a smart teacher, kids hated his class and always wanted to transfer out. On the other hand, teachers who had high standards that were reachable through revision and mastery did very well.

What I try to do with everyone — students, student teachers, my daughters, and grandchildren — is respect them so that they can respect themselves. Amazing things happen when you have self-respect. Self-respect gives you the confidence to take risks and become independent. Without self-respect, you're afraid. You're obsessed with what other people think instead of following your own moral compass and your own passions. The number one regret people have on their deathbed is not pursuing their dreams and instead living a life someone else expected of them. Nobody wants this for their child.

I remember watching Anne ice-skating when she was only three years old. Stan and I couldn't skate to save our lives — Stan couldn't even walk on the ice without falling. But there was Anne, twirling and spinning around the rink, this tiny little girl who would grow up to be on a synchronized ice-skating team and play ice hockey in college and face all challenges with the fearlessness she displayed on the ice, doing something she loved — becoming who she was meant to be. The same thing happens with students. Sammy, the son of Mexican immigrants and a student beloved by the whole journalism program for his exceptional graphics, transformed before my eyes. He used the self-respect and confidence he gained in my program and through an advanced academic research program in which students pick their own topic to study for a year with the support of a community mentor to become an expert in graphic design, and went on to study it at San Francisco State University. He is the first person in his family to attend college.

As the poet Kahlil Gibran wrote: "Your children are not your children. / They are the sons and daughters of Life's longing for itself. / They come through you but not from you. / And though they are with you yet they belong not to you." Respect is what we want to give our children, but sometimes we are held back by our own insecurities. As parents, this is one of the most difficult obstacles to overcome, but we're all capable of treating our children respectfully if we keep the basics in mind. Honor their wishes and interests, which may be different from our own. Challenge them to be their best at whatever activities they choose. And above all, give them love and support so they gain the confidence they need to pursue their own path.

INDEPENDENCE

4

Don't Do Anything
for Your Children That They Can
Do for Themselves

IN THE FALL OF 2014, I found myself on a brightly lit stage in Puebla, Mexico. Seated next to me was Amy Chua, author of *Battle Hymn of the Tiger Mother* and a vocal proponent of tiger parenting, a form of strict child-rearing common in China and other Asian countries. We'd been invited to debate each other at the Ciudad de las Ideas Festival, an annual gathering of some of the world's brightest minds in education, public policy, and technology. The auditorium was filled with more than seven thousand people eager to hear how we'd raised our daughters.

It was a bit strange to be on a stage at such a large venue, but my innovative teaching philosophy and my daughters' success in Silicon Valley had gained me some recognition. I was voted California Teacher of the Year in 2002, and I helped to form GoogleEdu, a teacher and student resource platform. For years I consulted at the U.S. Department of Education, the Hewlett Foundation, and *Time* Magazine Education. I also cared deeply about empowering kids and was speaking out more and more about changes that needed to be made in the classroom and in the home.

I was concerned after reading Amy Chua's book, which was a bestseller. The stories she shared about her daughters troubled me. She represented a growing trend in parenting that I thought was, well, really wrong. I'm sure some parents were reading her book and disagreeing with it, but I suspect many of them thought they ought to be tigers themselves. Chua is well known for her controlling, top-down, demanding style. Essentially, her philosophy is that the parent knows best and it's their responsibility not only to guide their children but to *enforce* the kind of behavior that leads to success. A few examples: She forbade playdates because they were distracting and useless. She decided which activities her daughters would pursue, regardless of their preferences or interests. It wasn't good enough for her daughters to get an A– or to be number two in the class. They had to get As *and* be number one ("in every subject except gym and drama"). Doesn't sound like much fun, does it?

Once, while Chua was trying to teach her three-year-old daughter, Lulu, how to play the piano, Lulu only wanted to smash her fists on the keys. Of course she did: she was three! Chua grew frustrated and swung open the back door. It was a cold winter day. She gave her daughter the option of obeying her mother or going outside. The three-year-old considered her options and decided that being outside was less unpleasant.

I have to say, I admire this little girl's spirit. And I do admire Chua's serious devotion to her daughters. Obviously, she wouldn't have gone to these lengths if she didn't care deeply about them, just as I cared about mine. The question, though, was how much agency her daughters had in their own lives — in other words, independence.

It's true that they did have tremendous success at a young age. One of them even performed as a soloist at Carnegie Hall, which is quite an honor, but how happy did this make the child? Or was it more about Chua's happiness? The fact that Lulu rebelled, at one point growing so enraged over a dinner in Russia that she said she hated her life and threw a glass onto the ground, shattering it, shows that she felt trapped in an existence that wasn't her own.

Chua's views are not isolated. They are shared by many other parents. Every year in December, I receive gift cards, expensive presents from Bloomingdale's and Neiman Marcus, and delicious homemade foods from my students' parents. I'm grateful for these gifts, and I'm grateful for what they represent: serious appreciation for teachers. The issue, though, is that we differ in our ideas of what teachers are supposed to do. These parents are accustomed to a controlling educational environment, while I'm all about independence.

In the media coverage of our debate, I was labeled a "panda mother." Of course, the press needed a parallel to "tiger mother," but to me the metaphor doesn't fit. Pandas are famous for sleeping and eating, and not much else. They are called "lazy," which, of course, is silly, but that's the popular image. My parenting is not lazy, not hands-free. But I do believe strongly in independence. Parents should encourage their children to be independent and self-starting. Other variations on Chua's style include "snowplow parenting," the most evocative term, in my opinion, because it means clearing all obstacles, all challenges the child might encounter. Most of us by now have heard of helicopter parenting, sometimes called overparenting, which the author Julie Lythcott-Haims explores in depth in her best-selling book, *How to Raise an Adult*. She cites her years of experience as a dean of admissions at Stanford, increasingly working with college students who were "somehow not quite fully formed as humans. They seemed to be scanning the sidelines for Mom and Dad. Under-constructed. Existentially impotent."

Her diagnosis? These parents were so involved in their children's lives that the kids couldn't function on their own. This was due to a whole host of reasons, including a growing culture of fear, media misrepresentations of threats against children, decreasing family size, and the so-called self-esteem movement. It can go pretty far. Parents have been known to rent apartments in the cities where their children are enrolled as college students or even to accompany them on job interviews. I wish I were kidding.

When I spoke with Lythcott-Haims about this unfortunate trend in parenting, she emphasized, and I agree, that overinvolvement in a child's life usually comes from a good place. Parents want their kids to succeed, so it's very painful for them to see children fail. *What's the harm in stepping in,* they think, *and making sure my child doesn't struggle?* Well, there's a lot of harm. As Lythcott-Haims told me, "It renders kids useless. They're veal-like humans. Accomplished, lovely to look at, but they don't know how to think things through as adults." She makes a strong case in her book for how overprotective parenting has led to anxiety, depression, and an alarming inability to deal with adult life.

As a teacher, I've seen kids become less empowered, less independent, and more afraid each year. They're scared to take a stand, scared to be wrong, scared to investigate controversial stories, and especially scared to fail. Their main source of motivation seems to be fear: the fear of disappointing their (usually overprotective) parents. They've been taught that perfect grades and the perfect college are all that matters. Some kids in Beginning Journalism are horrified to have their names attached to their articles. Why? They're worried about what other people might think. They are not empowered. And they do not possess the skills to make it in the twenty-first century. Confronting this crisis in parenting was one of my main motivations for writing this book.

But back to the "debate." It didn't turn out to be much of one. Chua talked for the first fifteen of our thirty allotted minutes. She reflected on her own childhood, recalling how she was whacked on the hand with chopsticks if she uttered a single word in English at home, and how if she scored a 99 out of 100, her mother would focus on the one missed point to make sure the next score was perfect. Here's a glimpse of Chua's father from her book: "In eighth grade, I won second place in a history contest and brought my family to the awards ceremony. Somebody else had won the Kiwanis prize for the best all-around student. Afterward, my father said to me: 'Never, ever disgrace me like that again.'" Chua claimed in the book and onstage that her parents' methods worked, and that she has a wonderful relationship with them. I have no doubt that she learned a lot growing up in this kind of unforgiving environment. My question is whether it was worth repeating.

She also spent a fair amount of time defending how she'd applied these same techniques to her own daughters. At one point Chua admitted, "Parenting is the hardest thing I've ever done." For her, the experience was an extraordinary struggle. She'd felt torn between two cultures and seemed to be convinced that she had to control her daughters or risk losing them to the mediocrity that came with American privilege. "If you're not a policeperson in your own house," I told Chua, "then you don't end up having such a hard time parenting." You see, I had the opposite experience. I told the audience that parenting was fun for me, that it doesn't have to be such a grueling battle. Of course, that doesn't mean that parenting was without challenges, but I genuinely enjoyed it.

My main issue with Chua's method: It failed to instill a sense of independence or passion in her daughters. Her girls didn't really know what they were passionate about; they were too busy following directions. All instructions came from Chua, which meant her daughters weren't required to think independently. But in my household, we prized independent thinking above all else. The last thing I wanted were kids who couldn't function without my making all their decisions. Our goals had nothing to do with our daughters being number one in the class, which would mean that they had conformed and followed all the rules. I wanted them to find joy doing the things *they* cared about. I wanted them to confront problems in society and find innovative solutions. I wanted them to have warm and loving relationships with the people in their lives, including their parents.

Nobody is happy living a life that's dictated by someone else. If there's one thing I've learned as a mother and teacher, it's that kids of all ages need their independence.

So the question becomes: How?

THE BASICS OF BUILDING INDEPENDENCE

"My mother was determined to make us independent," Richard Branson wrote in his memoir *Losing My Virginity*. "When I was four years old, she stopped the car a few miles from our house and made me find my own way home across the fields." Four? Okay, this might not be the most appropriate way to teach a lesson, but Branson's mom was right about the importance of independence.

I felt the same way as a young mother. Perhaps this was a result of having been brought up in the 1950s when women had no rights . . . literally none. My mother had no money and no power. She always did what my father wanted. That's one of the reasons she didn't question the advice of the doctor who refused to treat my brother David. She never dared to challenge anyone who wielded power over her. The assumption was that I would live the same way.

But I rebelled — I learned how to sew my own clothes instead of waiting for hand-me-downs; I wrote articles for three cents a word as a teenager, dreaming of someday becoming a journalist, which I was told was a man's profession; I became a model to pay my way through college (those long, skinny legs came in handy after all). But in one way I did conform to the vision my parents had for me: I married young.

The night before my wedding, my mother-in-law showed me how to take care of my future husband's needs. "Here is how to make his bed," she told me, folding the top sheet with a kind of precision I had never seen and was pretty sure I couldn't replicate. Then we moved over to the dresser, where she showed me how to organize his clothing. And his breakfast order? I got that, too: scrambled eggs and poppy seed sweet rolls, with strong coffee. I am not making this up. There I was, about to become a wife and inheriting a caretaker role from a highly educated woman with a PhD, a pioneer in her own right.

I wanted a different kind of life for my daughters. That didn't mean they weren't going to be wives and mothers too; it just meant they weren't going to be held back because they'd been taught to be subservient. Their options wouldn't be limited because they were dependent on anyone, especially their parents. Independence, I decided, was going to start on day one. And I do mean from day one — from the very start, when they're babies and you think they need you hovering the most. That's when independence begins.

Let's revisit sleep: the single biggest source of confusion for parents of young children. Back in Chapter 2, I told you sleep was the first lesson in trust. It's also the first lesson in independence. Sleep is your child's first chance to self-soothe, to take care of her needs *on her own*. That last part is critical.

In Pamela Druckerman's international bestseller *Bringing Up Bébé*, she talks about the French "pause," the tradition in French parenting culture of waiting just a second before comforting a baby who wakes up in the night. Instead of immediately rushing in, French parents are told to pause, giving a child the chance to learn how to sleep on her own. Even newborns are thought of having responsibilities to the family. They have to learn how to sleep so the parents can sleep.

I didn't know anything about the "pause," but it turns out it's remarkably similar to what I did with my daughters. They spent some of their early years in France and Switzerland, so perhaps I was subconsciously influenced by those cultures.

New research supports what the French seem to understand intuitively: A 2017 study published in *Pediatrics* found that at four and nine months of age, babies who slept independently (in their own rooms) slept longer and had increased "sleep consolidation" (longer stretches of sleep).[5] Unfortunately, many of us never got this memo.

Dr. Janesta Noland, a well-known pediatrician based in Menlo

Park, California, says she commonly sees children at eight, nine, and ten months old who wake up throughout the night. There are even one-, two-, and three-year-olds who don't sleep through the night. Why? Because they haven't been taught. "Sometimes as parents we're frightened to give our kids the opportunity to learn," she says. "We feel like we're harming them, and that we're not supporting them in the way they need to be supported." Dr. Noland told me that at around three to four months of age, babies develop a kind of cognition that tells them they are an individual. "Suddenly they understand they're separate," she says, "and you want to get your baby out of your bed, and hopefully out of your room, before they learn this." According to Druckerman, the French have a similar theory about babies at four months of age: If they haven't learned to sleep by themselves at that point, it's going to be very difficult to teach them. They've learned that making a fuss means you'll rush in. Some babies (especially those with colic) can be more difficult. But the majority of children will benefit immensely from learning early on how to sleep through the night. And most important, it will put them firmly on the track to independence.

If you do have an older child who isn't sleeping through the night, the first thing I recommend is to talk to her. Explain that sleep is how kids grow. She may not understand completely, but communication is an important first step. It also helps to set an age-appropriate routine and follow it. Reading books (especially books about sleep) and singing songs are great rituals before bed — they're fun, and they make kids relaxed. Finally, and this is most important, do not rush in if they wake up in the middle of the night. Practice the "pause."

If sleep is about stepping back, then temper tantrums are about laying down the law. You know what temper tantrums are about? Control. That's right, a child wanting control over himself and his environment, which is a necessary step toward independence. What the child can't control as a toddler are his emotions. That's where the wailing and thrashing come in. But with time and a little patience, he can learn how to ask for something without falling to pieces.

Okay, so there are occasions when you probably should give your kids what they want without much discussion, as long as what they want has some value. If a child screamed because she wanted to go to the library, I'd tolerate that because I want to encourage a love of reading (though we would work on the screaming part). Once, we were at Disneyland when my girls decided they wanted to go on the "It's a Small World" water ride. *All afternoon.* Did you know that ride is only fifteen minutes long? We must have cycled through it a dozen times. It took days to get that song out of my head, yet my girls loved it, and I thought the song had a powerful message: it's a small world, and we're all alike. To me, they were learning an important lesson. I did have one rule that was non-negotiable, despite the anger it could cause: No public tantrums allowed, especially if they wanted something that I didn't consider important. One day we were at Macy's when Janet saw a toy she wanted, and she was going to have that toy or else. It was me against her. She had the wildest temper tantrum you've ever seen. She screamed like I had stuck a pin into her, and I had to march her out of the store and far away before she gave up. I'm not suggesting that parents can avoid this! But if you stick to a firm rule about it, eventually even the most willful child will learn.

Temper tantrums usually start around age two, when children are beginning to do things on their own. It can be putting on their shoes, brushing their hair, or dressing themselves. If you should dare to help them, watch out! They can easily fly into a tantrum and insist on starting all over and doing it *by themselves*. My advice? *Give them a chance*. It takes more time, it can be really, really frustrating, and they might end up with their shirt on backwards or their shoes on the wrong feet. I can't tell you how many times I let my daughters out of the house looking completely crazy, but I wanted them to feel they'd completed a task on their own. This is so important for instilling independence. You might not have time for this every day, but make a plan to occasionally give them the time they need. I suggest letting your child dress herself and do other simple tasks at least 20 percent of the time. Remember, it's a good sign that she wants to be independent.

For those really difficult tantrums, the kind where you find yourself dragging a thrashing child through Macy's, you have to reason with them. Children can be irrational. Really irrational. Sometimes logic doesn't work, especially with very young kids. But they need to learn to control themselves in order to learn independence. I encouraged my daughters to "use their words." I'd tell them, "I know you're sad and that you want something, but as long as you're having a tantrum, I can't help you." Young children are still human beings (with developing brains). "Tell Mommy what you want," I'd say, more than once. With time, kids learn to talk about their emotions. The one thing I knew for sure was that I couldn't give in. Otherwise they'd learn that acting out got a response from me, and then I'd really be in trouble. Parents: Watch out for this. Set clear boundaries. That cute little kid in the stroller knows exactly what he's doing! This is how children come to control *us* — but only if we let them.

On a more positive note, consider that your child feels safe enough with you to have a tantrum. Just think about it. They would never have a tantrum with someone they don't know or don't feel comfortable with. They wait until you come home to do it because they trust you. This is the road to independence, though it may be noisy and unpleasant. Don't take it personally.

And at times there's wisdom in a child's resistance. We lived in Switzerland from 1973–74, and both Janet and Susan attended the United Nations School in Geneva. (Susan was five at the time, and Janet was three.) They were both very independent and smart, but Janet was also determined to do everything Susan did. She even started talking at about the same time as Susan; she was that determined!

When it came to entering school, she did not like being assigned to a younger group. The UN school disagreed. If you were three, you were in the three-year-olds' class. But that didn't deter Janet.

Without permission, Janet moved herself to the five-year-olds' class. I still have no idea how she pulled this off. Janet was in that grade level for six weeks before the teachers figured out she wasn't in the right class, and this was only because someone overheard her saying she was three.

They moved her back with the three-year-olds. Janet was not happy. Never one to take an insult without a battle, she decided to quit school rather than be humiliated with those younger students. And she did. No matter what we said or did, she refused to go back. Eventually, we enrolled her in an all-French school. She was placed in her appropriate age group and wasn't thrilled about that but at least it was in French, which gave her a challenge.

By the time we got back to California the following year, she decided she was old enough to go to school. But the public school didn't take four-year-olds, so we enrolled her in the Ford Country Day School (a private school). She was right, and she excelled. She loved everything about reading, and by the end of first grade, she had nearly completed the math curriculum through grade five.

Janet showed me that children often know what's best for them. It's up to us as parents to listen — within reason. Yes, you need to step in when they want something dangerous or irrational: when a child wants to jump in a pool but can't swim, or if your daughter is having a crying fit because her ice cream is too cold. But if what they want is rational but inconvenient, consider striking a deal: "I'd love to let you go down the slide again, but we promised to meet Grandma for lunch and we don't want to be late. Let's make a plan to come back to the park tomorrow." And if they really want to take on a challenge or follow some passion that excites them, I say give them a chance.

When kids move past the toddler years, parents have to negotiate how to give the child control and where to lay down the law as they pursue new interests. For me, giving control was predicated on a foundation of safety. That was my first focus as a mother. We have a pool in our side yard — we're lucky to live in California — and I was always worried when the girls were young, even though the pool is fenced. So I decided they should learn how to swim as soon as possible, and I mean really swim, not just splash around. I wanted them to be able to jump in at one end of the pool, swim to the other end, and get out without assistance. I didn't think I needed to hire a teacher or take them to swimming lessons. I bought a book called *Teaching an Infant to Swim*. The black-and-white pictures made it look pretty easy. I learned that children hold their breath naturally, and that their attitude toward swimming, like so many things, is informed by their parents. We started with putting their heads underwater, then the doggie paddle, and then swimming the crawl. They weren't perfect, of course, but they were strong in the water. All of my daughters learned how to swim by the time they were two years old. Janet could swim at thirteen months (kids learn at different ages and rates, and parents should always take this into account and make safety their first priority).

Sometimes I'd take them to the Stanford Campus Recreation Association (SCRA), a faculty swim and tennis club, to meet friends. One April afternoon when Janet was about fifteen months, we were taking advantage of one of the first warm days in spring, and she was running around the pool area with Susan, who was then three. The next thing I knew, Janet jumped into the pool. I wasn't worried because she knew how to swim — I'd taught her myself — but an older gentleman sitting nearby sprang from his chair and leapt into the pool to "save" her. You should have seen Janet's face. She was shocked. It was great that he was so proactive, but Janet wanted to swim on her own. The man apologized to her — to a fifteen-month-old! — and swam off. After that, I made sure I told whomever was watching that Janet could swim.

Water safety was non-negotiable, but when it came to other activities, I put my girls in charge, for the most part. This is where I really differ from the tiger and helicopter parents. The last thing I want to do is force a kid into something he hates for hours on end. While we want to encourage children to try new things and not give up when they find an activity difficult, we still have to respect their feelings. We have to remember why our children have activities in the first place: to promote their interests and engagement in life and to develop their character. When it came to my daughters, any activity was okay — as long as they were doing *something*.

Though music was important to my husband and me, it never worked out for our girls. They took lessons in piano and violin for a while, but they didn't enjoy them. I pointed out that violins were portable, but that didn't work, and neither did cutting down from two lessons per week to one. Anne wanted to ice-skate. Janet liked swimming, and Susan liked tennis. So I let them choose their activities. The most important thing for me was that they pursue something they liked.

Appreciating *differences* is essential. My grandson Jacob is a talented musician and composer. During his senior year of high school, he staged an amazing musical at Menlo School called *Ones and Zeros*. He wrote the music and script and served as director and actor. But that doesn't mean that his siblings are the same. Jacob's sister Amelia doesn't play any instruments but for years took dance. Their brother Leon is great at chess, and he's a Lego master and plays golf. The youngest two, Emma and Ava, love ballet. There is so much to do in this world.

Another important point: Sticking with something is important, but parents need to allow for evolving interests. If the activity starts to feel like a chore, take a break and reevaluate. If they still want to quit, then I would let them look around for something else. Amelia is an incredible dancer who won national competitions for years. She used to train for hours a night and traveled around the country with her team. But last year she decided to focus on soccer instead. Her parents encouraged her to finish out the year — it was important to teach her not to quit mid-midseason. (This is one of many ways in which activities build character.) But they also asked her what she honestly preferred. Once she finished the dance season, she quit. A more controlling parent might have made her continue, arguing that she'd invested so much time and energy (and so much of the parents' money). Maybe she'd even become a professional dancer. But if that happened, whose life would she be living? How independent would she be, and would she be happy?

LAY OFF (IF AT ALL POSSIBLE)

For decades, fourth-graders in the state of California have participated in the California Mission Project. It's part of a social studies unit that teaches students about the history of the state. The assignment is simple: build a mission out of sugar cubes. Sounds like a fun project that can help bring history to life, right?

Wrong.

You should see some of these missions. They're elaborately engineered works of art. Arched corridors, bell towers, slanted tile roofs. But guess who's making them? It's not the students. It's usually the dads. Parents these days are highly competitive and controlling — it's hard to believe how much they feel they need to interfere. Some teachers have stopped the project altogether because they know the kids aren't making the missions, and why have a project for the parents? Other teachers warn the parents in advance that the kids should do the work. That seems an effective way to go — up to a point. A lot of parents cooperate, but there's still the occasional mission that belongs in a museum. We all know who did that one. When my daughters were in fourth grade, they made their own missions. It never occurred to me to help until I took their projects to class and saw the competition. Anne's mission looked like it had suffered an earthquake. She got points in my book for historical realism.

I always thought their homework was just that: *their* homework. They each had big desks in their rooms, and in the afternoons I knew they were there, doing homework. They did it without being prompted. It was part of the routine. Of course, there were no distractions like phones or tablets. But they liked doing their homework and keeping up in class. If they didn't do it, it was *their* problem. Though I did help on request, and it was usually fun for both of us. When it came to projects, I didn't concern myself with other parents who were stepping in way more than I did. I'd tell my daughters, "I believe in you, you can do this project well enough, and I'll like it no matter what." If they wanted my assistance, I would agree to help, but only if *they* directed *me*. I refused to do it for them.

In talking with my friend Maye Musk, a nutritionist and successful model and the mother of Elon Musk, I learned that we were on the same page. She never checked her kids' homework. She couldn't. She was working five jobs to make ends meet. When their assignments required a parent's approval, she had them practice her signature so they could sign for her. "I didn't have time," she told me, "and it was their work."

That's what kids need: not constantly being controlled or overprotected, but allowed to take responsibility for their own lives.

For parents, that means giving kids responsibility — early and often. To say it another way, this means *laying off.* You have to offer guidance and instruction, but they can do a lot more — and at a much younger age — than you think. When Susan was eighteen months old, she was my official helper. There were no baby monitors back then, and we lived in a big house. Her responsibility was to *be* the baby monitor. When Janet cried, Susan called out, "Mommy, Janet is crying!" Susan couldn't speak clearly, but that didn't matter. She was in charge, and she was very proud of herself. And she felt like an important member of the family. She also helped fold diapers. She thought it was a game. Well, I made it into a game. While she wasn't that great at folding diapers, it was good enough for me. I just wanted her to be proud of the job she'd done. After all, they were just diapers. I suggest all children have a job that's theirs and theirs alone. They'll build skills toward independence and also learn how to help out around the house — a critical lesson for both girls and boys.

Later Susan took on the role of "Janet's teacher." She gave Janet toys, showed her how the rattles worked, and made sure Janet always had something to do. A few years later in Geneva, it was pretty funny to watch Susan try to feed Anne mashed banana. Most of the food ended up on Anne's face, but Susan was happy to contribute to the family, even in a small way.

Washing dishes was another important chore in our house. All my daughters stood on a little stool at the sink and washed the dishes after dinner. They didn't wash everything perfectly — but it did teach responsibility to the family. My grandkids carry on this tradition today. Ava, who's just four years old, will pull up a stool and help her brother Leon with the dishes. My daughters were also expected to make their beds every morning. Ha! A bed made by a kid can look like she's still asleep in it. But I didn't fight them. As long as they did it, I was okay with it.

When we went grocery shopping, I'd ask the girls to get two pounds of apples and put them in the cart. Today there are those child-sized shopping carts for kids. But they didn't exist back then; my daughters had to deal with the big carts! They had to measure two pounds, and they had to know how to pick good apples, which I'd taught them. They knew the budget, too. And when we went over our budget, they helped me figure out which items to put back.

I made a point of giving them certain freedoms, even when they were young. One thing I let them control was decorating their own rooms (at least to some extent). They got to decide what they wanted their rooms to look like, and then they had to live with it. In those days, wall-to-wall carpeting was in. We went to the carpet store and they got to choose. At age six, Susan chose to decorate her room with hot pink shag carpet. And she had to live with it. (Susan always loved the rug; I was the one who failed to appreciate its beauty.) Years later, when Susan bought her own home, she'd had some experience with interior design (and I'm thankful she opted for more versatile neutral tones). Janet, not to be left out of this decorating opportunity, picked royal blue for her rug. I liked that better, but it was her room so that is all that mattered. When Anne was six, she too got to pick her carpet: lime green shag.

To be clear: I'm not talking about giving kids responsibilities they don't understand or aren't capable of, nor am I talking about letting kids play in the street if it isn't safe, or walk to the store if the neighborhood is dangerous. I also wouldn't leave a small child alone with an older child unless that child was a teenager. This kind of premature independence can be counterproductive if not traumatizing. But sometimes we can take it way too far. In Maryland, a ten-year-old and six-year-old brother and sister were taken into custody as they were walking unsupervised a few blocks from their home. A mother in Chicago reports being "mom-shamed" after a neighbor called the police because her eight-year-old daughter was walking the dog on her own. A recent op-ed in the *New York Times* tells the story of a mother who was arrested for leaving her four-year-old son alone in a car for five minutes (it was a cool day, the windows were cracked, the doors child-locked, and the alarm turned on). She went into a store to quickly buy something, and a passerby called 911. Thankfully, there has been some pushback. In May of 2018, Utah passed a "free-range kids" bill that allows children to enjoy previously illegal activities — like walking to school or playing outside alone. The state decided to redefine "neglect" so that it didn't include what a lot of people think are just basic freedoms for kids.

For me, independence has scaffolding and support. Chores and responsibilities require teaching and allow imperfect results. Freedom to roam the neighborhood (if it is indeed safe) comes with the obligation to call and check in. My daughters used to call me from the pay phone at the local pool. They had to stand on their tippy-toes to reach. It's a lot easier now with cell phones. Children should always have access to emergency numbers — they can be posted on the wall, but it's better if the child memorizes important numbers as well as your address. They should know emergency procedures in general, not only for when they're alone, but for when they're with their parents (what if something happens to you?). Don't forget your neighbors; they can be a wonderful source of extra support as your child is building independence. If you're leaving your child alone for the first time, make sure they have your cell number. Give them suggestions of what to do and tell them when you will be back. Structure it for them. In time, they will learn how to take care of themselves, but at first they need some guidance. Remember, kids are adults in training.

Something else you need to understand: When kids start to take control, a little chaos ensues. I'm reminded of this every time I enter the Media Arts Center during production week for our school newspaper. The building itself looks like it belongs on a college campus, but here it is, at a public high school in Palo Alto. It opened in 2015. All the journalism teachers in the program are eternally grateful to the school board and the citizens of Palo Alto for supporting its construction. Before the Media Arts Center was built, I spent thirty years in a portable classroom with erratically functioning air conditioning and scuffed linoleum flooring. For those who don't know, a portable is like a trailer. Well, it isn't like a trailer. It *is* a trailer. The school rolls them onto campus, hooks them up to electricity, and calls them classrooms.

On a typical production day, the madness begins at around three thirty p.m. That's when the kids start filing in, if they haven't been there all day already or half the previous night. They're lounging in beanbag chairs with their laptops or huddling around a computer in the lab, discovering errors that were supposed to have been corrected, complaining about how the color looks on the SpotLight page, or worrying about the ad that didn't come in on time. Many types of music are blaring, but these teenagers are concentrating in a way that can be impossible for adults to understand. There's also food: lots of food. I make sure they have snacks all afternoon (I love Costco!), and our dinners are provided by teams of parents. Sometimes we have In-N-Out burgers. Other nights it can be anything from Indian food to Egyptian food to homemade spaghetti and lasagna. We've had legendary meals over the years, including all-organic dinners brought and served by Steve Jobs and Laurene Powell Jobs, whose daughter, Lisa, was in the program in the mid-1990s.

It looks (and sounds) chaotic, but it's productive. I'm proud to report that in thirty-six years, there has never been a paper that failed to be published — not once. Okay, there were a few times where the paper came out a day late because the students missed the deadline, in which case they had to raise additional funds to cover the printer's five-hundred-dollar late fee, but it always comes out, and it always looks good. Almost always. One night more than twenty-five years ago, a student thought it would be funny to draw horns and a mustache on a school board member pictured in that week's paper. It was a joke, and he planned to take it off before the paper was published. Well, he forgot. I remember looking at the copies and thinking, *Oh my god! What are we going to do?* I drove to Target and bought one hundred black Sharpies. The kids sat there all afternoon and night, blocking out every single horn and mustache on all 2,500 copies. It wasn't funny at the time, but now I can see the humor.

The horns incident brings me to one of the most important aspects of my philosophy for both parents and teachers: the mastery system. The mastery system is based on how learning actually works, something a surprising number of parents and teachers don't understand. Here's the deal: Failure is part of learning. If you do something perfectly the first time, *there is no learning.* Mistakes are encouraged. Remember the motto of Silicon Valley? Fail fast, fail often, fail forward. Kids are *supposed* to screw up when they're kids so they screw up less as adults. Home and school are environments that should support learning, which means allowing for failure. But too many kids are afraid that if they do poorly on one math quiz, they'll never get into college. If they don't get elected class president, their parents will be disappointed. So many kids are suffering from the conflict of wanting to do something on their own and wanting to get it right. When does it end? How much perfection do we need? How long do we want to delay the actual process of learning? How can our kids function, let alone become independent, if they're completely afraid to fail?

Mastery means doing something as many times as it takes to get it right. Mastery doesn't happen automatically. It's a process. Being a teacher of writing taught me this. In the eighties and nineties, when I was developing my methods, one of the supposed characteristics of a good teacher — in addition to being in total control of the class — was that your class was so hard that many students failed. Your performance was based on the number of students you failed each semester. This sounds unbelievable today, but it was true.

I couldn't abide by this. It went against my gut and sense of decency. Kids who got an F on the first paper found it impossible to recover. And they were de-motivated to improve since they were starting out so far behind. I gave my students an opportunity to revise their work as many times as they wanted — imagine that! Their final grade was based on the final product. It was the learning and the hard work that I wanted to reward, not getting it right the first time. "Writer's block" completely disappeared. Students weren't afraid to make mistakes, so they could write without as much struggle. The English department accused me of being too easy, saying that my students weren't learning enough. But when time came for testing, my students performed in the ninetieth percentile on the state exams.

I realized along the way that it was important for the kids to know that I made mistakes too. After all, we never stop learning. If I'm confusing when I teach something, I'll apologize, say I messed up, and start over. Sometimes my students challenge me on my revisions or my thoughts on which articles to include in the newspaper, and I'll admit that I was wrong. Over the years, I've had the kids try all kinds of new software that didn't work out. Oops. So what? I can't tell you how helpful it is to demonstrate that you don't have all the answers. Kids tend to put teachers and parents on a pedestal, assuming we're perfect, that we never screw up. They're much better off once they learn the truth: Nobody's perfect, and everyone can learn.

Yes, we all make mistakes, especially kids, but you know what? Kids often come up with the best solutions — even better than yours. A few years ago my whole family — including all nine grandkids — went on a vacation to an absolutely beautiful resort in Napa Valley called Carneros. There were all kinds of activities for the kids. The only problem was that the kids were constantly on their phones. All parents know what it feels like to show your children something special only to have them glued to a device. It can drive you mad.

Some of my family members thought the best option was to confiscate the phones. That's what Rio de Janeiro and the whole country of France decided to do in their schools. In 2017, the French government announced that phones would be banned in all elementary and middle school classrooms. Though I agree with studies that show phones should be banned in elementary schools, I don't believe in confiscation for older kids, because technology provides a perfect way to teach them self-control. If we try to ban something, it only makes people want it more. Remember Prohibition?

I decided to talk to my grandkids. "Why don't you come up with a plan for how we should regulate these phones?" I said. You should have seen them light up when I suggested that *they* make the decision. They huddled together, talked about it, fought about it, and finally came up with a plan. Do you want to know what they decided? To ban phones all day long, from nine a.m. to nine p.m.! Can you believe that? It was way more restrictive than I would have proposed, and we all followed the choice they made for themselves.

Tech is one of the things parents ask me about the most. They're right to be concerned. A 2017 study found that both depressive symptoms and the rate of suicide increased in parallel with adolescents' screen time.[6] It's a crisis, and it's something we all have to learn to control. To that end, I hope it helps to share my Ten Commandments for Tech:

1. Set up a plan *with* your kids, not *for* your kids.
2. No phones during meals, whether in your house or someone else's. A 2018 study found that subjects who used their phones during dinner felt more distracted and experienced less enjoyment.[7]
3. No phones after bedtime. Children need to sleep, and phones are a distraction. Explain the critical importance of sleep for their brain development, and remind them that they grow when they sleep.
4. Use your discretion with small children. Younger kids, starting at age four, should be taught to use cell phones in case of an emergency. Show them how to call for help — they're smart and capable of learning. Starting in the third grade, children can be taught appropriate cell phone use for school assignments and at home.
5. Children should come up with their own cell phone policies for

family vacations, weekend events, or any kind of social activity where they need to be present. Be sure they also choose a penalty for disobeying their own policy (losing a certain amount of time on a device is a good way to teach them how to stick to the rules).

6. Parental controls can be important for young children. But after eight years of age, kids can learn self-control. If they violate your trust or your agreement, the parental control switches back on.

7. Parents should model how they expect their kids to behave around technology. I have seen parents on their cell phones nonstop, and they call that "family time." That is *not* family time.

8. Discuss with your kids what pictures are appropriate to take and what audio is appropriate to record. Sometimes kids lack common sense. Explain that whatever you do online (in written form or any type of media) leaves a digital footprint that you should be proud to share with the world.

9. Explain cyberbullying and help them understand its negative impact not only on others but on them. You never know what kids think or consider funny. Teaching children what defines humor is hard, but it's important. My rule: Laugh with your friends, not at them.

10. Teach kids not to give out personal identification information.

THE FRUITS OF INDEPENDENCE

Back in the eighties, my daughters were known in our Tolman Drive neighborhood as the lemon girls. One day they noticed our neighbor's lemon tree, and she nicely agreed to their plan of using it to start a business. They came up with a price (fifty cents per lemon), and sold their goods door-to-door. They even sold lemons back to the neighbor with the lemon tree. Once they filled up their piggy banks, they'd spend their earnings at their favorite dime store, Patterson's on California Avenue.

I guess being an entrepreneur runs in the family, because my granddaughter Mia has a successful business making and selling slime. Yes, slime. It's exactly what you think it is. Gooey, stringy, a total mess. But kids love it, especially when it has sparkles and rainbow colors. Mia was talented at designing new types of slime and got the bright idea to market it at age nine. My grandson Leon started working at a local arcade in Los Altos called Area 151 when he was thirteen years old. It was his idea to get a job there, not his parents'. Leon sells tokens to the customers, teaches them how to play the games, and even resets and repairs some of the machines. His latest obsession is bitcoins. Trust me, he is a self-made expert on cryptocurrency.

All of these projects came from a spark of curiosity, which itself arises from independent thinking. Do you want to know the single hardest assignment for my students? Coming up with their own topics. They find basic free-writing almost impossible. They complain that they don't know what's interesting. The main thing they want to know is if their "interesting idea" will earn an A. I tell them any idea is an A idea as long as they are interested in it, because if they're not, why would anyone else want to read it?

Lack of curiosity and the inability to free-write were such widespread issues in the 1990s, when I was an instructional supervisor for English, that I instituted a department-wide policy of daily free-writing for every student at Palo Alto High. I waited for the back-to-school sale at Target and bought two thousand notebooks. I don't think they expected a customer like me. They didn't have a limit at that time (they do now!), but they were surprised that I wanted to buy that many and asked if I was a reseller. "No," I said. "I'm a teacher and I'm buying these for all the kids at the high school." Once they heard that, they couldn't have been more helpful.

For the first few weeks, you'd have thought I was asking them to solve a difficult math problem. All I wanted them to do was free-write about any topic for the first ten minutes of the class. How hard could that be? Really hard, it turns out. Sometimes I brought up topics from the newspaper. "Look what happened yesterday," I'd say. "What do you think about this story?" They didn't even know what those stories were. But suddenly they were paying attention, taking an interest in the world around them, and forming their own opinions. They learned to love those notebooks, and writing every day became a welcome ritual that increased confidence and fluency. This exercise was the beginning of their independent thinking.

Students often don't know *why* they're learning something. Asking *why* is so important to kids and they deserve a better answer than "because it will be on the test." By the time kids reach middle school, they give up asking and focus on getting a good grade. To increase curiosity, it is important to address the "why" questions. Why are we reading *Hamlet*? Why are we solving quadratic equations? When teachers answer these questions, it prompts kids to think more deeply about the implications of what they're learning.

Parents can elicit curiosity in their children through similar methods. We don't need to have the right answers all the time, but we need to encourage kids to ask the right questions. If we don't know the answer, we can say, "Let's find out. Do some research on Google, and we can go from there." My grandson Noah is always asking about the stars, the planets, and the world around him, difficult questions like "What are black holes?" and "What does it mean to have a sound barrier?" Those are for my husband, the physicist. Noah asks questions about math, too — complex, philosophical questions. Again, those questions are for my husband, or, better yet, for Noah's father, Sergey.

When we support curiosity, what we're really developing is a child's imagination. Which brings me to creativity, a wonderful by-product of independence and curiosity. Unfortunately, when it comes to creativity and innovation, our kids are suffering. In one study, a test based on NASA's recruiting process for engineers and rocket scientists was used to measure creativity and innovative thinking in small children. At age five, 98 percent of the kids had genius-level imaginative abilities. But at age ten, only 30 percent of the children fell into that category. Want to guess how many adults maintain their creative thinking skills after making it through our educational system? Just 2 percent. No wonder Elon Musk says, "I hated going to school when I was a kid. It was torture." He hated it so much, in fact, that when it came to educating his sons, he decided to start his own school. It's called the Ad Astra School, and — you guessed it — the focus is on self-motivated learning, problem-solving, and an entrepreneurial mind-set. There's even a class on the ethics of artificial intelligence. Musk's solution is unique to his family; other families are pursuing their own solutions, including homeschooling, which has grown in popularity over the past few decades. Why? Because the parents had negative experiences in school themselves and are looking for a better alternative for their children.

Eddy Zhong, CEO of Leangap, a unique incubator for teen start-ups, sold his first tech company for $1.2 million at age sixteen and had a similar experience as a student. He claims that schools make kids less intelligent and less creative. As he says in his TED Talk, "The fact is, there are way too many people out there right now who are obsessed with telling kids to go to college, to find a good job, to be successful. There are not enough who are telling kids to explore more possibilities, to become entrepreneurs . . . No one has ever changed the world by doing what the world has told them to do."

Here's what you can do as a parent, even if your child's creativity isn't being encouraged at school: I used to set up all kinds of art supplies for my daughters on the kitchen table. There would be markers, colored paper, books, Play-Doh, yarn for braiding, and other arts and crafts. When they came home from school, they got to make whatever they wanted. I was always on the lookout for toys that they could assemble and design themselves. The YouTube Kids app now has instructional videos for any kind of creative project you can think of. My granddaughter Emma drew some pretty incredible pictures of animals — she probably could have sold them at age seven. How did she learn to do that? Following a YouTube video. There's also no shortage of videos on scientific experiments for kids, like the optical illusions that my grandson Leon loves. Dan Russell, a computer scientist in charge of search quality and user happiness at Google, was upset with his young daughter for spending too much time online — until he realized that she had taught herself five languages!

Projects like these allow kids to imagine and experiment and, most important, play. Creativity flows from a sense of play, and it's one of the easiest things to teach your child. Here's a tip: *Let them be*. They will create their own imaginary worlds without any help from you. Think of a child on a beach and all the wonderful games and adventures he creates on his own — collecting shells and rocks, building sandcastles, skipping stones, splashing in the waves. This is what makes kids happiest (and builds the right skills). Following the rules is not play, ever, unless you're pretending to be a policeman. And don't forget to play *with* them. One of my grandkids recently rated me the "craziest person" in my family because I get down to their level. I have been known to crawl under the table with the kids and bark with the dogs and have a sincere conversation with the cats. Sergey has the same playful spirit and for that reason was voted second craziest in the family. Steve Jobs had a similar attitude toward life, and even told his daughter, Lisa, that schools kill creativity. I remember him in our cramped classroom, camped out on the beige corduroy beanbag chair. He'd talk to the students, play on the computers, and, well, hang out. He never stopped playing and exploring, and we all know what came of his incredible imagination.

MAKE YOURSELF OBSOLETE

Now, I know this will sound crazy to some people, but here's my ultimate goal as a teacher and parent: to make myself obsolete. That's right. I want kids to be so independent that they no longer need me. Traditional education made the teacher into a "sage on the stage." The teacher knows all; the child's role is to listen. That is not my goal or my style. Well, maybe I was more of a teacher when they were young, but even then my goal was to point them toward ideas of their own. Passively receiving instructions or watching someone else performing are the worst ways to learn. As John Dewey, the famous educational psychologist, claimed at the beginning of the twentieth century, "Learning is doing." Dewey's ideas make a lot of sense. If you can't experience something, you can't fully understand it. *And you can't do it independently.* That's why I made myself a "guide on the side." My philosophy is not to have them ignore or not appreciate me; it's that they feel empowered to do everything themselves. That doesn't mean I don't want to be part of their lives, or that they don't love or respect me. It means that I want them to be so empowered that they feel comfortable acting independently. I help, I facilitate. But I'm not in charge, and I do not take over.

So what does this look like? My editors in chief run my classes. They take roll, open the class, set the tone, and determine the structure of the day. Why not? These are tasks they can do without me, and it gives them agency. They sit in five chairs at the head of the class and lead the discussions. They decide which stories to include, which to cut, which last-minute revisions need to be made. The students are always shocked when they realize this is how I conduct my classes.

I remember my very first editors in chief. The whole concept was new, for my students but also for me. One of the first stories the students wrote back in 1991 was about the alarming increase in teen pregnancies, an issue that mattered to them. In fact, one of the articles they wrote discussed how students need to learn to use protection. It felt a little daring for all of us, but we also knew it was important.

This was just after the 1988 Supreme Court *Hazelwood v.*

Kuhlmeier decision that limited the First Amendment rights of student journalists. Basically, anything they wanted to publish in the school newspaper could legally be censored by the principal or paper advisor. I thought this kind of censorship was absurd and un-American. So I disregarded the ruling, and so did the state of California. I was thankful when the state senate voted in an anti-*Hazelwood* education law that invalidated the decision (though *Hazelwood* is still the law in 36 states). Why shouldn't students have the same rights as all citizens? How else will they develop a voice to make a contribution to society?

Those articles about sexual activity had a major impact on school policy. As a result of that series, the Palo Alto School District decided to start a new course for all district students called Skills for Living. This course is still a requirement some thirty years later. The primary focus is how to protect yourself from sexually transmitted diseases and unwanted pregnancies, though it also teaches other important life skills, such as cooking and managing finances.

All because these students were free to write about what mattered.

Once students are engaged and empowered, there's no limit to what they can achieve. One of the most amazing things about seeing my daughters grow up is how they've turned into passionate, creative revolutionaries. Their goals are to make the world a better place for all people, all nations, all economic groups. Susan saw YouTube as a life-changing platform, which is why she convinced Google to buy it and worked hard to become its CEO. Her vision is to democratize video, to give people all over the world the chance to share their lives, their work, their opinions and ideas and products and services. The goal is to give everyone a voice. YouTube believes that the world is a better place when we listen, share, and build community through stories. This message is equally important in education, and I've been honored to collaborate with Susan on bringing YouTube into the classroom.

Meanwhile, Janet is on a radical mission to eradicate obesity in children and adults, and her number one target is the soda industry. She travels all over the world, to some of the most marginalized and needy communities, spreading this message about the dangers of sugar. She focuses on the health of pregnant women, infants, toddlers, and children, as well as the negative impact of sugar on the future population. To date, she has published more than a hundred research papers on various health-related topics ranging from the effects of obesity on breastfeeding to chronic disease in Alaska Native villages.

And then there's Anne, who left the man's world of Wall Street to forge her path in the medical world with 23andMe. Her focus is on empowering consumers to get the information they need about their health so they can make intelligent choices. One of her mottos is "No one cares more about your body than you." It was a major effort to convince the American Association of Physicians and the FDA of her mission, but she worked with them and showed them the power of giving each patient information about their risks for chronic diseases like Parkinson's, Alzheimer's, and breast cancer. Her idea is that once we are armed with this information, we can make lifestyle choices to dramatically reduce those risks. 23andMe is completely changing the landscape of patient knowledge and empowerment. It's a groundbreaking concept, and she's just getting started.

The thing is, we need creative, independent thinkers and revolutionaries now more than ever. Our kids will face so many challenges. They'll need to experiment and take risks and think for themselves just to survive. But they won't be able to do any of this if we control and overprotect them. We owe our kids their freedom so they can thrive in the most unpredictable century we've ever faced.

5

Give Your Child Grit

GADY EPSTEIN WOULDN'T TAKE no for an answer. His older brother, Amir, had been in my class, and Gady wanted to join too. The problem was, he couldn't fit Beginning Journalism into his schedule, but that didn't stop him from wanting to take it *now*. He was just fourteen, but he was so inquisitive and energetic. And persistent. I liked him right away.

We agreed to do an independent study, just the two of us, during his free period. It was great for him and fun for me. I love working with independent students because I really get to know them and their interests. Gady would find me at lunch and ask for feedback on a new paragraph he'd written. He was a fast runner who could spot me from the other side of the campus. I was impressed with his dedication.

From day one, he loved writing and reporting. He also loved reading the paper — I brought in sets of newspapers to class, local papers and sometimes the *New York Times*. Gady would always come to our meetings with ideas for articles — lots of ideas. And he was willing to revise as many times as necessary until he got it right.

As an eleventh-grader, Gady joined the Advanced Journalism

class. He did a great job working with the team, and in the spring of that year he decided to run for one of five editor in chief positions. It seemed logical because of his passion and hard work. He was really talented. I guess I assumed he would be elected. So did Gady. The election process, completely in the hands of the journalism students, includes a vote by the current editors, and while Gady was rated highly by his peers in his writing and leadership skills, he ended up losing the election.

This happens no matter how talented the student is. Gady was clearly upset, and so was I, but I have to honor the students' opinions.

For a couple weeks I was a bit worried about Gady. He was really bummed. After all, he wanted to be a journalist. But then one day he said, "I'm still going to work to make the *Campanile* the best it can be." "Okay," I said, impressed but still cautious. Teenagers change their minds all the time. But Gady did exactly what he said he would. He dove into the work with so much purpose that he became the go-to person on the staff. Everyone consulted with him. He wrote the best articles and assisted everyone who asked for help. Along with his classmate, Oliver Weisberg, he even mounted a sting operation at a local video store that was selling pornography to minors. As a result of the article they wrote, the police raided the store and shut it down for good.

The fall of his senior year, Gady decided to apply to Harvard. He didn't have a 4.0, and no, he hadn't been elected editor in chief, but he decided to try. I was honored to write his recommendation, in which I shared the story of the editor race and his subsequent behavior and passion as a team player. I described how Gady excelled despite this setback, and what a great writer he was. I guess my enthusiasm came through, because Harvard called me to talk about

Gady. I was stunned. I had never been called by the admissions office before. I explained how Gady performed at the highest level no matter the obstacles.

Harvard liked the sound of this — a lot. Gady got in without the fancy title, even without the 4.0 grade point average. He was accepted because they were more impressed by his character and his determination.

I have many stories about the editor in chief elections, which have become a litmus test for how children deal with loss and adversity. Every year, I tell my students about Gady Epstein. His is a story about how to cope with losing, how not to be defeated, even if you didn't win, and most important, how not to lose sight of your goals no matter what. It is a lesson for all of us, because we face disappointments constantly. Your reaction to those disappointments is what matters, and your reaction is something you can control. In fact, it's the only thing you can control.

Gady went off to Harvard, where he majored in international relations and followed his dream of becoming a journalist. After making his way through several jobs in the industry, including at the *Baltimore Sun* and *Forbes*, where he served as the Beijing bureau chief, he is now the *Economist*'s media editor.

Gady Epstein is not an isolated case. There are always students like him in my classes, and it's what keeps me excited about teaching after all these years. Driven by a meaningful goal, Gady pursued his devotion to journalism. What he had was a vision, and grit.

Grit is a popular buzzword in parenting and education. It means sticking with something no matter how hard it is or how much adversity you must face to achieve it. That's my definition. In her best-selling 2014 book *Grit: The Power of Passion and Perseverance*, the psychologist and researcher Angela Duckworth studied West Point cadets, inner-city Chicago high school students, salespeople, and contestants in the Scripps National Spelling Bee. As she searched for what made people in all walks of life successful over time, Duckworth found that "no matter the domain, the highly successful had a kind of ferocious determination that played out in two ways. First, these exemplars were unusually resilient and hardworking. Second, they knew in a very, very deep way what it was they wanted. They not only had determination, they had direction. It was this combination of passion and perseverance that made high achievers special. In a word, they had grit." More recently, other researchers have argued that grit is a combination of conscientiousness and perseverance, two traits long studied in the field of personality psychology. I agree that conscientiousness and perseverance are integral to grit, but when I think about grit, I also think about self-control, delayed gratification, patience, and courage, all aspects of grit that we'll explore in the coming pages. Duckworth's theory reflects my own: the most powerful kind of grit is coupled with passion.

Sometimes that passion or drive is automatic. Think of immigrants, like my own parents and so many others, who are known for having tremendous drive. The idea behind "immigrant grit" is that those who fought to leave their countries and remake their lives are by definition determined and focused. Amy Chua was worried about her daughters losing the edge that helped shape her own success. In *Battle Hymn of the Tiger Mother*, she writes of third-generation immigrants:

> This generation will be born into the great comforts of the upper middle class . . . They will have wealthy friends who get paid

for B-pluses. They may or may not attend private schools, but in either case they will expect expensive, brand-name clothes. Finally and most problematically, they will feel that they have individual rights guaranteed by the U.S. Constitution and therefore be much more likely to disobey their parents and ignore career advice. In short, all factors point to this generation being headed straight for decline.

Okay, maybe these kids aren't "headed straight for decline," but their lives aren't automatically filled with experiences that build grit. It's a variation on the old saying "shirtsleeves to shirtsleeves in three generations," referring to farmer's sons who made it to college and white-collar work, and whose children obediently followed suit, until the grandchildren, raised in too much comfort, lacking motivation, reverted back to manual labor. And there's some evidence showing that third-generation children of immigrants can lag behind previous generations and recent immigrants. One study of 10,795 adolescents found that children born outside the United States had higher academic achievement and school engagement than children born in the United States to both foreign-born and native-born parents.[8] Not surprising. There's a certain passion to make it here in America that dissipates over time. Shifts in the business sector show similar trends. Looking to the tech industry, we know that in 2016, immigrants in the United States founded or co-founded half of the billion-dollar startups. A 2017 study by the Center for American Entrepreneurship found that of the top thirty-five companies in the Fortune 500, 57 percent were founded or co-founded by an immigrant or the child of an immigrant. Sergey Brin is an immigrant. So is Elon Musk. And don't forget Albert Einstein. Sure, there are many variables to consider, but the inborn grit of immigrants and the success it leads to cannot be ignored.

Adversity itself can build a kind of automatic grit. Either you succumb to your circumstances or you fight tooth and nail to overcome them. In this case, grit is essentially your will to survive. Studies in "post-traumatic growth" have shown that children who suffered severe illnesses in their early years are more positive and resilient as adults. There's no shortage of examples that prove this point. Look at Oprah Winfrey. She survived childhood sexual abuse and inner-city poverty only to become a multi-billionaire media mogul widely considered one of the most powerful women in the world. Or Sonia Sotomayor. She developed Type 1 diabetes at seven years old and had to give herself insulin injections. Her father, an alcoholic with a third-grade education, died when she was nine. Her way out was education, just as it had been for me, and in 2009 she became the first Latina Supreme Court justice.

In the summer of 2018, the whole world was gripped as news broke of a Thai soccer team that was trapped in the Tham Luang cave due to flash floods. One of the soccer team members, fourteen-year-old Adul Sam-on, a stateless scholarship student whose parents sent him from Myanmar to Thailand in the hopes that he'd find a better life, played an instrumental role in the rescue because he could speak English with the British cave divers. His whole life up to that point had been an exercise in grit: He came from an impoverished, illiterate family, immigrated to Thailand, left his parents to live with a pastor and his wife so he could attend school, and against all odds flourished there, becoming the top student and winning numerous athletic awards. Is there any question that all the adversity he faced made him tough, resilient, and incredibly courageous?

I'm inspired by all of these people, perhaps because I see a hint of my own journey in theirs. As my daughter Anne says, I'm a believer. I had a real fighter mentality growing up. A lot of bad things happened in my life, but I taught my daughters that you can either let them control you, or you can make the rest of your life great.

I'm not arguing for imposing trauma or suffering on children. Obviously, adversity can have tremendous negative effects — physical and psychological — that can last well into adulthood. But I do want to point out that overcoming hardships can make us stronger, that sometimes it happens automatically, and that kids in difficult situations often end up building grit, resilience, patience, and other vital life skills.

But what about the rest of us? How do children raised in comfortable households develop grit? Are you praising your child's effort over his talent? Are you teaching him that setbacks are a necessary part of learning?

The answer: Probably not. Overprotective helicopter parenting has resulted in children who don't know how to do anything for themselves, let alone overcome fears and challenges and failures. They cry when they don't get the snack or toy they want. This is not a tragedy, but they can make you feel like it is. They're used to their parents giving in, and in some cases, catering to their every whim. They're not asked to do anything uncomfortable, so as adolescents they're way more conservative, and way more afraid. They're absolutely terrified to take risks.

Schools aren't helping matters when the system praises only the end result. Most teachers today are completely focused on assessments and numbers because their evaluation depends on their students' scores. They're trained to follow instructions, to obey. The whole educational model is based on not failing, not taking risks. If the students come to school with any grit at all, it is the grit to endure the system, not the grit of passion for something they love. I'm not saying all students lack determination and persistence, because it's clear to me and all teachers that many kids do have an admirable fighting spirit that serves them well, but I meet fewer and fewer kids who approach challenges the way Gady did. If they don't succeed, they look around for someone to blame. I swear, every semester my students walk into the beginning class looking like lambs. They're terrified. And they need help to find themselves and feel empowered. Learning comes when students are willing to take risks. Otherwise, it is called memorizing.

I'm not the only one who has noticed this change in student behavior. Recently, I visited Carol Dweck in her office at Stanford University. Dweck is one of the foremost experts when it comes to how we deal with setbacks. Her book, *Mindset*, first published in 2006, offered groundbreaking insights into the psychology of human success. Dweck describes two different belief systems, or mind-sets: *fixed* and *growth*. People with fixed mind-sets believe that our innate abilities are set. There are geniuses, and, well, not-geniuses, and there isn't anything they can do to change that. Why do they believe this? Because that's what parents and teachers taught them. As Dweck's research revealed, these subjects assumed "You were smart or you weren't, and failure meant you weren't. It was that simple."

On the other hand, people with growth mind-sets believe success is achieved through hard work and focus, and that failure is no reason to quit. People with this mind-set have been praised for their effort and dedication rather than their "brilliance." Subjects with growth mind-sets, Dweck explains, "knew that human qualities, such as intellectual skills, could be cultivated through effort ... Not only weren't they discouraged by failure, they didn't even think they were failing. They thought they were learning." It sounds a lot like my mastery system: learning involves failure, and you should keep working until you get it right. Dweck's research has shown that teaching people how to have a growth mind-set completely changes their idea about the meaning of challenge and failure. The growth mind-set gives us grit — and it can be learned.

Dweck talked with me about a trend she's observed in her students. "I don't think helicopter parenting is making kids stupid," she told me. "It's making them ineffective. They've been chauffeured everywhere, given little to no freedom. So how are they supposed to do something in the world later? A lot of them aren't going for careers. They're doing little gigs here and there. And I don't blame them. Because all your life you've had to live up to this standard, you've been anxious, all you want to do is not be anxious anymore." Does avoiding anxiety sound like a good source of motivation, or the right mind-set for pursuing meaningful goals? Is it giving kids grit?

Dweck went on to tell me about a freshman writing seminar that she began teaching in 2005. She assigns her students a private essay each week — read only by her — and when she first started, she would have an occasional student who wrote about being nervous and afraid. "But around five years ago," Dweck told me, "all of them, male and female, were saying they were terrified of making a mistake, terrified of exposing inadequacies, terrified of being found out." The exact same thing has happened in my classes. Dweck's advice to those fearful freshmen: "You're terrified because you think Stanford admitted you because they thought you were a genius. Wrong. You're not a genius. Stanford thinks you have a *contribution* to make to the school, and then the world." When she says this to her classes, there's a huge, collective sigh of relief.

Business leaders tell me a similar story. Stacey Bendet Eisner, an accomplished fashion designer and the owner of Alice + Olivia, a high-end women's clothing store, believes it is harder than ever to hire the right people. "I always talk about wanting to bring up a generation underneath me that's better, that knows more than I do," she said. "I want to hire better workers. But there's been this generation of parenting that's about doing everything for your children whether you have the financial means or not. And then these kids get into the world and can't accept criticism, can't do things for themselves, they expect someone to hand them everything, and it's a workplace disaster."

Jamie Simon is the executive director of Camp Tawonga, an incredible wilderness camp near Yosemite National Park. The whole camp is built on grit: Kids are responsible to their groups and are given tasks ranging from making sure everyone is wearing sunscreen and has taken their medications to scheduling the group's activities and coming up with policies that encourage both fun and kindness. They even have seven-year-olds doing overnight camping where they pack and carry their own gear (including cans of bear spray), and prepare and cook their own food. I wish every kid could have an experience like this. Ironically, for such a grit-focused camp, Simon has noticed changes in her college-aged counselors. In the past, the resident psychologist would work exclusively with young campers, but now she has to see the counselors as well. Why? Because they're disempowered and depressed and, well, gritless. It's not their fault; it's how they've been raised.

There's another equally troubling problem, which is the extreme *inverse* of gritlessness. Picture your average tiger or helicopter parents who set countless, sky-high goals for their children. Sometimes it works. They do instill a brand of grit in a child who's expected to be number one in all activities. She will be the perfect student and get into the perfect college. She will be the next Mozart. There are many kids who rise to the challenge despite all the pressure. They meet these insane goals and even surpass them. They're incredibly tough and resilient and high-achieving. But for almost all kids in these circumstances, the source of their grit is fear. Fear of failure. Fear of not being loved by their parents if they bring home a B+. Fear of not actually being the next Mozart (which is virtually certain to be the case). Grit and determination work against them living with purpose and being happy. They are overprogrammed and overcontrolled, forced into a life where goals are supplied for them, where stepping off the track of predetermined achievement means they completely fall apart.

Contrast this with grit that arises from the child's own passion. These kids have parents who see their child as a human being with his own opinions and interests and purpose. That purpose might disagree with theirs, but it's his to choose. He's encouraged to pursue his fascinations and set his own goals. When he inevitably fails, he's taught that mistakes are a natural part of learning and that he should stay focused. Obstacles don't deter him. He becomes strong enough to tolerate anything in his path — failure, boredom, distraction, intimidation. He just keeps going, no matter what, because he's driven by passion instead of fear. His motivation comes from inner goals, not external forces. The kind of grit that results is what drives the most remarkable kids I meet today, like the seventeen-year-old software developer from Cairo who's making an app to assist deaf people. It's not an easy process, and I'm sure he's been discouraged more than once, but he's determined to succeed and determined to help the hearing-impaired. Basically, he's unstoppable.

This is what we want to bring out in our kids: grit that flows from unbreakable and keen drive and carries them through any obstacle. With resilience. Toughness. Never giving up.

This, to me, is the kind of grit our children need.

GRIT IS A TEACHABLE SKILL

On the east side of Stanford's campus sits Bing Nursery School, beloved for its classrooms filled with games and toys and a massive outdoor play area. In the spring of 1972, Susan had been a student at Bing for almost two years when she was asked to participate in an educational experiment that sounded like fun. Susan was four years old at the time.

"We had marshmallows today," Susan announced as we walked to the parking lot, "and I got *two*." She told me she had been in a special game room and had been given a marshmallow. "If I could wait and not eat it right away, I'd get a second one," she said. She was super proud of herself for her restraint being rewarded. She couldn't stop talking about those marshmallows.

I later found out that Susan had been a participant in the famous marshmallow experiment. If you Google it, you'll find over two million hits describing Walter Mischel's groundbreaking research. Mischel wanted to test children's ability to delay gratification and assert self-control, and he wondered how these qualities affected them in adult life. In a way, he decided to torture the nursery school students — but nicely. His team of researchers would lead children ages four to five into an empty room at the school. A treat — often a marshmallow, but M&M's, Oreos, and other goodies were sometimes used — was placed on the table. The child was told they could eat the marshmallow right then, or they could wait by themselves until the researcher returned (after fifteen minutes, practically a lifetime for a little kid) and get two marshmallows instead of one. Some kids succumbed right away. The marshmallow was just too tempting. The kids who waited the longest found all kinds of creative ways to distract themselves — singing songs, dancing, sitting on their hands, looking anywhere but at the marshmallow. But what was most striking were the follow-up studies. Mischel and his research team found over the course of forty years that children who could delay gratification at a young age were "more cognitively and socially competent adolescents," had lower BMIs (body mass index), and fewer interpersonal problems as adults.[9]

Just as I was about to pull away from the nursery school, one of the researchers ran up to the car and told me that of all the students at Bing, Susan had waited the longest for her marshmallow. He seemed very proud. Though I didn't understand the experiment at the time, it makes sense now. Susan is one of the most patient and logical people I know. She's also tremendously calm under pressure. Nothing fazes her. She has enormous self-control. She surrounds herself with employees that she trusts and respects. She had all these traits as a young girl, and not because she'd been born that way, but because she'd been practicing for years.

Grit is made up of many different skills. I think of them as pieces of a puzzle: each is important. One major key is knowing yourself well enough to control your emotions and your behavior so that you can stay the course and not be swayed. I didn't set out to do it, but I had inadvertently been teaching delayed gratification at home long before Susan was tested with a marshmallow. For instance, when it came to food, my daughters knew there was a particular order to follow. I'd give them a small piece of candy with their main course, but they could only eat it after they finished their dinner. No exceptions. Another tactic: Whenever they wanted something, I always suggested a way to get it — but it usually took time. If they wanted to go swimming, for example, I would say, "Should we wait until it's a little warmer outside before we go to the pool?" Or another common request would be, "Can we go outside and play now?" My response: "Did you feed Truffle (the dog)?" or "Did you finish the drawing you started last night?" I can't really say why I did this, but I had a hunch that they should learn to control themselves as early as possible, even when tempted with candy or other treats.

Patience is another piece of the puzzle. I taught that, too: waiting and saving were part of our lives. We didn't have much money when the girls were growing up, so we saved for what we wanted. They each had their own piggy bank, and they filled them penny by penny. Every Sunday we cut coupons from the newspaper. Anne even developed a special coupon organizing system so they were easy to find while we were shopping.

Here's the opposite of teaching patience: letting a kid be online twenty-four/seven, with her device, in the car, in restaurants, at the dinner table. If I recommended that you take away your kids' devices in the car and teach them patience instead, I would be going against what 90 percent of parents are doing on a daily basis. I understand.

In today's world it's just not practical or realistic. But my method might be worth a try every once in a while. Have your child share with you what she's doing on her phone, or make a movie about your trip. Try a "Go Back in Time" day where you pretend there are no phones or iPads and see what your kids come up with. You could announce: "Let's pretend we are Grandma or Grandpa when they were little. What do you think they did in the car?" Make sure you're ready to sing.

Even as you pursue goals you're passionate about, you're bound to encounter boredom. Learning to deal with it is another important step in building grit. In class, especially during lectures (yes, I do give lectures in my Beginning Journalism class, to teach basic skills) students would sometimes complain that I couldn't hold their attention. I have an open enough relationship with my kids that they feel comfortable coming right out and telling me, "You've talked for such a long time. I'm bored. Can't we do something else?" Okay, so that's not very encouraging when you're standing in front of the class, but I never get mad at them. I seize this as a learning opportunity. Here's what I say: "I want you to go home and ask your parents something important . . . Ask them if they are ever bored at their jobs. If you come back tomorrow with the answer that they are never bored, then you can skip my lecture." This usually gets their attention. "Being bored is preparation for life," I tell them. "You are practicing right now." They laugh, but they all get it. Life is sometimes, or often, *boring*.

But I also teach them that we can make the most of these kinds of moments. You can count dots on the ceiling, or you can dream. You can think about your goals. What are your next steps? What obstacles might get in your way? What are new things to reach for? Where do you feel the most excitement, the most hope? All of this thinking can happen during so-called boring moments. Boredom could in fact lead you to surprising places and your next, big passion.

LEARNING TO FIGHT BACK

Courage is one of the most powerful expressions of grit. It's a kind of selfless determination. It can involve self-restraint and patience, and it always requires a strong sense of self and a willingness to stand up for what's right.

After the horrific school shooting in Parkland, Florida, many students there and elsewhere started to stand up for the cause of safety. It takes courage for them to protest, courage to become public figures, and courage to enter into political debates with adults. Kids everywhere are now seeing what is possible; they too can stand up for what they believe in. They don't have to just accept what adults tell them. Another important lesson for all schools is the power of debate, journalism, and drama in the curriculum. These subjects taught the Parkland students skills that enabled them to speak out and exert some control. They wrote in blogs and online. They spoke at vigils. They took to the streets to demonstrate. A group of Parkland students are on a mission called March for Our Lives, traveling around the country demanding gun law reform, trying to bring the nation together. They are now powerful participants in the democratic process, and powerful examples for other students.

Six weeks after the Parkland shooting, on March 29, 2018, the office at Palo Alto High School got a dramatic call. Jenny in the main office answered the phone. On the other end there was a male voice that warned, "Someone on campus has a gun, and they are going to shoot up the school this afternoon."

The school went into lockdown. It was ninety minutes of hell for the students, waiting to see if their classroom, their school, would be the next in a string of shootings. The call turned out to be a hoax, but the students suffered during that ninety-minute period. *Verde* magazine, one of the ten publications put out by the Palo Alto High Media Arts Center, published its next issue with what looked like a bullet hole through the entire eighty-page magazine. No matter which page you turned to, you found that bullet hole. That is how we all felt — tragically affected. The magazine, edited by Julie Cornfield, Emma Cockerell, Saurin Holdheim (all seventeen years old), and their advisor, Paul Kandell, went national. It was featured on CNN, CNBC, and ABC. It illustrated the stress and fear that students nationwide feel on a daily basis. And it showed their courage to think critically, take control, and stand up with an unexpected and creative response to senseless violence.

We want to raise our kids to be the courageous ones, the ones who have what it takes to speak out, to stand up, to be heard. We can start by talking about brave people and having them share their stories of courage. All you have to do is watch TV any night to find examples of people standing up for what they believe. You as a parent can demonstrate courage by speaking out to protect the values you believe in, even if they are not popular. No need to be nasty about it; in fact, the impact is far greater if you are polite but persistent. That way your kids can see courage in action.

Encourage your child to stand up for what is right — from an early age. It's okay for kids to talk back, as long as they're being respectful.

Parents who silence their kids are teaching the wrong skills. They are teaching them not to speak up about things that matter to them. Respect is important, but so is having a voice. Teach your child to be friends with the kid no one else wants to be friends with; to be friends with the kid who may have different ideas than he does, to talk about them. Teach your child to help the teacher when it isn't seen as cool and to share with other students in class. When your child is courageous, be sure to acknowledge it. If he sticks up for the kid everyone is ridiculing, that shows courage and empathy.

Sometimes, though, despite all our tenacity and courage, grit means knowing when to quit. Grittiness is needed even when it's time to back down gracefully. It's the skill that gives us the strength to make a change. Susan learned this when she was working on Google Video, a free video hosting service from Google that launched on January 25, 2005. In 2006, she realized that there was a product out there called YouTube — and it was growing faster than Google Video. It was also a free video hosting service, but with some features Google Video didn't have. Susan had to make a very difficult decision: keep working on Google Video, on which Google had already spent a lot of time and millions of dollars, or acquire YouTube, the faster-growing product. Looking at the facts, she admitted that she had to change her plans. It was then up to her to convince Google management that they should buy YouTube. It was no small feat, because the price tag was $1.65 billion. It was the right decision, as we all know today, but at the time it took a lot of grit for Susan to give up her own project and risk buying the competition.

We need to let our children know that it's okay to give up and to fail if something isn't working out. There's wisdom in learning how to fail fast, figuring out and admitting quickly if a project won't work. Remember my mastery system in teaching writing? I assume that an essay will not be perfect the first time or even the second time. The same is true for coding; most of the time there are bugs at the start. Some parents have heard about the importance of failure and have actually asked me, "How can I help arrange a failure for my child?" I'm not kidding. This is coming from a good place, but this is not how learning works. It's not up to us to orchestrate a failure. What we have to do is allow kids to work on their own projects and make their own decisions about when to try something else.

Failure is a necessary part of learning, and learning involves doing it yourself. If you fail, you are not alone. The majority of people will fail at something at some point. It's the ones who get back up and continue who ultimately succeed.

GRIT AND ABUNDANCE

According to the National Center for Children in Poverty, 21 percent of American children live in households with incomes below the poverty threshold, and 43 percent of children come from low-income families that struggle to cover basic living expenses. Poverty is devastating; I know firsthand. But there is a silver lining in every cloud, and the silver lining of poverty is grit. If you have limited resources, or no resources at all, whatever you want is going to take a lot of imagination, and you have no choice but to use your creativity. When I was a teenager, I wanted a nightstand, and we had no money to buy one. So I took free orange crates from the grocery store, painted them in exciting colors, and made them into nightstands. They looked pretty nice. I only got one pair of shoes as a child because shoes were expensive. My father used to say: "Why do you need two pairs? You only have one pair of feet." I polished my one pair of shoes every single night. I was still poor, but my shoes always looked new. I am sure kids in poverty today can tell you better stories than mine about how they innovate.

The grit I developed as a child has stayed with me for life. It is a way of thinking about the world and how to make it better. If your family is in this situation, it's a constant struggle and a problem all of us should be working together to solve, but know that your children are developing important coping skills and grit skills as long as they stick with it. These are skills that will serve them their whole lives.

It's at the other end of the wealth spectrum where we have a grit deficit. Too many kids have too many toys. Electronic games, Lego sets, high-tech bikes, rooms so full of stuff that they can't use it all. Even some low-income kids have an abundance of toys. We all want to give our kids a better or abundant life, but overindulgence can rob them of the desire to work hard for something. If kids get whatever they want, they never struggle, they never understand the real value of pursuing something, and they don't develop their creativity and grit.

But it doesn't have to be this way. For one, stop buying all those toys! (A lesson I needed to relearn as a grandmother.) First make sure they enjoy the ones they already have. Since when did shopping become a principal activity with children? Just taking them to the store tempts them into wanting more than they already have. What about going to the park or on a hike? What about letting them do projects around the house or hanging out with their friends? What about simply spending time with them playing board games or cooking?

And if they like cooking, let them bake their own birthday cakes. It's tempting to plan an extravagant party, but some birthday events today border on weddings. I have seen full-fledged *Frozen* princess parties that included an actress posing as Elsa, and an elaborate circus party with ponies. Okay, the kids loved these parties, but you know what they would love just as much? Planning their own day, coming up with the concept, helping decorate, being in charge. Give them a budget, and let them decide how to put the day together. Let them go online and search for what they want. Make them compare prices and be smart shoppers. If they want a magic show, see if they can hire a neighborhood kid.

Children should be in charge of their education, too — no matter who's paying. When kids are in charge, they care. How well do you treat a rented apartment? How does your behavior change if you actually own that apartment? I'm not arguing that you shouldn't pay your child's college tuition. We were fortunate enough to be able to pay for our daughters to go to college, and we believed in the value of education. Yet we made them pay for their own graduate school. I remember Susan being upset when we told her we wouldn't finance her graduate education. We knew she could get scholarships or teaching assistantships. And if it wouldn't have been possible for her to find funding, I would have *loaned* her the money. Not *given* it to her. That's an important difference. She was our first child, and so what we did for her is what we would have to do for all three. We figured that they were old enough to manage, and they did. Both Susan and Janet paid for graduate education, or got scholarships. While it was tough for Susan, she learned a heck of a lot more balancing graduate studies and work than if we had paid for it. Not to mention that she also has an incredible sense of accomplishment, rightfully proud of herself. She did it.

If you've spent decades saving to pay for your child's college, do it. But here's my tip: Have the kid pay the tuition bill, even if it's from your account. They can write the check, and you can sign it. Just the act of writing that amount of money makes them realize what you're sacrificing. They'll see the real costs. It makes such a psychological impact. They will never forget that. I wish I would have thought of this back when my daughters were in college (even though they didn't really need it — they took their education seriously).

No matter the family income, I strongly suggest all teens get jobs. There is no better way to learn about how the real world works. All three of my girls worked during high school. Susan coordinated garbage trucks (as mentioned) and she worked as a hostess at the Fish Market in Palo Alto, a fun job because all of her friends came to eat there. Janet and Anne both babysat. Heidi Roizen, now a venture capitalist and entrepreneur, was doing puppet shows at birthday parties when she was in high school. She earned eight hundred dollars a month doing those shows, and only made a bit more — a thousand dollars a month — in her first job out of Stanford.

I love employing teenagers — they're some of the most enthusiastic, creative, forthright workers out there. They tell you what they think. My students designed my website, and I just hired a local teenager to water the garden. I love being a launching pad. They get their first job with me, and then they're off and running. Early on,

23andMe, Anne's genomic testing company, hired teams of my students to run conferences. My students even organized a swim meet at Stanford for competitors over age fifty. I'm proud that my grandson Jacob landed a job as a camp cook for ten weeks before heading off to college. He's on his feet eight hours a day, serving three hundred kids per session. I saw him in action — it's hard work. But he has a fantastic attitude, and he's learning a lot about grit.

Remember, too, that you get to decide what you model for your child. Money was tight in our household, and a lot of what I did was out of necessity. But these ideas will work with any child, from any background.

Grit was just part of my character. Living in Los Angeles in the late fifties meant you had to have a car. On my sixteenth birthday, I got my driver's license and I celebrated like all sixteen-year-olds in the L.A. area: my parents bought me a 1948 olive green Studebaker — heavily used — for three hundred dollars, and my dad, an amateur mechanic, taught me how to take care of it. His philosophy was that I had to do everything myself, since we could not afford to service the car. I learned how to change the oil, tires, and spark plugs, and do a pretty decent tune-up. Years later, when we were living on the Stanford campus, the neighbors were shocked to see me on the street under the car, changing the oil. I was known for climbing up onto the roof and cleaning the gutters. It was how I had been raised. My daughters were watching all of this. They saw their mother as someone who could do (almost) anything.

They also saw me as someone with a lot of persistence and self-control. I have enormous self-control when it comes to eating. I guess I learned how to value food growing up, when there was never enough for the whole family. I also realize that this is one thing I can control about my health: what I put into my mouth. No one else is in control but me. I can sit at a fancy dinner with amazing food and not eat it. My reasoning is that if I'm not hungry, I'm not going to eat. Period. I taught my daughters this same self-control. I didn't want them to use food as an emotional escape. Food was nutrition and sustenance in our house.

Another lesson in grit for my daughters: When I got an idea in my head, I would pursue it no matter what. My determination was unstoppable. Our kitchen and family room had linoleum floors when we moved in. It was my fault: I picked that linoleum, but I didn't know what high-quality flooring looked like. After a couple of years, I began to dislike those floors. I really, really hated those floors. I wanted them out — and I wanted hardwood. But there was no way we could afford expensive floors. We barely had any furniture; our budget was maxed out. Stan didn't see anything wrong with the linoleum, so it was hard to get him to support my idea. Then I took matters into my own hands. Slowly, over the course of a year, I saved a little money every week from our food budget. My daughters observed the whole process, all of my persistence and determination (in secret, of course). That summer, Stan went to Europe for two weeks, and it was time to execute my plan. I didn't want to give Stan a chance to argue, so I did it all myself. I had shopped around beforehand for the best price, I found a great company to do the work, and I scheduled the work to start the day he left. When he came back, he went into the kitchen/family room area and was absolutely shocked to see the beautiful hardwood floors. "Looks great, doesn't it?" I said. Stan was speechless. He was afraid to say he liked it at first, probably because he wasn't sure where I had gotten the money to do it, but he admitted I'd done a nice job and he was thrilled when he learned that I had paid for it. We have those same floors forty years later, and they still look great.

I also tried to show my daughters the value of being an intelligent shopper and how to speak up when they saw a problem in the store. I always had this attitude that you want to improve the experience for yourself but also for other people. Sometimes a store would advertise an item for a discounted price, but by the time we got to the register, the clerk would try to charge me more. "Sorry," they'd say. "The price has been updated," or "It must have been mismarked." That never worked for me. I fought, called in the manager, and insisted on the advertised price. I always brought in the ad with me. I figured that if no one complained, then the store would continue to do this to all the customers, not just me. I thought, *Why is it okay for them to misadvertise, to bring in a customer on false pretense?* My daughters would hide, they were so embarrassed. Now stores are very careful about the listed prices, and often if they ring up the wrong price, you get a discount. I think those policies came from people like me! And I like to think my daughters learned how to avoid being misled, and how to stand up for yourself and for the little guy, that a company has an obligation to advertise with integrity and treat customers fairly.

Perhaps the most powerful aspect of grit is that it becomes *you*. But while it's tempting to view grit as an individual quality, it's much more inspiring when we recognize how it can change not only us but the world — in both small and large ways. Gady did this by giving his all to everyone working on the paper, and the Parkland kids did it by using the enormous platform they had in an attempt to finally change the laws that affect us all. Success does not exist in isolation. Grit, then, is about fluidity and going beyond self-interest into the strength we can create in the world at large. When we have the flexibility to find strength in numbers, all boats lift on a rising tide.

COLLABORATION

6

Don't Dictate, Collaborate

IT WAS MY FIRST YEAR of teaching, and I was at a breaking point. Each day I taught 125 students in five classes of English and journalism, and I was supposed to police every one of them. They had to listen to me lecture — on anything from essay writing to grammar to journalism ethics — and I had to pretend I was interested in what I was saying. I love grammar as much as any English teacher, but I was forced to give the same lecture five times a day. That's what high school teachers do: You repeat yourself every period (if you're teaching the same subject). Some people are really good at that. I'm not. I get bored. I never did well with a script that tells me exactly what to do each day. It didn't matter if a certain class needed more of a challenge, or more time to understand a new concept. But even worse was having to present myself as the "authority" day in and day out. I wanted to work with my students, not against them.

When I wasn't lecturing, they were supposed to work independently. They all had their books, they (mostly) took notes, and they were to do the exercises at the end of each chapter. My hands were constantly stained purple from churning out extra exercises I made myself using a typewriter and running off copies on a mimeograph machine in the mornings. Why go through the trouble? Because if the kids finished the exercises in the book, I needed something to occupy them. You should have seen their faces when they finally finished the most boring exercises ever designed (the people who write grammar books should be required to take a class in creativity), only to see me approaching their desks with more drills on the same topics. "Learning" was memorizing, and we were all suffering through it together.

By November, I was so stressed out that I had stomach problems and a series of colds. One of the older teachers said to me, "You should take some time off. You look pretty sick." Well, I *was* sick, and I looked as bad as I felt. But most of all, I was confused. I'd been dutifully following the administration's instructions and what I'd learned in graduate school. I had the training that all teachers at the UC Berkeley School of Education had back in the 1960s. The main takeaway: The teacher is the boss. I took numerous classes on how to manage students. In fact, we had a book called *How to Maintain Control of Your Classes*. We were graded on classroom management — how well mannered the students were, how "on task," how often they raised their hands before speaking. The idea was for students to know without a doubt that the teacher is in charge. No question ever. One of the most memorable tips from my administration was "Don't smile until Christmas." I'm not making this up. Ask teachers trained before 2000, at UC Berkeley or any other school.

My students weren't just unengaged; they were afraid. Afraid of me punishing and maybe even failing them. I was supposed to be afraid too — of the mask slipping, of exposing my inner goofball, who was dying to make a joke, but I figured I'd get fired if I did.

When one student saw me coming and grabbed a pencil to look excited about another grammar exercise, I returned to my desk and took a deep breath. Right then and there I decided I had to make a change. I couldn't remain in control of everything and everyone while keeping my sanity. I considered my options: Quit to save my health, go to therapy to save my mind, or do what I wanted and wait to be fired.

Surprisingly, the decision was pretty easy. My first step: Stop lecturing full-time and let the students work in groups for some of the class. If they had to learn grammar from *Warriner's English Grammar and Composition,* which was about as exciting as it sounds, at least they could do it together. Mind you, this was not traditional or acceptable. It was sacrilege. Here I was the new teacher on the block, already trying to break some of the rules. Not a smart idea. But I couldn't teach these kids anything if I didn't make learning more interesting. So they picked partners and worked on grammar and spelling in groups.

I felt a little freer. My wild sense of humor started coming through. I made up crazy stories that belonged on some kind of sitcom and had them add the punctuation. I also had the students generate their own material. They'd walk into class on a Monday, and I'd say, "Tell me what you did this weekend. Write it out, and punctuate it with your partner." Kids had the option of telling the truth or wildly exaggerating. Either was fine with me. I got a lot of stories about beer pong (I now consider myself an expert, though I've never played the game), accounts of strange accomplishments (like a kid who ate twenty-five candy bars in a row), and — you guessed it — sex stories. That's where I drew the line, despite their protests. "Your parents think you don't even know what sex is," I said, "so don't get me in trouble!" There was a lot of laughter in that classroom, but I wasn't afraid of disciplining them. I had their attention — because I was always doing such wacky things — and I had their trust.

Then one day the principal entered my classroom unannounced, made his way to the back row, and took a seat. Scanning the room, he noted that my students were working in pairs, or in groups of three. I panicked. All I could think was: Lecture! So I ran to the front of the class and started expounding upon the beauty of semi-colons. The kids looked at me like I was crazy. I mean, they always looked at me like I was crazy, but this time was different. They had no idea what was going on. I knew control was supposedly the most important thing, so I said, "Put down your pencils and listen to me," in my best Graduate School of Education style. Some kids listened, but two did not. The principal noted it on my "observation." "Class out of control and many students talking and not on task," he wrote. This was considered a serious problem.

The principal gave me three weeks to "get my classes under control." That meant silent students sitting in rows. No one talking when I was talking. Everyone taking notes. All period long. I was upset and again wondered if I should quit. Maybe I wasn't cut out to be a teacher. Many teachers today feel the same way. They're so pressured by the system to improve test scores that all they can do is teach the same material over and over. Today they use computers to help repeat the material, but the method remains the same. No flexibility, little creativity, and very few opportunities for the teacher to collaborate with the kids.

The rebel in me came up with an unusual idea. I decided to tell my students what was happening to me. The next time the principal came to evaluate me, they needed to be totally quiet or I was going to be fired. I actually told them that. I trusted them, and I had nothing to lose. "If you don't want the class to change, if you still want me as your teacher, you have to help me out," I said. It was a bold move to make them part of my scheme. But if we could work together, I thought, we just might pull it off.

The plan was to teach my way — collaboratively — until the first sign of the principal. At that moment, all students were to stop talking and face the front, where I would begin to lecture. We did a drill a few days later when I spotted the principal walking down the hallway. I bolted to the front of the class, and the kids stopped talking in an instant. Success! They loved the idea of being in on the plan. As my former student, now an assistant professor of sculpture at CSU Chico, Lauren Ruth, said: "One of the main things Woj did was deconstruct the hierarchy in the classroom. She was always breaking down systems. There was a special place that Woj could occupy that was different from a parent. She was a partner in crime. She trusted *us* enough to be that partner in crime. And there was something delightful about that experience."

Three weeks later the principal returned to observe me again, and the class was silent. I mean *silent*. It was like a morgue. And I passed with flying colors. "Glad to see you're in control," he said. He wanted to know how I had transformed my students in just a few weeks. I told him it was easy: "I made sure they knew I was in charge, and I stopped smiling, like they taught me in graduate school."

I got pretty gutsy after that.

In 1986, I walked past a store in the Los Altos Shopping Center that had a Macintosh computer in the window. "Hello" came up on its screen, like it was talking just to me. I had never seen anything like it, but I was pretty sure it was better than the Just-O-Writer typewriter that my students were using. It took hours to type up the stories in the school newspaper that they produced. I had to hire a student for a dollar per hour to type the stories for the kids who couldn't type. When there were mistakes, the stories had to be re-typed. That Macintosh looked like a godsend.

But I didn't have the funding. Then, purely by accident, I came across a State of California grant application for special funding. I filled out the request for seven Macintosh computers. My administration warned me that those grants were competitive. Not very encouraging, but guess who got the grant in the fall of 1987? Seven beautiful computers arrived at my portable classroom. I was thrilled, even though I couldn't figure out how to turn them on. For several weeks they sat in the back of my classroom until I announced to my students, "I'm so happy to tell you that I got a grant from the state, and now we have seven new computers!" They knew what computers were, but they'd never seen a Macintosh up close. No one at the school knew how to use them. The administration told me that these devices were "just a fad" and that they didn't have anyone to help me. Maybe I should have been discouraged, or even afraid — I had studied political science and English, not tech. Here's how ignorant I was: The first time I tried to use a Macintosh, I couldn't figure out where the words on my screen had gone. Turns out I scrolled too much. I didn't even know what scrolling was! But my students were way more skilled than I was, and they were excited to help.

"No problem," I told the administrators. "The kids and I will figure it out."

All of us spent extra hours after school and on weekends working on setting up the computers and learning to use them. I remember the Gill brothers — twins — and how they worked with the other students to figure out the mysterious science of Macs. Their father worked for Aldus Corporation and came in one Saturday to demonstrate how to use a program called PageMaker. It was perfect for the layout of the newspaper. We gladly took those Aldus disks — remember floppy disks? — and started using what would become a powerful digital platform for designing our newspaper, the *Campanile*. Then we had to figure out how to store our data. The kids did that, too.

It took us about six weeks to set up the seven computers, find a printer, network the machines, and organize our files. We were truly computer pioneers. Whenever something broke or we needed help (which was often), I would take a few kids and go to Fry's, the local electronics store. We got to know the store really well, and the kids became incredibly skilled in IT, way before that term became well known. If you haven't ever been to Fry's in Palo Alto, it is quite an experience. In the entrance there was a huge statue of a horse bucking on its hind legs. To me it represented the excitement about the coming tech revolution. Something big was happening, and we were part of it.

During that year I first got the idea to make T-shirts for the journalism program. Kids in sports got T-shirts, and we had a team, too. I'm proud to say there have been some amazing designs over the past thirty years, always done by the students: a graphic of me stomping on the school administration building, a shirt with a big coin on the front and TRUST IN WOJ on the back, and, recently, WOJ YOURSELF. The kids wear their shirts all over campus and Palo Alto.

What has happened in my classroom, from my first days teaching grammar to today's high-tech journalism, is all about collaboration.

Collaboration is only possible with a strong foundation of trust, respect, and independence. Kids also need a defined goal, one they feel passionate about. These elements have to be in place for students to work with one another, and mentor each other. My students practice these skills every day, and they've blown me away with their ability to support, educate, and inspire one another.

To produce a high-quality publication, my kids have to know journalism inside out. It isn't theoretical. They aren't memorizing material for a test and then forgetting it a few days later. They're writing and designing a complete newspaper, and they have to master the skills involved. I used to lecture on Adobe PageMaker and Photoshop, but the students would listen, take notes, and then go into the computer lab and have no idea how to use the programs. It never worked. You simply can't learn how to use a program by listening to somebody telling you how to do it. So I switched to a more interactive lecture where I would explain one aspect of the program and have them work on that function, and then we'd move on to the next step, alternating between lecture and practice. That worked better — but what worked best of all was having the students teach each other.

My idea was to pair each beginning student with an advanced student. We called the beginning students "cubbies." It was an affectionate term. Everyone had their cubbie. The advanced students got to pick whom they worked with, and they were responsible for making sure the beginning student knew how to do everything. I'd provide the structure, announcing, "Today we're working on improving our features," or, "Today we're improving our opinion pieces." Then we'd read examples together, and the cubbies would sketch a draft with an older student's help. Most of the time it worked perfectly, but not always. If a cubbie turned in work that needed further revision, I'd tell the older student, "Hey, your cubbie didn't write a very good news lead. Please go back and help him." Many times they would, but if they said, "I can't," or "I don't get it," then we'd talk about it some more — until they understood everything. Basically, I kept pawning off as much work as possible onto the students, and it turned out to be a tremendous success. Byron Zhang, one of my current students, who immigrated from China when he was in seventh grade, told me how important this mentorship was to his overall education. He was always a little shy about his written and spoken English, but his mentor helped him gain confidence in his abilities. He also valued the chance to be friends with students in other grade levels, which was rare outside of my class.

In all the years I've been doing this, I've never had a kid who didn't rise to the occasion. When you trust your students, and you help them structure their time and tasks, they can do it. But if you're fearful and don't believe in their abilities, well, they often can't.

Later I expanded this mentoring system to writing itself. It was impossible for me to give personal critiques to 150 students per day, but they could critique each other. And over the course of a year, students made significant improvements that both they and their partners could celebrate. Luckily, I got to provide feedback to Google on what was then called Writely, a new program that allowed my students to collaborate on their writing, and to edit each other's work. My students were some of the first users of what eventually became Google Docs, an application they, and millions of other students, still use today.

Again, I'm not saying it's always smooth sailing. There's an uncertainty factor anytime you're working with teenagers. Working with large, collaborative classes means you're going to have some chaos. But I happen to like the chaos. I guess I've developed a tolerance for it over time. There are times during production week when the kids play loud music and yell across the room and pay attention to three devices at once. I sit in the middle of it and do my own work.

It's hard to describe the impact this method of teaching has on kids. When students feel they can collaborate with their teachers, their self-image skyrockets and they feel absolutely empowered. They can do anything, because someone has their back. They can also weather disappointments, because they know they're a valuable member of the team no matter what. This year I have a very talented student who ran for editor in chief but lost. Sure, she was disappointed, but not for long. She has an important role as the school board representative, which means she attends all school board meetings and reports on the decisions that directly affect students. She also serves as a counselor in our journalism summer camp. She knows she's valuable to me and everyone else on the paper, and that's all the motivation she needs.

WORK WITH YOUR CHILDREN, NOT AGAINST THEM

It's unfortunate but true: A lot of people think the best way to educate kids both at home and at school is to be in total control. We think, *Children are young and know nothing. The parent has to show the way.* While kids like structure, too much structure doesn't bode well for their psychological health, according to some of the most important research done on parenting styles and their effects on children's behavior. In 1971, the developmental psychology researcher Diana Baumrind analyzed a group of 146 preschool children and their parents. She observed four distinct parenting styles: **authoritarian**, **authoritative**, **permissive**, and **uninvolved**. Let's break down the first two categories.

Authoritarian parents act like dictators. They focus primarily on obedience and following the rules. This is the parent who says it's my way or the highway, who is totally inflexible. By contrast, **authoritative** parents create a positive, warm, but firm relationship with the child. Most notably, these parents are willing to consider the child's opinions and engage in discussions and debates, which likely contributes to the development of social skills. As the Silicon Valley pediatrician Janesta Noland says, "An authoritative parent is one who sets some boundaries but does so through engagement — not your best friend, not a person who doesn't care about you, not a person who just wants to control you, but a person who is scaffolding you with expectations." Baumrind's original study found that authoritative parenting is associated with independent, purposeful behavior and social responsibility in both boys and girls.[10] Similarly, her follow-up study from 1991 found that authoritative parenting protected adolescents from problem drug use, proving that parenting styles have long-lasting influences on children.[11]

The last two categories are more self-explanatory: The **permissive** parent is prone to overindulgence and fails to enforce rules or expectations, taking a back seat in the child's life. Some people may misinterpret my philosophy as permissive or free-range parenting, but they're missing one important point: I never offer freedom without structure. I don't want my students to run wild in the Media Center; I want them to run wild with ideas for articles with a strong foundation in newswriting and a clear deadline. Big difference. I set high expectations. I just want the students to figure out how to meet them. The **uninvolved** parent backs away from his or her responsibilities, neglecting the child when it comes to attention, love, and guidance. Obviously a poor collaborator and a problematic caretaker.

There's a time and place for each kind of parenting, though the extremes are often excessive on a day-to-day basis. If you're in a dangerous situation, you might have to act like a dictator to command the attention and obedience you need from your child in the moment. You don't want to be consistently uninvolved, shoving your kids out the door and not knowing where they're going or when they'll be back, but there are moments when you do need to back off and keep your mouth shut. As far as authoritative parenting, I agree that you have to be firm with children when they're young and just starting to learn the elements of TRICK. It calms little kids knowing that someone is in charge. It gives them structure and direction.

But I think there might be another category. I'd like to call it the **collaborative** parent, someone who builds a relationship of mutual respect with their child once he or she is old enough to grasp the basics. For instance, if I were painting a child's bedroom, the authoritative style might be: "Here is the paint. Watch me paint first, and then you can do it the same way," while the collaborative style would give the child much more agency: "Let's go to the paint store and pick out a color. What color do you like? Now let's pick out brushes." This approach takes more time, but the child feels more like a collaborator than a worker. Giving them even a little choice can have a profound impact.

Kids seem to understand this naturally. We tend to think of toddlers as fixated on asserting their independence, but a study from 2017 found that kids as young as two experienced the same amount of joy when they achieved their own goals as when they helped another child achieve her goal.[12] Other research has shown that as children approach the age of three, they understand what it means to have obligations to a partner, and they can see their own perspective alongside others' perspectives.[13] It makes sense that collaboration is a natural impulse. Humans only survived because they figured out how to work together: there's strength in numbers. Collaboration is that powerful.

So why do we insist on dictating? Why are we so controlling? Aren't we trying to teach our children to function in a democratic society, to be able to live and work with others? The answer is we forget how important it is to let them practice having control, but that's what we have to do as parents, for the health of our children and the whole family.

THE PATH TO COLLABORATION

Like all the TRICK principles, collaboration starts with you, the parent. It's pretty hard to model collaboration if you don't know how to listen to others' opinions or if you're constantly attacking your partner because you think you know best. Remember, it's a team effort to conceive and raise a child. Your partner is your partner, not your adversary. And what you model is what you get. Kids are always watching.

But there will be disagreements. Kids misbehave and act completely crazy. They're not born with manners, and they are very self-centered. But as they grow they learn to think about others if that is what they observe. It's up to you to react in the moment, and that can be quite a challenge when your kid is throwing his food on the floor or having a meltdown in the toy store. Here's my suggestion: Try to avoid nasty fights with your partner (count to ten) and certainly don't have them in front of your child. But the annoyances and disagreements of daily life? Don't hide them. Seeing how you deal with them is exactly what your child needs. Kids learn from observing people airing their grievances and coming to some resolution. Don't hide the fact that you're upset, but model how to disagree in a way that helps resolve the issue.

Let's say your spouse comes home and wants to go out to dinner, but you have been cooking all day. Your spouse insists, "I'm tired of eating the same food all the time. I want to go out." A typical disagreement for couples. It's late in the day, you are both cranky. Your kids are watching! Your main objective? Find a compromise. That's what relationships are all about. Maybe you go out tomorrow night, or you save the leftovers for tomorrow and go out tonight. Don't blow the situation out of proportion. Keep your cool and find a solution. After all, this is really not an earth-shattering disagreement. Remember, kids watch us for a living. What kind of lessons are you teaching through your actions?

Collaboration in the home also depends on establishing the right pattern of communication. Talking to your child as a collaborator makes them feel like part of the team, and that's what families should be. This might seem subtle, especially when you're talking to little kids, but it makes a huge difference. Instead of commanding, "Put on your swimsuit. You're going swimming now," try a suggestion: "It's hot outside. Do you want to come swimming with us now?" Of course, sometimes you have to dictate. Some two- or three-year-olds would take over running the house if they could. But rather than dictating a child's afternoon activities, give him a say in the matter.

You are teaching them that they are heard and valued, even if they are little. "Do you want to go to the park or to the zoo? Would you like to play with your Legos or help Mommy prepare your snack?" I can just hear the likely answer: "I want to go get ice cream." And those kinds of answers have to be rejected. But the responses from kids can often be helpful. We need to avoid talking to them in ways we would never talk to our friends, especially when we're bossing them around. I see this all the time in public. I know how frustrated parents can get, but there are more collaborative ways to say "Get in the car," "Get off your phone," "Get over here." Also avoid saying things that can be hurtful long term, like "That was a stupid thing to do." We all make stupid choices, but saying this makes it worse. Keep the golden rule in mind: Would you want to be talked to the way you're talking to your child?

Collaboration doesn't have to be earth-shattering or huge in scope. Make it part of your daily living. For example, Susan and her family have dinner together every night. They go around the table and they all share one thing that happened to them that day. Even Ava, the four-year-old, reports on her day. It's a ritual that brings the family together and celebrates the importance of each child.

When it comes to chores and responsibilities, almost any task can be broken down into collaborative parts. At home, kids can play an important role in planning dinners: They can set the table, choose the recipes and help cook, and also clean up afterward. Keeping a home clean is a collaborative process, and the child should have a clear role in it. Who vacuums? Who does the laundry? Who takes the garbage out? Who's going to wash the car? Who's responsible for shoveling the snow? The overall idea should be that the house belongs to all of us, and we all need to work together to keep it nice. I'm not a servant, and you aren't either. Each of us has a responsibility to keep up our end of the bargain.

The same goes for school. I'm so impressed by the students in Japan who collaborate with each other to clean the classrooms, sweep the floors, and take out the trash. There are no custodians. They work together to keep their schools clean. We are a long way from the outstanding job that the Japanese kids do, but we at least try in most American schools by having the kids clean up after lunch. In the Palo Alto schools, students are responsible for separating their trash into the right bin (recycling or trash) and helping the custodians make sure the campus is in order. The kids in the journalism program take full responsibility for setting up the food for production nights when they stay late, and they clean up afterward. For the most part, they do a great job. And I make sure they know and value our custodians — we all share the responsibility, and we all care.

My favorite activity for teaching family collaboration is vacation planning — kids love it. You can offer a few options, and then the kids can research, pick a location, and choose activities. Here's the best part: Then you won't have to force them to do things. They will have planned it. In our family, Stan took the lead in planning our vacations. He had good ideas, and we trusted him to plan some pretty exceptional trips. We never took tours. Stan was the tour director, but always with input from the kids. Our daughters made suggestions every step of the way. We traveled to Spain when Susan was five years old, and I remember her picking out the restaurants. That kept her interested and excited. I'm not really sure how she made up her mind, but the meals we had were good. When we took hikes in the Swiss Alps, there were always choices, and we left it to the girls to make up their minds. "Should we take the longer route or the shorter one? Keep in mind, the shorter one is steeper. What's it going to be, kids?" They also chose which museums we would visit based on brochures. When they were part of the decision-making, they loved the museums. But I remember times when we didn't ask them. That was a mistake. Getting them into the museum was like taking them to the dentist! There were things Stan and I wanted to do too, so I would let the girls choose their time slot and activity. I'd say, "There's a whole day for us to plan, morning, noon, and night. You get to have input on one part — which part do you want?" They'd have an intense discussion and come to some consensus. We always honored it, though there was occasionally an exception when Stan argued, "I'm the oldest, and I might not ever get back here." The girls usually let him win that round.

I can't overemphasize the importance of friendships for children. Life is a series of collaborative relationships: first with parents, then with family and friends, then with teachers, and later on with mentors, colleagues, and the greater community. Every day my daughters had some kind of playdate or an art or science project with neighborhood kids. They were learning how to be a friend, how to share, how to get along. Most neighbors are a good and often unnoticed resource, easy to overlook in today's busy, overscheduled world.

And it doesn't always have to be kids. Children can be friends with people of all ages. We were great friends with an older couple next door who loved the girls, and so they would go over to visit whenever they felt like it. Turns out that our neighbor, George Dantzig, was a groundbreaking leader in the tech world, only we didn't know it for years, and he certainly never told us. He and his wife, Anne, were so friendly and down to earth. You never would have guessed.

But one day I noticed George had a study full of awards and honorary doctorates from countries around the world. *Hmm,* I wondered, *what did he do?* I learned that he'd developed the simplex algorithm, which solved the Internet's linear program problems, which then made the development of the Web possible. He was a humble man.

One evening when Anne was about two years old, she decided to take her doll for a walk and visit the Dantzigs. Our front door was unlocked, so she went out. The only problem was that she was stark naked, at a stage where she refused to put on clothing. Absolutely refused. It was summer, and it was hot. After hearing the door open from upstairs, I looked out the window and saw her wheeling her stroller up their driveway. At that moment I didn't have any more energy to explain the importance of clothes, so I just let her go. I figured they wouldn't mind. But later I found out they'd had dinner guests, some very distinguished people from France. Anne rang the doorbell, announced, "I am here to play," and then walked right in, naked, and sat down at the table. She created quite a sensation, and that story became a neighborhood classic.

As kids get older, sports become a perfect vehicle for teaching teamwork and being accountable to others. All kids should be involved in sports at some point. Individual sports teach grit, perseverance, and technical skills, but group sports are even better because kids learn that they're part of the team and that their performance matters to the group. My daughters joined the Stanford Campus Recreation Association swim team starting at about five years old. They would swim laps for an hour each evening. That really made them sleep well. On the weekends, they swam in relay races as part of the official team. Imagine a relay team of five-year-olds trying their best to swim the breaststroke, butterfly, backstroke, or crawl. It was pretty hilarious, but it was also great training for the real world.

Over the years, I watched how the attitudes they learned in swimming, tennis, and soccer carried over into other parts of their lives. They became more aware of each other, more understanding in the midst of disagreements, and more apt to help out. Though sometimes other parents worked against these lessons. Sports can become the parents' way of competing, if we allow our egos to get involved — insulting other teams, taunting other parents, or screaming at our own child because he missed a goal. Let's not forget to teach good sportsmanship, to always congratulate the other team on a good game, no matter the score. Easier said than done, but when in doubt, remind yourself: It's not about you.

Finally, don't miss giving advice as a chance to collaborate (*not* dictate). During high school, my daughters were not doing well in physics, of all things. You can imagine with their dad as a professor of physics, that was not cool. They didn't feel they were learning anything.

So I proposed three options and asked them to choose the best one: 1) Stay after school and get help from the physics teacher; 2) Have their dad help them, though he was very busy and didn't have a lot of time; or 3) Hire a tutor. They chose the tutor, so we posted an ad in the physics department and soon had a graduate student coming to the house three afternoons a week. Problem solved, together.

The same problem-solving happened when Janet decided to try out to be a cheerleader. She made the squad, and I was very proud of her. But there was a small problem: turns out she didn't like it. Again, I was the sounding board. "Well, what do you want to do?"

I asked. "I want to quit," she said. We talked about it. "How would it impact the team if you quit now?" I asked her. "And how would it feel to quit? They chose you for the year, so you might want to stick with it to hold up your end of the bargain." She understood my argument, and in the end she did finish the season.

There's no shortage of challenges that kids face on a daily basis. Every parent knows this: there's always some kind of problem to solve. The best thing we can do for our kids is to guide them and support them in their decision-making instead of telling them what to do. We have to be patient, and we need to stop being so judgmental.

COLLABORATIVE DISCIPLINE

All of this working together sounds good, but kids are still going to make mistakes, because they're learning. That's what kids do. They learn the most when they make mistakes. When problems arise, as they inevitably will, it pays to have an educational mind-set. Every issue, every misstep means a lesson has to be learned. And you guessed it: You're the teacher.

One of my grandkids was a biter. He actually bit one of his friends at school. This is more common than you might think. Biting, hair pulling, hitting — kids do all this because they don't know how to control themselves and are still learning how to interact. It's tempting to get mad. Really tempting. But you have to remain calm and reason with the child. And you have to be willing to talk with them.

That's what my daughter did with my grandson. She took him to a separate room, sat him down, and asked why he was doing it. She wanted to know what was making him so frustrated. Frustration is behind a lot of unwanted behaviors in little kids. In this case, he was upset because another kid was playing with his toys. For a toddler, that's tough. So she talked about how important it is to share with others so that they'll share with you. This is a critical skill for getting along in the world, and biting is not an acceptable way of voicing an opinion. While nothing works overnight, eventually this solved the problem.

When kids are a little older, I recommend they take some quiet time to write about what they're feeling and how they're behaving, in addition to having a discussion with parents. Reflective writing is a wonderful teaching tool; I used it all the time with my daughters. And if they can't yet write, have them draw a picture of what they're feeling. The point is to get them to reflect and express. Have them write a story from the perspective of the kid who is being bitten. That helps them have empathy and stop the unwanted behavior.

After that, move forward together. Don't carry grudges, especially against young children. They are learning. Instead, be your child's partner in learning. And if it happens again, repeat the process (without getting nasty). Identify the mistake, do your best to understand where the child is coming from, and have him write more about why he's acting out. He will learn, but it might take some time.

That is my way of solving many problems, but especially when dealing with plagiarism, which plagues teachers everywhere. When I used to teach English classes, I'd assign really unusual topics that made plagiarizing hard. But some kids still managed. I'm thankful I don't have a lot of problems with this in my journalism classes. I remind my students to think about all the eyeballs that will be on their story — and that does it. That's the beauty of a journalism program with real-world consequences. But when I had to deal with students who plagiarized, the main thing I did was talk to them. I gave them a zero on the paper and met with them after school, but I didn't give them a referral to the vice principal or they would have been dropped from the class or given an F. The school takes the issue pretty seriously. I figured it was between me and the student, not the administration and the student. Here's what I learned: Kids who plagiarize, like kids who cheat, are under a lot of pressure. I always treated it as a symptom of stress. Where is the stress coming from? Usually it's parental stress that the kid has to get an A or there's some kind of penalty. They're living in fear of punishment and fear of not knowing how to make the paper better.

I saw any kind of plagiarism as a teaching moment. First, I figured out why they did it, why they felt they couldn't complete the assignment themselves. Then I taught them what they needed to know to write the essay on their own. I explained why plagiarism is so bad, why it's unethical to take another person's words and thoughts and claim them as your own. "I want to know what *you* have to say," I'd tell them. "Not what CliffsNotes says." I also tried to help them see the bigger picture, the fact that the city was paying me to teach them. "Just think of all the money and time and effort you're wasting because you aren't taking advantage of this opportunity to learn," I'd tell them. This method was surprisingly effective.

The thing is, they were terrified. Terrified is an understatement. They were beside themselves. The penalty for plagiarizing at Palo Alto High School was harsh. But I never wanted them to learn that one mistake could ruin their school careers. I wanted to show them they were smart and didn't need to copy. That is why I don't give grades until they have revised sufficiently to get an A. Some kids revise twice and others revise ten times, but it doesn't matter. Each time they revise, they are learning. When I started this system, about twenty-five years ago, plagiarism disappeared from my classes and the motivation — and trust — went up.

But sometimes even if you trust kids, they do crazy things that damage the relationship, at least for a while. One such situation took place in the spring of Susan's sophomore year. It must have been 1994. My husband and I went away for the weekend and left our daughters home alone to take care of the house. They promised they would follow the routines, feed our dog, Truffle, and take good care of each other. Susan was sixteen, Janet, fifteen, and Anne, thirteen. Stan and I had a great time on our weekend trip and were so happy that we could finally leave our kids alone.

We were shocked to see how clean the house was when we came back on Sunday night. It looked spotless. Someone had vacuumed every room in the house. Wonderful, I thought. What great daughters. I was right to trust them. They even cleaned! The next morning was Monday, and I went to school as usual. In my first-period class there was a lot of giggling. I noticed a student wearing the exact same outfit that I owned — a matching blue shirt and skirt from Macy's, one of my favorite outfits. It looked great on her. I asked her where she got it. There was even more laughing.

"Janet gave it to me," she said.

"Really?" I asked. "Where did Janet get it?"

"In your closet. Didn't you hear about the rager?"

"What rager?"

"The one at your house this past weekend. I spilled a drink on my shirt, so Janet let me wear your clothes."

I almost fainted right there. I had a reputation of being a nice teacher, so I guess this student felt comfortable enough to tell me the truth. I think she enjoyed telling everyone that she had been invited to the party and was now wearing my clothes. How cool was that?

Well, it was pretty tense at our house that evening. Some of Stan's clothes were missing too. I wasn't sure how to tell my daughters I knew what had happened. I was fuming but trying to be calm, and I was not doing such a great job.

They all came into the kitchen for dinner, and I said, "Is there anything you guys want to tell me about this past weekend?"

They looked at each other, paused, and shook their heads no.

"Really? Well, in my first-period class today, I heard something about a rager."

"We didn't have a party," Janet said.

"Yeah," Susan chimed in. "We just wanted to clean the house."

"You had a party while we were gone," I said. "And I have evidence."

I told them about the girl in my class who was wearing my matching skirt and shirt. After that, well, I got mad. Finally, they admitted that more than a hundred kids had been partying at our house with no adult supervision.

"We're not leaving you home alone again," I told them. "You're having a sitter." They didn't fight back. Because they knew they had violated our trust, they were grounded for a month. We felt we had to make that point. But what was more important was having a serious conversation. Grounding wasn't the end of the process. "Let me tell you why it's dangerous to have a huge party," I said. "You have no control of these people, and you're really lucky that something didn't happen, because if someone gets hurt at your home, you're liable." They hadn't thought of that. Of course they hadn't. Teenagers don't think like lawyers.

In time I saw how clever they had been, and I had to laugh about how I figured it out. At least there hadn't been any damage to the house, beyond our missing clothes. And I had no idea their cleaning skills were so well honed. I also realized that leaving them alone for the weekend was a bad idea. Their friends knew we were out of town, so the pressure was on. By the way, we weren't the only parents who had this experience. If you have teenage kids, expect that they'll throw a party when you leave. Try to set them up for success by having a sitter. And make sure your favorite outfits are out of sight! (I did get my outfit back, by the way, but Stan's clothes were never returned.)

But let's say your child does something worse than throw a party, something like shoplifting, a common enough offense for teenagers. In these cases, discipline is in the hands of the police. All you can do is cooperate with law enforcement and let your child face the consequences. But afterward, it's again an occasion to talk and get to the bottom of what happened. Was your child acting out because of anger, stress, or lack of control? Or maybe they shoplifted because they wanted something and didn't have the resources. Those are problems that need to be addressed collaboratively, as a family. Sometimes teenagers are just after thrills, especially teenage boys, and they end up taking stupid risks. I've worked with dozens of parents over the years in this situation. Here, too, it's up to you to find the lesson you need to teach, and to work with your child to make sure he learns it.

It was 2005, during the week before school started, that a popular gym teacher at our local middle school was arrested for inappropriate sexual activity with a student. Everyone in our community was shocked and upset, especially his former students, many of whom were now at Palo Alto High. It was the kind of story that we absolutely had to cover in the paper. But the gym teacher's son had just joined the *Campanile* staff. He was a great student and a popular kid, and it was hard for the students and for him. As my former student Chris Lewis, then an editor in chief, says: "'Elephant in the room' doesn't begin to describe it." None of us wanted to make this student feel bad about himself. He was already devastated. What were we supposed to do? My students didn't know. I didn't either, but I told them they had a paper to run and they had to figure it out.

That led to many afterschool discussions. Lewis recalls: "I was surprised when Woj told us, 'You guys are the editors, this is your paper. It's your choice.' Never had I been given this much input or power — we could take the newspaper seriously and all, but this was a real-life, real-relationships, real-people situation with huge implications. We struggled with finding a decision, talked about it, and reached out for counsel. But eventually, the choice was ours." The editors had a talk with the gym teacher's son and asked how he felt. They let him be as involved or uninvolved as he wanted. In the end, they published a cover story about the gym teacher, but the son also wrote an editorial about the importance of presumption of innocence. It was a perfect solution to an almost impossible problem, but they figured it out on their own, and they did it as a group. If we give kids the opportunity to figure things out on a regular basis in high school, they will be ready for the adult world.

REAL-WORLD COLLABORATION

There's a misconception that life starts at eighteen years old when you can vote, that everything before then is just practice. Funny how you can vote at eighteen but not drink until twenty-one. Does anyone really believe that kids don't drink until twenty-one? Children are part of the real world from the day they are born. We just don't tend to think of them that way. Your child's life is already under way — they are running on a parallel track to yours, only on a different level, so why not have them join activities that reinforce this idea of parallels, that help them think in terms of the larger working world, that show them they are already a valuable participant?

In the summer of 2015, I got an email from my former student James Franco. He said he was interested in making a film with me and a group of teenagers from our community. I loved the idea . . . having kids make a full-length feature film with James and me as the teachers/coaches. Before I knew it, I was standing in the Media Center with James; his mother, Betsy, a children's book author; his brother Tom, an actor and artist; and Tom's girlfriend, Iris Torres, an accomplished film producer. The film was based on Betsy's young adult novel, *Metamorphosis: Junior Year*. It's a coming-of-age tale about the struggles of a sixteen-year-old boy, filtered through art and the myths of Ovid, the famous Roman poet. A perfect project for high school students.

On the first day, James and I started the workshop by handing out a script that Betsy had created from the book. The kids weren't afraid to share their opinions: "It doesn't sound real." "Teenagers would never talk that way." "The plot needs to be changed."

"Okay, guys, you rewrite the script," Betsy said. She's been teaching at the Children's Theatre in Palo Alto for years, so she knew a thing or two about working with teens.

The next time we met, the kids had revised the script. We went over it scene by scene, with James and Betsy leading the way. Then they read it out loud and continued to make changes, but only if they were approved by the whole group. It took time, a lot of time, but the script was amazing. They were all excited about it, and Betsy agreed that the revision was a major improvement on the original.

Then we had a movie to make. James, Tom, Iris, and I created forty roles — one for each kid. They all had a title of some kind, just like what would happen in professional films. We wanted them to have their own responsibilities and to contribute something important to the team. I'll tell you right now that this movie was probably the most complex project I've ever taken on, and it lasted a year. We had five directors, multiple actors and screenwriters, and kids running all kinds of departments, including casting, music, cinematography, editing, costume design, production design, cameras, animation, sound, and stunts. They were all working three days a week after school and on the weekends during the filming. I quickly learned that not only did we all need to work together, but we needed the equipment and the weather to cooperate too. Every day something went wrong: a kid showed up in the wrong place, brought the wrong camera, couldn't figure out how to work the lighting equipment. But they were all learning some of life's hardest lessons: how to make something work even when it doesn't work, how to work together with so many moving pieces, so many conflicting opinions. It was a real film, not a little attempt at a film, and in the end it turned out beautifully. It was even entered in multiple film festivals, including the Mill Valley Film Festival in the Bay Area.

This kind of experience is the real-world training ground we need for the professional world, where collaboration works in unexpected (and complicated) ways. As the CEO of 23andMe, Anne did a tremendous job of hiring top talent, but she never thought she'd be collaborating with her adversary. Yet in November of 2013, Anne learned that the FDA had deemed 23andMe's saliva-testing kit a "medical device" that needed to pass a daunting marketing approval process. Overnight, and after six years of business, she was banned from selling her product.

If Anne didn't have more grit than anyone I know, she never would have survived this. But she refused to fall apart. She was extremely strategic. And more than her toughness, it was her ability to collaborate that ultimately saved her company. In essence, she had to convince the FDA of the importance and validity of the idea behind her product, the fact that consumers could and should have their own genetic information and be able to make decisions about their health. There was no precedent for this type of product, so it was up to her to collaborate with the FDA about what she was doing and why.

Tracy Keim, 23andMe's vice president of brand and consumer marketing, recalls that Anne had "a constant drive to seek out the opinions of those within the FDA system and to understand them, to respect them. The realization that she never quite knew them at a human level made her want to get to know, understand, and respect those individuals." She set out to show the FDA that it was possible to educate consumers about the probability involved in calculating genetic risk. It was a major, company-wide effort. "The amount of collaboration and kindness that came out of that one moment in the company's history was unbelievable," Keim says. "While Anne balanced leadership with listening, this heightened sense of collaboration among the employees came into effect. Everyone wanted to win. Everyone wanted to win together."

23andMe successfully made their case, and in the spring of 2017, they received authorization from the FDA to sell tests that assess genetic risk for a number of diseases, and since have added other genetic markers, including the BRCA 1 and 2 genes associated with breast, ovarian, and prostate cancer. This was not only a victory for 23andMe but a victory for those who now had direct consumer access to their genetic information.

Anne realized through all of this that the FDA wasn't her adversary at all. It was a group of people with a different opinion about medical care, but like her, their objective was to protect the consumer. She wasn't a bulldozer, and she wasn't a dictator. She was a true collaborator.

In the current political climate, it wouldn't hurt any of us to take these lessons to heart: Respect your adversaries, understand where they're coming from, find common ground, and pursue collaborative solutions. We all want our country to be great, whether we live in the United States, Mexico, or China, and working collaboratively is really the only way to get there.

Finding common ground is more crucial than many of us realize. Perhaps today more than ever. It involves patience, flexibility, giving, and listening. It means noticing one another and taking each other into account. It also means tolerating chaos and uncertainty, especially when kids are involved. If we can do this, if we can learn to work together, we can solve complicated problems, navigate morally fraught decisions, and harness the power of many (often competing) opinions and ideas. We'll also become more aware of how we treat our children. Are they truly our collaborators? Do we value their ideas and passions? And what are we teaching them, through our own actions, about how to live in the adult world? This is one of the most important collaborations of all, because who we are as parents determines the people our children become.

And, of course, the people our children become determine the future of everything.

7

Children Hear What You Do,
Not What You Say

CLAUDIA STOOD AT THE DOOR to my office, holding back tears. The prior weekend I'd had to break the news that she hadn't won the editor in chief election. I dread making those calls or having my editors make them. During my first few years of teaching, selecting the editors was easy because the class was so small, and usually one clear candidate emerged. Today is another story. In a recent election there were twenty-eight students competing for just five editor in chief roles. The campaigning is fierce. And consoling the losers? It's getting harder every year.

"I can't believe I didn't win," Claudia managed through sobs. She was a bright, accomplished student who'd written many important articles for the paper. I hated to see her so upset.

I let her cry and tried to reassure her that in the long run it didn't matter. "You'll get into college and do well even without having been editor," I said. I could tell she wasn't convinced.

The next day it was obvious that she was jealous of the kids who won. It was bad for class morale, and for her, so I decided to talk to her parents. When I got her mom on the phone, I was shocked to hear that she, too, was crying. "What did I do wrong?" she said. She interpreted this one election as a referendum on her own parenting and a reflection of her daughter's worth. I've seen this so many times, but it's always upsetting. She was obsessed with preventing this kind of failure from happening again. "How can I make sure my other children win?" she asked. I decided to break out my secret weapon: the Gady Epstein speech. I told her about how Gady lost the election, committed himself to making the paper great no matter his title, and ended up getting into Harvard. "It's all about learning to fail with grace," I kept saying. "That's so much more important than being editor."

But I wasn't sure that sank in, and I worried about whether Claudia would commit to the program for the whole school year. I've had students who couldn't recover and ended up quitting. I didn't want that to happen.

Claudia finally came through. She showed up smiling and ready to work and, as predicted, got into a good college. This was one of many instances in which I had to solve "the mother problem." Then, magically, the child was fine.

A few years later, I had a hardworking student who vomited every time she had to take a standardized test. She had a very challenging schedule with four Advanced Placement classes and afterschool tutoring. Her parents were immigrants from China, and she spoke highly of them, but she also overheard their discussions about her academic performance. She was under a lot of pressure. It didn't seem like a very positive situation.

The parents got so worried that they pursued the so-called 504 plan for their daughter, which provides testing accommodations for students with disabilities. They wanted her to be able to take the

SAT without the usual time limit. Alternative testing arrangements are necessary for students with learning disabilities — I'm not arguing with that. But there is an epidemic of worried parents who will do anything to make sure their children succeed. This student didn't have a learning disability; she had an emotional disability.

I met with the parents and suggested they might be projecting their own anxiety onto their daughter. They were immediately defensive. "It isn't us," they told me. "It's the school environment." This is a common defense — I hear it all the time. Parents don't want to think they're causing any problems for their children. I understand. But the truth is, they're wrong.

These parents eventually succeeded in establishing 504 status for their daughter. What was interesting is that as soon as she realized she could take tests untimed, her vomiting and anxiety disappeared. I didn't think it was about the timing at all. I saw that her parents relaxed, and in response, the daughter relaxed.

The parents in both of these stories made a common mistake: They forgot that when it comes to children, what you feel and what you model is what you get. This is so obvious, so automatic, that we just don't think about it. Both parents and teachers fall into this trap, despite the decades of research — and common sense — that prove this point. Kids pick up on subconscious cues as well as overt behaviors. Back in the 1960s, the famous Bobo doll study at Stanford found that kids who observed aggressive behaviors by adult models, like pounding a doll with a hammer, were more likely to exhibit aggression themselves. A 2010 study published in *Behavior Research and Therapy* found that children whose parents modeled anxious behavior and thinking showed greater anxiety and avoidance behaviors on academic tests — exactly what I've observed over the years.[14]

Other studies show that children learn to regulate their emotions through observing their parents, and that if parents are able to express a wide range of emotions, children are better equipped to manage their own emotions. Your child really is your mirror, for better or worse.

Modeling is often subconscious. We can see this in our own behavior as parents. For instance, my father had a rule: *Never bathe when you're sick*. It was a steadfast rule later in my own home, because I'd grown up with it. I never thought twice about it until my kids said, "What a silly rule, Mommy." Then I stopped and wondered why I was doing it, and where my father might have gotten that idea. Maybe it was wisdom from the Ukraine, where my father lived over a century ago. It probably was a bad idea to go outside in the frigid winter and take a bath if you were sick. But we were in California. We had heat and plenty of hot water. So the rule disappeared, but only because my daughters made me aware of its lack of sense.

Even if we're aware of what we're doing, we're pretty inconsistent. Some of us are downright hypocritical (myself included at times). We speed, but expect our teenage drivers not to go a mile over the speed limit. We check our phones during dinner, but yell at our children when they do the same. We lose our temper with them, and then wonder why they talk back. Any of this sound familiar?

And then there's anxiety and insecurity, some of the most debilitating behaviors we can model for our children, and unfortunately some of the most common. It starts when you first become a parent. I can't tell you how many times a new mother or father has come up to me at a conference and said, "I need to talk to you. I don't know how to be a parent. I need guidance." And they launch into question after question about sleeping, eating, discipline — you name it. I can see why. There's a real lack of understanding of what parenting is about. That's the reason I wanted to write this book. Because without the right support and information, we become insecure. We worry our child won't succeed because of our own deficiencies; we hover because we're afraid we've made a mistake. Test-taking anxiety among the children of parents who are obsessed with academic success is a perfect example of this — when parents project their own fears onto a child, the child can be so crippled by those fears that she can't perform. The same thing happens when young children are learning to sleep on their own. They pick up so many of the parents' insecurities that they can't do a simple, natural activity by themselves. It becomes a kind of codependency, a dysfunctional relationship where the boundaries between the two partners are blurred and each partner enables unhealthy behavior in the other. People usually think of codependency in the context of romantic partners, but the same thing can happen between parents and children. We can impair our children with our own anxiety. We can discourage and disempower them.

At the heart of all this anxiety and insecurity, all the inconsistency and confusion, is one simple wish: For our children to thrive. That's it. We want them to be better than we are, not to have the same hang-ups and habits, not to fail because of something we could have prevented. This is a noble goal, no question. But parents are only human. We all make mistakes. We all experience anxiety that our kids pick up on. We all have said or done something in front of our child that we later regretted. It's okay. It's bound to happen, and your children will turn out just fine. The last thing I want to do is make you more anxious. What I want to talk about is how we can be better models, and how we can make parenting a little easier for kids and adults. Because it's possible, as long as we're willing to examine our own behavior.

A CLOSER LOOK

One of the great gifts of parenting is that it makes you a better person. It's challenging and frustrating at times, of course. You have to grapple with long-held beliefs and patterns. You have to confront things about yourself that you might not like. But in the end, the experience of being a parent transforms you. It's the greatest opportunity available to us for positive change. With that in mind, I'd like you to consider the following behaviors. When it comes to this list, so many of us are modeling the opposite of what we'd like to see in our children. (I've done this plenty of times myself.) The point is to start to recognize what we're showing our kids and what we might want to change:

1) Are you generally punctual or often late to events and appointments? Punctuality shows respect for people's time. Being habitually late shows the opposite. Living in Silicon Valley, I'm pretty familiar with this. Wealth makes it worse. Somehow wealthy people think that just because they have money or fame, they can dictate the time they show up for appointments. It's as though they're saying, "I'm so busy and so important that I can set my own schedule, and the world will revolve around *me*." I've seen people show up two hours late or more and expect everything to go as planned. Unfortunately, they get away with it. And plenty of noncelebrities are habitually late and

disorganized. I try to teach all my students (and children, and grandchildren) that something as simple as being on time is important. If you can't make the appointment, at least call or text to let the other person know. It's common courtesy, and it's about being willing to see the situation from the other person's perspective.

2) Another simple thing: How do you present yourself in terms of clothing and grooming? The way you present yourself to the world says a lot about your confidence, capability, and respect for other people. If you wear basketball shorts to a cocktail party, that is showing lack of respect for the hosts. This has nothing to do with income or socioeconomic class — it has to do with self-esteem and respect for others, and understanding what's appropriate in a given situation.

The best way children learn this is by observing you. I'm not saying you need to teach them that looks are everything. I am saying you should teach them to look respectable and professional. I kept wondering why my daughters don't wear much makeup, and then I realized that I don't either, most of the time. This was never something I taught them or focused on when they were growing up. They didn't need to put on full makeup before leaving the house, but they did need to bathe, take care of themselves, and dress well. I always looked put together and professional, but never felt pressure to wear the latest high fashion outfit. That, too, influenced my daughters — except for that time Anne wore flip-flops to her interview. I guess she was still learning. Fortunately, they considered her accomplishments, not her clothes.

3) How do you interact with other people? Are you generally friendly? Do you invite guests into your home? How do you treat your children's friends and teachers? What about waiters and cashiers? How is your phone etiquette? Are you professional and courteous when someone calls?

   Phone etiquette is a pretty reliable measure of what kids are learning. I tried my best to model this and have my girls practice so they knew exactly what to say. Maybe it's because I come from a humble background, but I always made a point of recognizing and thanking all kinds of people doing their jobs around me. I can guarantee you that I wasn't always perfect. Sometimes I lost my patience or simply overlooked someone in the rush of another busy day. But I always tried my best.

4) Do you clean up after yourself or leave a mess? I realize that there are a lot of families where both parents work and need to hire outside help. That's okay, but you can still clean some of the house yourself and keep it tidy on your own. I also suggest that you take on a monthly cleaning or organizing project with your children. This will help you model these important skills and reinforce your children's respect for the home they live in.

   There will come a day when you leave the teens at home alone, responsible for taking care of the house and the pets. What if they don't know how to do it? One teenager I know who was left to take care of the house didn't know the difference between dishwasher soap and dish soap, and put the dish soap into the dishwasher. If you've never tried that, don't. It made such a sudsy mess that the floor had to be refinished.

When you treat your children as royalty, when you don't give them serious responsibilities, then you end up with a young adult who has no experience being responsible or keeping a house clean, and you're the one who has the pleasure of visiting them in their first apartment.

5) Do you have a healthy relationship with technology? This is a big one. Research shows that the average American checks their phone eighty times per day. Can you believe that? Actually, as a high school teacher, I can. This compulsive phone checking leads to what the technology expert Linda Stone calls "continuous partial attention." We're constantly in a state of doing many things at once, but we're not completely focused on any of them. We all know exactly what this feels like: eating lunch while typing an email while listening to a podcast. This behavior is bad for kids who need to concentrate on their homework, but it's even worse when it comes to parenting. A study published in *Developmental Science* found that young children whose mothers reported higher phone usage had more trouble recovering from emotional stress.[15] There's a clear connection between the amount of attention and care we receive and our ability to process our emotions. Additionally, a survey of over six thousand participants found that 54 percent of *kids* thought that their *parents* used their devices too frequently.[16] Thirty-two percent of kids felt "unimportant" when their parents were on their phones. *Unimportant.* That makes me really sad. And worried — and not just about children. How many of us adults have felt unimportant when someone

checked their phone during our conversation? I know phones are addictive, but for our children's sake and ours, we have to set some boundaries.

6) Do you have a healthy relationship with food? What about regular exercise and time in nature? Do you stay up late watching television and then wonder why your kid develops the same habit? Do you experience a lot of stress? If so, how do you manage it? Are you kind to yourself? Taking care of our own health is the best way to teach our kids how to do the same. Exercise, adequate sleep, and relaxation are so important. I've found that humor helps a lot in times of stress. And contrary to popular belief, we can actually say no when we're too overwhelmed to fit one more activity into our schedules. We also need to spend time with friends, do something fun once in a while, and have perspective when life gets difficult.

When it comes to food, a lot of us parents can make better choices. In my family, we teach the grandchildren that not all food is good for you. They learn to read labels early, and they know to avoid processed junk food. In my classes, students know that I confiscate soda. No exceptions! The whole class gets the "anti-soda lecture" at the beginning of the year and then at intervals throughout the year, whenever I think it's necessary. Their health is important to me because I care about them as human beings.

7) How do you treat your relatives? To what extent do you prioritize family? How do you treat your former spouse? What

is your child learning about the importance of familial relationships? Even in divorced households, parents should model collaboration and cooperation for the benefit of the kids.

We're lucky because all nine grandkids live close by and are friends. They eat together, play together, vacation together, and sleep over at each other's houses. But my daughters did not grow up with family close by. They had cousins in Ohio but saw them only a few times growing up. So our family consisted of friends and neighbors we adopted. We spent holidays with them, went camping together, and shared meals every week. Many of them did not have family nearby either. Today they are still like my family, and I'm glad I was able to show my daughters the importance of creating and maintaining a community.

Prioritizing family also means sharing experiences, good and bad. Family members are instrumental in modeling how to cope intelligently, and they form a strong support system for the child. It means having someone to talk to, someone who can help you work out any issue, someone who will be there for you.

I've always thought that positive family interactions are critical to a child's happiness. The best way to teach the importance of family is to have fun together. The more positive experiences, the more support the child feels. It can be just playing a board game, or going to the park, or jumping on a trampoline. We are lucky to have my granddaughter Amelia (now seventeen), who is a very social person and one of the best organizers of kid fun. She has led the kids in imagining they were all on Mars, and dressed everyone up in funny costumes that she found in some adult's closet. We all sit down in the family room and watch them play, which usually turns out to be hysterical. Sometimes we just see Amelia out on the lawn with the kids all following her as if she's the Pied Piper.

8) Are you willing to discuss controversial topics? Do you model for your child how to talk about important issues, how to respectfully disagree with someone? Do you demonstrate the ability to listen and negotiate?

We always talk about what is going on in the world with the grandkids. We listen to and respect their opinions. Conversations around the table are lively. The current political climate means there is never a dull day — no one sits passively. A lot of the time we're debating with Ethan and Leon, both thirteen, who read the *Economist* every week. It isn't something we told them to read. They want to know what is happening in the world and they think the *Economist* is the best source. Inevitably, someone gets out-argued or proven wrong. Emma and Mia always add to the conversation by providing the devil's advocate view. These are the most instructive moments. As adults, we try our best to demonstrate our ability to change our minds and consider new information. We never shy away from a passionate argument, but we want to show that insights and ideas evolve, just as people do.

9) What about lying to your children? I think all parents lie to their children at times. We say things like "Don't think the ice cream store is open now," or "Daddy's really tired and wants to go home" when he really wants to do something else. After a

while, kids catch on — they're not stupid — but these types of lies aren't really harmful. It's the lies about significant issues that create lack of trust. Telling your child that no one else is going to the show is a big problem when they find out that everyone else went to the show. They will tend not to trust you, and we know that trust is the foundation of all our relationships.

10) Do you yell? Okay, we all yell at some point, but are you inadvertently teaching your children that yelling is an acceptable way of communicating? Do you curse but get mad when your kids use foul language?

No one is perfect, no one has total control, but some people yell more than others just because they are irritated. Yelling means raising your voice. Speaking in an agitated negative way might not be yelling, but it can still create an unpleasant situation for kids. We all need to be real with our kids — it does no good to fake or withhold your emotions — but it would help to realize that anger doesn't make things better. It's a choice and a way of life that we'd like our children to avoid.

11) How do you react to adversity? If you encounter an obstacle, do you stay committed to your goal and find another way to achieve it? Or are you easily defeated?

There are times in life when things go wrong. You turn right instead of left and end up in an accident. You break off a relationship when you should strive to keep it. We all make these kinds of "mistakes." But they aren't really mistakes; they're fate. Luck plays an important role in our lives. It is luck that puts you in the right place at the right time. I can certainly say that about Susan, who ended up buying a house in Menlo Park and then having to rent part of it to make the mortgage payments. If she hadn't needed to rent the garage, she never would have met Larry and Sergey, the co-founders of Google. There is a silver lining to almost everything, a lesson to be learned, even when that's hard to find.

12) Are you willing to learn and admit you're wrong? Are you willing to forgive? Many people aren't. But pride stands in the way of reconciliation. We all talk about kindness and forgiveness, but that doesn't mean we know how to practice them. In all my decades of teaching, I've learned to forgive my students no matter what. That doesn't mean no punishments, but it does mean that I always give them a chance to make something right. Though it's painful to admit I'm wrong, I've found it's less painful than trying to cover up a mistake I've made. No one can be right all the time, or even most of the time. This is where humility and open-mindedness come in. We can't be perfect models, but we can be aware of these qualities and how we illustrate them for our children.

WHAT TO DO IF YOU'RE NOT THE IDEAL MODEL (HINT: NO ONE IS)

So you have some flaws. You've identified some behaviors you want to change. Maybe you get irritated easily and often. Instead of feeling guilty or defeated, think about this: You are the best model possible for your child. Why? Because the process of change is an incredibly powerful lesson. A child can't learn this from a parent who's perfect all the time (and of course no parent is), and they won't learn it from a parent who repeats the same bad behavior over and over again. Consider yourself lucky: You have a golden opportunity. You can teach your child how to become a better person by being a living example. I'm not saying it's easy. Sorry to break it to you. It probably won't happen overnight. It might take a few months. But with time and patience, I believe anything is possible. If your child sees you working on your anger, she will learn to work on her own issues. Having the mind-set that behavior can be changed and then showing your children that you are working on it with their help proves to them it can be done.

There are all kinds of theories and methods out there, but change for parents comes down to these three principles:

BE AWARE AND WILLING. The first step to making any kind of change is awareness. You have to recognize the problem before you set out to solve it. Pause for a moment and study the problematic behavior. Why are you doing it? Is it largely unconscious? Did you pick it up from your own parents? Is it coming out of some anxiety or insecurity you feel about yourself when it comes to parenting? No matter the reason, try to learn from it. Identify a pattern that you might be stuck in. But then let it go. Forgive yourself. You'll save a lot of time and pain. I remember how difficult it was to admit to myself that I'd made mistakes with my daughters (and I made so many of them). I wasn't always who I wanted to be as a mother. There were times when I got mad, or punished my daughters the wrong way. I completely lost my patience. But this happens to all of us.

And, for my part, I realized I'd inherited this behavior over generations. Once I was aware of what I wanted to change, though, I was committed. I believed in myself. I started by asking their forgiveness and admitting that I was wrong (just like the time I looked at Janet's diary). We keep learning as parents — in fact, we never stop learning until we die. We can change if we set our minds to it. We can always be better. Think about your children and how important they are to you. They are worth the effort.

IDENTIFY AND SHARE YOUR GOAL. Pick just one thing to change at a time, not everything. I suggest you start with the behavior that most impacts your child. Maybe you need to be more patient when your son is getting ready for school. Maybe you need to start exercising and showing your daughter the power of healthy habits. Or you want to repair your relationship with your mother, and in doing so, teach your children a profound lesson in forgiveness. Whatever it is, share this goal with your child. You can say something like, "My goal is to be more patient with you in the morning. Can you help me figure out what I should focus on first? What bothers you the most? Why are mornings so difficult for us?" This definitely makes you vulnerable and caring, and will get your child's attention. This is an opportunity for them to see that Mom and Dad are real people with hopes and dreams and failures and imperfections. And most kids want to help their parents. Sophie, Anne's daughter, always has great suggestions even though she's only seven. She'll say, "Mommy, you can let me do more things with my friends by myself," or "Kids know what they want to do. You just need to let them do it." Explain that everyone is trying to improve, and so are you as a parent. Also say *why* you want to make a change. What do you want to show your child, what lessons do you want to impart? And why is this so important to you? Why start with this goal? Why start now?

BE FLEXIBLE AS YOU PURSUE A SOLUTION. So you had the best of intentions, but you lost your cool with your son again. You worked overtime and didn't jog with your daughter like you'd promised. Things with your mother are even harder than you'd thought. It's okay. Like so many things, behavior change might not work on the first try. But that's not a reason to abandon your goal. Changing our behavior as adults is a lot like writing. You have to sketch out a first draft to get a feel for what you want to say. Then you have to go over it again and again, finding those run-on sentences and errors in logic. You'll feel a lot saner if you don't expect perfection out of the gate. Stick to your goal, but be flexible. Maybe the strategy you designed isn't working. Why not? What's getting in your way? How can you fix the problem and move forward? Is there a creative solution you haven't thought of? Can your children help you troubleshoot? Can they play an important role in the process? Maybe the night before school, your son can set out the clothes he wants to wear, or you can have him remind you to take a deep breath when he's running a few minutes late. Don't be afraid to enlist your child's help and support. In doing so, you'll show him how much determination it takes to change. And don't forget to keep a journal of your progress so you can look back and see how much change you've made. A written rec- ord will keep you motivated and committed, and writing can spark even more ideas about smart revisions to your plan.

THE SINGLE MOST IMPORTANT BEHAVIOR
YOU MODEL FOR YOUR CHILDREN

If you ask me, the single most important life skill we model for our children is our ability to have functional relationships with other people. The happiness we experience in life is determined by the quality of our relationships. This, perhaps more than anything else, sets our children up for success or failure as adults. For many of us, our most significant relationship is with a spouse or partner. But not everyone today has a long-term partner or fits into traditional definitions of family. If you're widowed, or a single parent by choice or circumstance, the same idea applies to you. The quality of your interpersonal relationships — with friends, family members, colleagues, and other caregivers — will deeply influence the relationships your child forges in his own life. Through observing you, your child learns how the world works, how people get along, and how conflicts are resolved. If you have acrimonious relationships in your life, your children will suffer the consequences. But if you relate positively to your spouse, partner, colleagues, and friends, you'll give your children the best chance to live happy, fulfilling lives.

I'm the first to admit that long-term partnerships aren't easy. No one who's been married for fifty-five years hasn't struggled. My marriage to Stan is still a work in progress, and by that I mean we work on the relationship every single day. When we were raising our daughters, we fought — over religion (Stan is Catholic; I'm Jewish), parenting styles (Stan is naturally more strict; I was more collaborative), and all the time we had to spend apart because of Stan's work. But we were committed to each other, and our goal was always the same: to provide a loving home for our children. We didn't have a perfect home, but it was a good home, and we built a good life for our daughters. As for our marriage, it isn't perfect either. But we love each other and are committed. There is no perfect marriage. Hollywood love stories only exist on film. That's one thing that young people have to understand. We fool ourselves by thinking there is "just one person for us" or that "love solves everything." Real life doesn't work like that.

Marriage is a compromise. This might sound basic, but it's worth repeating. In a marriage, both partners have to sacrifice. It's a partnership, not a competition. You shouldn't be keeping score: *I won that argument about the dishwasher, but he spent more of our money last month*. Sometimes one of you will give more than the other, but maybe the next year the situation is reversed. If you're constantly keeping score, you'll lose perspective of your goal, which is to get along and raise your children in a loving environment.

But marriage is also an incredible way to live a satisfying life. Stan and I share more than fifty years of memories: people we knew, trips we took, mistakes we made, ridiculous ideas we had. We can sit together and page through more than a hundred photo albums documenting our lives. It wouldn't be the same with a partner of five or ten years — we've accumulated so much life and experience, and we've done it together. We have memories of the early days, riding around Berkeley on Stan's Vespa scooter or the first car we bought (a VW Bug, so small that when I hurt my knee skiing, I couldn't even fit my leg in it). We drove around Europe, with Stan the driver while I was the navigator, though I couldn't for the life of me figure out where we were (sometimes it was Stan's fault, because he drove off the map!). And then there's the family we built with our girls, watching them grow up, our family then expanding with nine beautiful grandchildren. Who else can I talk to about all this? Who else can fill in the gaps in my own memory? No one. I hate to think what it would feel like to cut Stan out of my life. We would both lose so much. The whole arc of our lives would dissolve.

But so many relationships do end. I've seen it with my friends and family, and I'm sure you have too. Based on all my years, and all the relationships I've observed — marriages, friendships, parent-child relationships — I can tell you that no relationship functions without the principles of TRICK. You can see the deterioration of these fundamental values in all kinds of relationships, but especially between spouses. When couples separate, it's not always the big bomb everyone thinks about: infidelity. Sometimes it is, but infidelity usually happens because TRICK is missing. There are many other reasons that relationships fail — disagreement on common goals, different sexual needs, growing apart — but they're all a result of the absence of these basic human values.

LACK OF TRUST. The minute you stop trusting your partner is the minute the relationship starts to fall apart. But have they given you reason to be jealous and suspicious? If not, trust that you both have the other's best interests at heart. Trust in the commitment you made to each other. If there is an issue, resolve it. Remember, broken trust can be repaired.

LACK OF RESPECT AND LOVE. The number one cause of divorce is loss of respect, and once you lose respect, it is hard to get it back. Respect means that you value and admire someone. You are their number one supporter in all situations. You don't suddenly turn on that person because they made a mistake. When there's a problem, you first try to understand the issue and always give them the benefit of the doubt before accusing them. You don't jump to conclusions; you give them an opportunity to explain.

LACK OF INDEPENDENCE AND PRIVACY. Adults need some privacy, even if they are married. One of the fallacies of marriage is that everything has to be done in tandem all the time. In fact, people need some breathing room and independence. Too much togetherness is constricting. I've been married for more than half a century, and I realized long ago that my husband and I don't have to do everything together. We can go to dinner with friends without our spouse, and even travel with friends without our spouse. Many people wonder if that's a good idea. I think it is. Of course, my husband and I are together a lot of the time, but we have the freedom to act independently if we want. We also give each other privacy, but that doesn't mean we keep important secrets. It means we value a sense of autonomy and freedom.

LACK OF COLLABORATION AND COMMUNICATION. Relationships that involve parenting require so much collaboration, especially regarding how to take care of the child. Living together is nothing if not a collaboration, but sometimes people get so mad that they stop collaborating. They try the silent treatment, which avoids discussion, resolution, and continuing to communicate. One of the worst things a couple can do is to go to bed mad. Then in addition to not resolving their differences, they can't even sleep well. So many people know this rule, and yet they violate it. Too many of these negative memories, without forgiveness, mean the beginning of the end. The lines of communication have broken down, and no one wants to apologize or accept an apology. These are also the reasons that friendships and parent-child relationships break down. No matter the age, the causes are the same.

LACK OF KINDNESS. FAILURE TO FORGIVE. Kindness should be a daily habit in relationships. Smiling, helping carry heavy groceries, holding the door, cooking your partner's favorite meal — common courtesy. It's so important, so why do we tend to neglect the people closest to us when it comes to the basics? I guess because life gets busy, but really, how much time does it take to be kind? And how about forgiveness? If you can't forgive, you can forget being in any kind of relationship. Forgiving means being humble. It means letting go of grudges. It means prizing the relationship and the family over some petty disagreement, or even a bigger argument. In the end, what's more important?

Even if you and your spouse are working hard to keep the elements of TRICK alive in your relationship, children will cause strain. An eight-year longitudinal study found that parents showed a "sudden deterioration" in their marriage that was more drastic than married couples who didn't have kids, and this strain persisted throughout the length of the study.[17] Even the best relationships are put to the test. But additional research has shown that intervention programs and couples' workshops can help parents deal with the pressures of raising a family. In other words, you can work it out, as long as you're willing.

But it doesn't seem like a lot of us are: So many children have divorced parents these days. It's an epidemic. When I was growing up, divorce was rare, very rare. But today the national average is roughly one in two. It makes me wonder: Do we really value our marriage vows? People make a promise, but they don't prepare themselves for the major disruption kids cause. Then they're blindsided and come to the painful conclusion that separating is the only answer. But is that what's best for the partnership? And more important, is that what's best for kids?

I have witnessed how continuously painful divorce can be. It seems rampant in Silicon Valley, where sudden wealth contributes to the problem. That is why many children in divorced families are psychologically distressed. Experts say that younger children are negatively affected because they're still so attached to their parents, and adolescents, who are already in a rebellious stage, tend to feel betrayed, which only makes them pull away more. In a 2014 analysis of three decades of research on family structure and the well-being of children, Dr. Jane Anderson concludes that with the exception of abusive relationships, "children fare better when parents work at maintaining the marriage."[18] Dozens of studies point to the adverse effects of divorce, including reduced time with each parent, loss of economic and emotional security, decreased social and psychological development, impaired cognitive and academic development, and a decrease in physical health. Interestingly, additional research has found many of these same effects in the parents. This should certainly cause us concern, though there are other researchers who argue that children experience short-term negative effects of divorce that are usually not long-lasting. They argue that it's not the act of divorce itself that is so damaging to children but exposure to high levels of parental conflict during and after a divorce. I'm not a social scientist, but I'm not sure I agree with these researchers.

I have rarely seen a divorce where kids were happy about it; in fact, I have seen divorce destroy a child's motivation in life. I have seen divorce cause long-term depression. I have seen high school students fall apart when they hear that their parents are getting divorced. They're suddenly plunged into a situation of missing one parent or the other. Many couples today have joint custody, which means the children travel between houses and the burden is on them to move every few days or weeks. Some kids stop caring about school and start having dysfunctional relationships. They are looking for support and a group that cares about them. They are looking for stability. I have also seen incredible anger and conflict among divorcing couples. Divorce seems to bring out the worst, most vindictive nature in people. It's like we're trying to be so nasty that the other person — whom we once loved — completely falls apart.

And this is what we're modeling for our children: How to live an angry life. There are many things in life that make us mad. It happens all the time. The key is how you recover from these breakdowns and whether you hold grudges. Sometimes the breakdowns are small, but other times they are big. Either way, what lesson do you want your child to learn? Divorce shows kids that no relationship in life is forever; no relationship can be trusted. It's a sad and scary message for many children, especially younger ones. Divorce also teaches kids that if you don't like something, then you can run away from it instead of staying and solving the problem. We live in a society where everything happens quickly, where information travels at the speed of light, where the primary source of news is served in messages of 140 characters or fewer, and this all affects our willingness to put up with hard times. We're losing grit, and that's affecting our ability to deal with the challenges of long-term relationships.

So what am I recommending? Avoid divorce if at all possible (except in the case of abuse, untreatable addiction, or violence). I know that may be controversial to some people, but I mean it. At some point you loved your partner enough to marry them. Maybe you can still be civil to each other and fix things. Being civil doesn't mean you agree with everything your partner says or does, but it's important to show your kids that you can get along despite disagreements, that when a relationship is broken, it can be repaired. Everything, and I mean everything, can be forgiven — even infidelity. As the psychologist and best-selling author Esther Perel says, divorce is no place for haste: "The rush to divorce makes no allowance for error, for human fragility. It also makes no allowance for repair, resilience, and recovery." There is so much infidelity these days, and so much stigma. A woman is a slut for straying from her husband. A man is weak for staying. In the end, it's up to the couple and the couple alone. They should listen to what they think, listen to their hearts, and not be influenced by their friends.

And consider the fallout. If kids are involved, think twice. And it isn't just the kids who'll be upended. It's the whole family, the social network, the grandchildren. A divorce lingers for generations. It has an impact on years and years of your life. Reassess and ask whether this breach of trust, this breakdown of communication, is worth trading for a lifetime of alienation and discord, a lifetime that affects the happiness of you and your children. The pain does not go away after divorce. In many cases it intensifies. It's better to repair and forgive. So much unhappiness can be avoided for so many people. Of course, I realize that it's not always possible to fix things. My daughter Anne went through a very public divorce. When she told me there were problems in her marriage, I encouraged her to work it out. Both she and her partner tried, but the relationship couldn't be saved. It was time to move on, and to focus on making sure the children are affected as little as possible.

If you have already divorced, or if you have an acrimonious relationship with your former partner, it isn't too late to start to collaborate, to start to cooperate. Make it clear that you want to improve the lives of the kids and consequently your own lives. It is so much easier to drop the anger and look toward a positive future. That doesn't mean re-establishing the relationship; it means getting along. Your former partner wants the same thing you do — happy, healthy, productive kids. That is something you can agree on without concern about conflicts. Usually the conflicts arise from *how* to achieve this. Model those collaboration and negotiation skills that you want your kids to have. Everyone will be happier and you will be teaching them skills for their adult life. And if you have already reached a point where collaboration is no longer possible, then be kind to yourself, forgive yourself, and move on. That is also important to model for your children: moving on in life and being optimistic in the face of really difficult times.

It is important for kids to know that people change and that change is just part of life, sometimes in ways you do not expect. Some people change so much, they are unrecognizable. They want another life. There are illnesses, accidents, financial problems — so many changes that could happen. Most of the time these changes can be worked out with your partner, but if they can't, then there are always sensible ways to cope. That is the first thing you need to model and teach your child. *No matter what, you will find a good way to work it out and solve the problem.* We all have a choice: to be depressed or to be an optimist — and I choose to be an optimist and an activist. Take the necessary steps to feel better and to plan for the future. The alternative leads nowhere. I believe that things will get better, people will be nicer, and overall, human beings are fundamentally good — just believing it seems to make it happen.

On a positive note, divorce rates in the United States dropped between 2008 and 2015, and recently reached a forty-year low, according to the National Center for Family and Marriage Research. More people are aware of the importance of working it out for the benefit of the kids and for their own long-term happiness. The decline in divorce rates can be attributed to a number of factors, including the trend of marrying later in life, couples living together before getting married, and — thanks to feminism — the ability to marry for love rather than for financial support. People who find partners on dating websites also tend to have lower divorce rates. Perhaps it is because they look for people who have similar interests and backgrounds.

There are so many lessons in parenting and in relationships. Some are difficult, no doubt, but each one is an opportunity. An opportunity to make our own lives better, and to be better models for our children. All of us are capable of making positive changes. We just have to be willing.

KINDNESS

8

Kindness: Model It. It's Contagious

CARING IS KINDNESS; that is my mantra. In the fall of 2002, I got a call from my mother's doctor telling me she'd been admitted to the hospital. She was ninety-one, and she'd been sick and unable to walk for years. Recently, she'd been suffering from urinary tract infections and needed antibiotics almost all the time. I was really worried, so I flew down to see her at Eisenhower Hospital in Palm Desert. I remember how small she looked in that big hospital bed, but she was so happy to see me. My mother always had such a wonderful smile.

It didn't seem like much could be done for her. The doctor suggested that she be moved to a nursing home with a hospice wing. I didn't know at the time that "hospice" means palliative care for those considered terminally ill. I should have asked more questions. "They take care of the patient," he explained, "but they don't do any dramatic medical interventions." It seemed like the right decision for someone in her nineties. He promised they would take good care of her.

Once she was settled at the hospice, I flew home. A few weeks later, my daughter Anne decided to visit her. Anne always had a special relationship with my mother. After college, she went to Kras-noyarsk, Siberia, and visited my mother's hometown to see it for herself. My other daughters were close to their grandmother too. How could they not be? She was the kindest, most caring person I've ever met.

I always included my mother in as much as I could, but it wasn't easy. She couldn't travel because of her multiple sclerosis. It mainly affected her legs. First she used a cane, then a walker, until she couldn't walk at all. Anne, Susan, and Janet went to visit my mom in Palm Desert at least once a year, where she was living with my brother Lee. They'd all drive around together in a golf cart. They knew their grandmother wasn't well. They spent as much time with her as possible, wrote her letters, and called when they weren't with her. I tried to teach my daughters to be loving and kind to all people, especially the elderly. I made it clear that every single person is im-portant, no matter what, and I modeled that behavior. I didn't just talk about it.

When Anne entered the hospice she saw the opposite of kindness. She heard a number of patients crying out and moaning. People in hospitals didn't normally cry out. Something was the matter. She scrambled to locate her grandmother. Then she realized that one of the patients in distress was her grandmother. Anne couldn't find any nurses. But when she did, they went the other way. None of the per-sonnel seemed concerned. (Most hospice care is not like this, thank-fully — it turns out we just had a really bad experience.)

This was not okay with Anne: her grandmother was not going to be treated like this. She took action. She called an ambulance, and it arrived within six minutes. She told them that her grandmother was on the verge of dying and needed to be transferred back to Eisenhower Hospital, that she was completely dehydrated and needed emergency care. The shocked nursing staff watched the entire process, dumbfounded. They said nothing as my mother was wheeled out. "Hard to believe you call this care," Anne said. "You're not taking proper care of your patients." And she was off with the ambulance.

At the hospital, my mother got an IV for fluid and was given some food. Apparently she hadn't eaten or had any water for hours. No wonder she was so incoherent. She started to regain some strength, and that was encouraging, but Anne knew from her work in the ER at San Francisco General Hospital that there was still more that could be done. She decided she needed new doctors on the case, so she found two and removed the previous one who had sent her to the hospice in the first place. The new doctors changed her medications, and within two days there was dramatic improvement. She was alert and talking.

Now the big question was how to care for her once she was released. How could we make sure this did not happen again? We lived in the Bay Area, and it was hard to monitor the situation from hundreds of miles away. My mother needed a family member who could oversee her care. She couldn't advocate for herself.

Always creative, Anne came up with a plan. We had to move my mother, but the cost of an ambulance was prohibitive. So she decided that we would drive her ourselves, with her IV drip and other medications. The hospital was shocked. "You are transferring a patient five hundred miles, and not in an ambulance?" they said. "That's dangerous."

"Well, not as dangerous as leaving her with people who don't care about her," Anne said. She figured out a way to do it, took responsibility for the medications, and rented a van and a stretcher. A few days later, at five in the morning, we got on Interstate 5 and drove my mother from Palm Desert all the way to the Bay Area, to a nursing home in Los Altos. It took eight hours, but my mother was fine the whole way. I had called them earlier to see if they would accept my mother, and they'd said yes, even though they had a waiting list. They were struck by the drama of the story.

Her new nursing home in Los Altos turned out to be great. They had daily activities, physical therapy, and a social hour, and they took good care of the patients. Our whole family celebrated Thanksgiving with her at the nursing home, a wonderful memory we never would have had if Anne hadn't stepped in. My mother lived another two years before passing away at ninety-three.

Anne's kindness, compassion, and persistence saved my mother's life. She came up with this innovative way to save her grandmother, and she took two weeks out of her work schedule to do it. Kindness is part of Anne's character. She doesn't just talk about it or think about it; she shows it. She was a very loving child, always socially aware, always concerned about the smallest kitten in the litter, or the dog that had a broken leg, or kids who didn't seem to have friends. In kindergarten, when she was asked what she was thankful for, she wrote, "I am thankful for Kenji," her friend. She is also a very caring mother.

Empathy and kindness had always been part of my way of looking at the world. I realized many years later that I was inadvertently teaching my daughters empathy, gratitude, and forgiveness by the way I behaved, the books I picked to read to them, the shows I suggested they see. Perhaps it also had to do with my childhood and hearing all those stories from my parents about their difficult lives surviving the pogroms in Russia, or perhaps it was because of losing my brother David. Whatever the reason, it was part of my life: warmth, concern, and empathy were a way of being.

Anne took those lessons to heart, but she wasn't the only one. Susan and Janet did too. They all worked in some way after college trying to make the world a better place. Susan was in India; Janet in South Africa. They did this on their own — no suggestions from me. During college, Anne volunteered in the emergency room of a local hospital and was shocked by the problems patients encountered. It made her want to volunteer even more. Patients couldn't advocate for themselves because they were too sick, and that often meant they didn't get the right treatment. Later she worked at San Francisco General Hospital and Stanford Hospital, thinking she would be a doctor. In the end, she decided that she would have more of an impact if she did something other than be a doctor confined to an examination room. She first wanted to establish a patient advocacy service to advocate for each patient since they were usually too sick to do so. She saw a real lack of kindness and concern. It wasn't that the doctors and nurses didn't care. It was more that they were overworked and just didn't have time. They were in medicine to be kind, but their grueling schedules didn't permit it. It is a major problem today.

Instead of establishing a patient advocacy service, she went way beyond that. She did something that would have a greater impact for all patients worldwide by starting a company that put people in charge of their DNA, the building blocks of their body. Understanding your DNA is the key to understanding your health and how to prevent disease. As the co-founder and CEO of 23andMe, she gives millions of people access to their own health information based on the belief that no one cares more about you than you, yourself. And she continues to fight for the best care for everyone. Someone she was particularly concerned about was her former mother-in-law, Genia Brin, who has Parkinson's disease. One of Anne's earliest actions was to join forces with the Michael J. Fox Foundation to study Parkinson's and find treatments. The company recently published the largest meta-analysis of Parkinson's disease to date.

One question I have is, *Are kids today learning how to be kind?* What is our national model when they read daily stories about an ICE raid, about infants and children being separated from their parents, about immigrants stalled at the border for days? I hope all parents, regardless of political affiliation, have empathy for immigrants and talk about it with their kids. But several studies suggest they aren't. When researchers at the Harvard Graduate School of Education surveyed ten thousand kids for the Making Caring Common Project, an initiative to help make kids more caring and community-minded, they found that 80 percent of children identified achievement or happiness as their top priority. Only 20 percent said "caring for others" was their top priority. This survey also revealed, "Youth are three times more likely to agree than disagree with this statement: 'My parents are prouder if I get good grades than if I'm a caring community member.'" Not very encouraging. Another study at the University of Michigan found a sharp drop in empathy in American college students after the year 2000.[19] One of my teaching colleagues had a similar finding when he did an informal poll with his students at a public school in the United States. He asked kids to raise their hands if they experienced TRICK in their classes. Starting with trust, most of the kids raised their hands — a great sign. Respect and independence: about half. Two-thirds of the kids said they had experienced collaboration. But no one raised their hands when asked about kindness.

We've fallen victim to the dominant style of parenting — helicopter parenting — that places no importance on kindness. Too many parents are focused on winning. Our main goal is to make our kids successful, and our main fear is that they can't succeed without our help. We're convinced that if they're not perfect, they'll fail in life, which is bad for them but even worse for our own anxieties and insecurities. When they fail, we fail — and we can't let that happen. Kindness has disappeared from our parenting goals. Amy Chua, Tiger Mom, even said in her talk with me in Puebla, Mexico, that she never worried about kindness or happiness. She just wanted her daughters to be number one.

But we're paying a price by focusing on individual success and perfection. We are inadvertently raising narcissistic children who lack kindness and empathy. We don't mean to do that, but that is what is happening. They don't have time to think about other people: they're too focused on performing. If they don't excel, they might not receive the love and acceptance they need from you, the parent. How kind is that? So they funnel all their energy into succeeding, which might produce perfect grades but does nothing for their independence and sense of empowerment, let alone their kindness toward others. And when it's all over, our kids end up entitled and self-obsessed in a society that values individual achievement above almost anything else.

Kindness doesn't factor anywhere into this kind of parenting, or this kind of society. I think it's because kindness gets a bad rap. It's often seen as weakness. When you're kind, the thinking goes, people will walk all over you. I have heard that throughout my decades as a teacher who tries to work with students instead of police them. When I was running the English department at Palo Alto High, at least half the faculty questioned my treatment of students. They didn't like my "punishments," in which I tried to understand where students were coming from and give them a second chance. My colleagues always told me, "They're walking all over you. They'll just break the rules again. You know what you are? A pushover." They didn't realize that kindness gets results. It makes your life better while improving the lives of everyone around you. I'm not saying you shouldn't be discerning when someone asks for help. Sure, some people are out to manipulate you, but you can usually sense when a person has ulterior motives (they're overly solicitous, they're asking for a lot of money, something they promise seems too good to be true). There is bad in the world, but that shouldn't stop us from trying to make the world better. We just have to be cautious.

Some of my students' parents have the same attitude as the teachers. How is kindness going to help their child get into college? I recently met with Marc Tessier-Lavigne, the president of Stanford University, and he told me the number one quality they're looking for in applicants is kindness and caring about others. These are the skills that determine a student's success both at Stanford and as a citizen of the world. Colleges say they don't want kids who are cutthroat and nasty. We may have fallen into a cruel and overly competitive system that rewards affluent students with top scores and top grades, but the tide is turning. Many colleges are dropping standardized tests and looking at the student as a whole, considering how their unique talents might benefit the community.

Kindness is now critical in the business world, too. When Google conducted an internal survey (called Project Oxygen), they found it was these so-called soft skills — not STEM skills — that separated their high-ranking managers from other Google employees. In fact, four of the seven top managerial skills were directly related to kindness: empathy, consideration for employees as individuals with different values and points of view, coaching and providing helpful feedback, and meaningful discussion of career development. Many companies today focus on kindness for employees and customers. Zappos is one, and another is Whole Foods. Jeff Bezos, CEO of Amazon, wants customers to be happy (though he freely admits that his employees face a demanding workplace — you don't hear much about kindness toward employees at Amazon). They are doing everything to be kind to customers. My daughters have taught me the importance of kindness at work firsthand. Janet has a similar story to Anne's in terms of fighting for people's health and well-being. She saw underserved communities decimated by chronic disease and wanted to do something about it. Her caring gave her access to real people in these communities, whom she has helped with advice about breastfeeding, managing HIV and AIDS, and tackling childhood obesity and other difficult health problems.

In Susan's professional life, kindness means taking better care of her employees. One important thing she did at Google was to help set up a daycare program. She wanted a top-notch program not just for her own kids but for as many employees as possible. She knew parents would be happier and perform better if their children were in good hands. She also fought for longer maternity leave for employees. It was major news when she succeeded in getting a fully paid eight-week maternity leave for parents at Google. She kept working to improve the policy over the years, and Google now awards eighteen weeks of paid leave for mothers and twelve weeks for fathers.

Google is a great example of how the best businesses are focusing on kindness for their employees. All people want to work in places where they feel the management genuinely cares about their health and happiness, and where they have a passion project. Google takes this idea to heart and provides free food, places to nap, and a collaborative work environment, and that's why it's consistently ranked one of the top companies to work for in the United States. Their generous policies have motivated other companies to change, and they've ushered in a whole new way of thinking about what it means to be an employee.

Kindness brings so much more than a college acceptance letter and a good job. Being kind makes the people around us happy, and ourselves as well. All kind acts have a bit of self-interest in them: they give us a sense of peace and meaning that can't be bought. We all have to go through life — why not make everyone's journey more pleasant, especially when we're so interconnected?

Today's drug addiction epidemic affords many opportunities for kindness. More people than ever are becoming addicted to prescription opioids, and more people are dying from drug overdoses than died from AIDS at the peak of that epidemic. It is a national tragedy. Finding a solution should be a national priority. So what does this have to do with kindness? Research shows that what addicts need most is kindness and love to help them cope and overcome their dependence. They need support from people they care about, not just support from therapists. Johann Hari's bestseller *Lost Connections* discusses the real causes of depression and anxiety, both of which can lead to addiction. Some of the risk factors he cites include disconnection from other people, from meaningful work and values, from status and respect, and from hope.

While everyone appreciates therapists and the care provided by treatment programs, another solution that works is a support network of friends and family. Sadly, many people struggle to find it because we all assume that the treatment program will take care of the problem. It just doesn't, as we can see from the statistics: Some studies have found that more than 85 percent of people who receive drug addiction treatment relapse within the first year. Twelve-step programs have helped many — and continue to do so — because they teach you to believe in yourself, but these programs need much more support from the outside world. One of the reasons people take drugs even though they know it is terrible for them is to alleviate emotional or physical pain; if family and friends can help mitigate the emotional pain, that, along with professional treatment, would make a difference. The true miracle cure for addiction is kindness.

I have seen tragic situations with teenagers addicted to drugs, which is why I always give my anti-drug talk in class. I don't call it that. It is a talk about how the most important organ in your body is not your heart; it is your brain. That is why you wear a helmet when you ride a bike. That is why you never want to do anything that impacts your brain, such as taking drugs. There are many other ways to get thrills that don't damage you for a lifetime. I also make sure they know that while they feel really empowered (which is good), they need to remember that their brain development continues through the midtwenties. Try bungee jumping or skydiving or car racing (on a track), but dump the idea of using drugs for excitement.

As parents, we can't brush off kindness as some nice-sounding but unnecessary skill. It's at the heart of what parenting really is: bringing children into the world and hoping they'll make it a better place.

INSTILLING KINDNESS

Kindness is a way of living. It's not something you do a few times a year, on Christmas, Thanksgiving, and Valentine's Day. It's an attitude, and it starts with common courtesy. Courtesy is an acknowledgment of someone else's presence. It's the perfect antidote to our self-obsessed culture.

"Good morning. How are you doing today?" So simple, but so effective. This should be a typical greeting when we walk into school or the office or someone's house. Say hello when your spouse, parents, relatives, or friends come in. Make sure your kids do that too. Sounds so easy, but it is missing in many families. Look people in the eye. Eye contact is important. And don't forget to smile. Here's a strange fact about families: Many people who practice these common courtesies outside the home don't carry them over to their own families. They walk in the door without a greeting. They watch a family member carrying groceries without offering to help.

Other easy acts on a daily basis include helping someone unload their car, holding the door for a mother and baby, making sure an elderly person gets off the bus safely, letting someone get in front of you in traffic, being a good listener. Even sending an email saying thank you is an important act of kindness. It seems so small — and it is — but it makes a difference.

As parents, we can teach our children by modeling common courtesy ourselves and guiding our children in making it part of their everyday lives. "Thank you" should be a common phrase in the home. I taught my daughters to thank me, thank each other, and thank everyone who did something for them, whether that was in person, on the phone, or in a letter. Every child should realize that even when they are little, they, too, can say nice things — to their friends, their parents, the adults in their lives. It starts with saying "Hello," progressing to "How are you?" and then to active listening.

Gratitude is part of kindness. It requires that you notice others, consider the ways in which they make your life better, and do something to show your appreciation. Based on what I've seen, a lot of kids today don't know what gratitude is. Perhaps it is because we are so focused on making sure our kids are happy. We do things for them all the time, and they take us for granted. One of the main issues that parents of teenagers have is that they regret having spoiled their kids by giving them too much. It is a common problem. The kids are not grateful for anything because they just expect all. They want more. It happens even in low-income families.

Gratitude makes everyone happy: the giver and the receiver. Many studies have found a connection between expressing gratitude and a general sense of well-being. A new study from 2018 found that being in a grateful state of mind increases levels of hope and happiness.[20] Another study published in the *Journal of School Psychology* found that adolescents who reported greater levels of gratitude were more optimistic, experienced higher life satisfaction, and had a decreased risk of developing depression.[21] Gratitude also improves our relationships with friends, parents, colleagues, business partners. When you are grateful for the people in your life, people want to be with you. It really is a powerful tool for not only creating kindness in the world, but becoming a better person.

To teach gratitude, model it yourself, the same way you do with courtesy and politeness. Those kids are watching you. You are the most powerful teacher. If you are grateful for what you have, your kids will be too. If you are always complaining, well, expect them to do the same. Here's a lesson that many parents need to take to heart: Make sure your kids appreciate the presents they receive for birthdays or holidays. I'm not saying giving gifts is bad. For some families, tons of presents under the Christmas tree could be a stroke of good luck because there wasn't enough money for presents the year before. In other families, kids open gift after gift without ever once saying thank you or understanding the time and effort that went into buying those gifts. We need to teach our kids that when someone gives you a present, you should always be grateful (even if you don't like it or you already have something similar).

Have children talk about their gratitude with you. What are they grateful for? Most kids are grateful for their parents. My daughters were grateful for their grandparents and wrote letters and thank-you notes to their grandfather in Poland on a regular basis (unfortunately, we couldn't thank him in person, and we couldn't call him, either, because he didn't have a phone). Some of the letters were pretty trivial, but they were sharing their lives with him. "I went to the park today and played with my friend Jessica. I missed you." They wrote to my parents and Stan's mother, too. They were always writing little notes, gift or not. It was a way to acknowledge someone else's effort, and to appreciate all the people who loved them. The art of writing thank-you notes needs to be revived.

The act of writing itself helps us to reflect on our life and actions. My daughters kept diaries, especially while we were traveling, and they learned to reflect on and be grateful for all their experiences. I recommend that kids write about their day and what they're grateful for every night before bed. It is a good way to practice writing, a good way to think about what you are grateful for, and a good way to keep a diary. It will be fun to read years later. Some of the entries can be pretty hilarious.

"I am grateful that I found a ladybug today."

"I am happy that my brother shared his ice cream."

"I am so excited that I went to a birthday party with a bouncy house."

It's a powerful ritual, and it's even been shown to increase gratitude-related activity in the brain. I also made sure to acknowledge my kids' actions when they did something around the house. "You did a good job of cleaning up with Mommy" was something I always said. "Your room looks very neat today. Good work." Even though it was far from perfect. It would be wonderful if we could all be grateful for what we have in life each and every day. I am like most people — I don't always have the time. Life is too busy. But my family celebrates Shabbat every Friday night, and that's when we think about our gratitude for the whole week.

At school, I tell the students that when they interview people for the paper, they should double-check all quotes for accuracy, and they should thank everyone who took the time to talk with them. We make a point of thanking our advertisers. So many wonderful businesses, including small ones, have supported the journalism program for years both with advertising and donations of food or services. I also remind the students to thank their parents for helping out with group dinners. Every three weeks, the students have dinner together for three nights in a row during production — sixty super-hungry students. The parents are so great to provide these meals. You can imagine the mess. Even though they clean up after themselves, there's still a lot of trash, so we make sure to thank our custodians, who are an important part of our program.

THE DEEPEST FORM OF KINDNESS

When my daughters were growing up, we had a Christmas tradition of buying the saddest tree we could find at the "Lucky National Forest," the lot at our Lucky grocery store. We'd buy the tree no one else wanted, the one left behind, and we'd take that tree home and do our best to make it beautiful. My daughters loved decorating our trees. The original ornaments were just cut-up egg cartons that they painted and put sparkles on, but as the years went by, the ornaments got more sophisticated. What we were building, without really realizing it, was a sense of empathy. Stan and I were teaching them to look beyond themselves and try to understand what another person (or, in this case, living being) was feeling. They comforted and cared for animals just as they did our Christmas trees. And those patterns naturally extended to all people, whether family, friends, a random patient in the ER who needed help, or a young mother in an impoverished neighborhood struggling to take care of her child.

There are many simple and enjoyable activities that teach kids about empathy. At home, parents can encourage pretend play. All you have to do is give a child the start of a story, a piece of clothing, or a toy, and she will invent her own characters, worlds, universes. It's free and kids love it. When kids pretend to be someone else, they learn what it feels like to be in another person's shoes. It gets them outside of themselves, a necessary state for having empathy. As the child development researchers Dorothy Singer and Jerome Singer point out, "Taking on different roles allows children the unique opportunity to learn social skills such as communication, problem solving, and empathy." So all those dress-up clothes, and that running around the house doing what looks like "crazy things," actually help your kids learn a very important skill.

Reading to your kids on a regular basis, especially books about kindness and empathy, is another helpful activity. We all need to remember the power of stories. Research has shown that reading fiction and considering other characters' feelings helps kids develop empathy. Some of my favorite books for children are *The Rainbow Fish*, about a beautiful fish who finds happiness when he learns to share, *Tikki Tikki Tembo*, in which a young boy rescues his brother, and Shel Silverstein's *The Giving Tree*, a classic story of love and selflessness. Kids love these books because the emotions feel familiar, and the characters are relatable. Just like with pretend play, they're able to imagine themselves in someone else's life. Be sure to talk about the characters and their decisions and feelings. Stan and I did this every night (well, almost every night). We'd read to the kids and reflect on the story. Talking about what you had read was what we did before the Internet. I didn't do it to build empathy specifically. I did it because I wanted to teach my kids about the world, other cultures, travel, history. But it had an added benefit.

Another tip for families: Get a pet. Pets are a wonderful way to teach compassion (and responsibility). We had multiple pets: a golden retriever named Truffle, two cats, and three rats. The girls had to take Truffle out every day. They took her for walks and fed her. They played with her, brushed her, and hugged her. They also took care of the cats and rats. Our pets were part of the family, included in everything. They even got Christmas gifts and birthday gifts. Because of this, my daughters were constantly thinking beyond themselves and making sure that everyone was well cared for.

One summer we decided to let Truffle become a mother. We bred her with a beautiful golden retriever in Oakland, and she gave birth to eight adorable puppies. It was so exciting. The girls couldn't believe their good luck, and they took this new responsibility very seriously. Every day they were taking care of the puppies and watching them grow up, and we moved our cars to let them spread out in luxury over the entire garage. The girls made sure that Truffle had plenty of food and water, that the puppies were nursing properly, and that they all had toys. We became the most popular house on the block. Two months later, my daughters helped find a home for each puppy and set up a way to keep in touch with the new owners. They wanted to make sure that all the dogs had good lives.

Empathy in children is natural. If we model it, our kids will follow.

HOW TO BE KIND WHEN KINDNESS IS HARD

Years ago I had a student, Dominic, who came from a poor family in East Palo Alto and accidentally entered my upper-lane English class as a freshman. He didn't really belong in that class, and he didn't sign up for it. The computer system had made an error. He performed below grade level, so he should have been in a remedial class.

Dominic was an angry kid, the kind of kid that the school considered hopeless. He was aggressive and unkind, seemingly for no reason. I could see that he was just reflecting the way he'd been treated all his life. I was worried about him from the start.

When I figured out the error two weeks into the semester, he had already bonded with me. I asked him if he wanted to move to the lower lane. "Absolutely not," he said.

"Well, you're going to have to do some catch-up work," I said. Dominic accepted the challenge. He was already beginning to see himself as another type of student, perhaps one who could make it in this world, just from receiving trust and respect in my class. I treated him like he was equal to everyone else, because he was. He'd just never been seen that way. The energy he was putting into being mean-spirited now went into catching up academically. It's amazing what a little kindness can do.

Dominic had more than a little catch-up work. He had to stay after school with me every day to work on his reading and writing for the whole year. Then he wanted to be in my journalism program. Here was a kid considered a below-average performer by the school district, now focused on not only getting to grade level but surpassing it. It was an amazing transformation.

Dominic did join the program. I gave him an old computer from home so he could keep up with the work, and he made a lot of new friends. The journalism program is a community of kids who all know each other and care about each other. He seemed pretty happy, but it wasn't all roses for him. Reaching the level of writing required by the paper was tough, and being evaluated by his peers was even tougher. But since everyone was in the same boat, Dominic did not take it personally and continued to work hard on his articles.

At a certain point, though, the pressure got to him. He wanted to perform, but he didn't think he could do it. One day, another kid in class reported that there was a plagiarized article. How did he know? He had read it online . . . the exact same article. I learned that it had been "written" by Dominic.

Dominic was embarrassed and apologized profusely. "I didn't have time and couldn't write it myself," he told me. "I never thought anyone would know."

We talked about the importance of doing your own work, and I decided to suspend him from the paper for one cycle. I had to make a point about the severity of plagiarism, but I didn't want to embarrass him or reignite the anger that he felt when he first arrived in my classroom. I knew why he'd done it. I could see things from his perspective. And what he needed most was some kindness and understanding if he was going to stick to this new path. He didn't need someone to lash out at him. He'd obviously gotten way too much of that in his life already. These are the most important moments in parenting and teaching: Instead of getting mad at the child, can you have a discussion and understand their point of view? Can you muster some compassion? Can you show them kindness even in the most extreme circumstances? I'm happy to say that my method worked: Dominic never plagiarized again.

As a senior, Dominic decided to go to college. He was the first person in his family to do so. I helped him get a scholarship to a college on the East Coast, and off he went. Today he works in retail in New York. He has not only changed his life, but the life and self-image of his family.

A few years after Dominic, I had another student on the verge of being expelled for drinking on campus. He and his girlfriend had been caught with alcohol in the darkroom. They were good kids, embarrassed by the situation. The campus supervisor was preparing to take them to the principal's office when I intervened and said, "Let me handle this one." If they went to the main office, they would be suspended for more than a week. Suspensions don't allow you to make up the work; this means you are permanently behind in your classes and all of your grades are affected. Imagine how devastating that is for kids.

Their punishment was my typical protocol: a conversation, writing, and staying after school and helping me. They also helped other students who needed additional support with their articles. I never took their behavior personally. Of course, I wasn't a pushover; I did have standards. It's just that my consequences were different from being suspended. I forgave their little adventure in the darkroom and allowed them a chance to make it right.

A big part of practicing kindness is remembering that kids are adults in training. They're learning—they're going to make mistakes. That's where forgiveness comes in. Teachers and parents need to know that violations and mistakes aren't necessarily attacks against us. Sometimes it's a case of typical teenager misjudgment. Yes, these mistakes can be hurtful and frustrating, but carrying a grudge, overreacting, and doling out harsh punishment only perpetuate the pain and anger. Try instead to show kindness and forgiveness. Remember what *you* did when you were that age. It doesn't mean you're weak; it doesn't mean you don't have standards. It means you stand firm but are also a big enough person to forgive.

But what if one child attacks another? It can happen in so many ways. I had a female student who was being bullied because she was overweight. She often wore unfashionable clothes to school—a T-shirt and ratty-looking jeans. Teenagers can be ruthless about appearance. They ridiculed her on Facebook. The student was crying and very upset. I tried to get the post removed, but that was pretty tough. (This was six years ago.) I submitted a request to Facebook to take down the comments, but they didn't respond. So I called up people I knew at Facebook, former students, and told them about the problem. The content was finally removed — and then we dealt with the bully. Not everyone has contacts at Facebook. I was lucky. Today Facebook and other social media platforms are working hard to decrease online bullying. Our children's mental health is at stake.

No one wants their child to be a bully. Most parents are horrified when their child is a perpetrator. Yet it happens all the time. According to the National Center for Education Statistics and the Bureau of Justice Statistics, 28 percent of sixth- through twelfth-graders in the United States have experienced bullying. It's likely much more common, since a lot of bullying goes unreported. And of course bullying now also extends into the digital sphere. A 2016 study by the Cyberbullying Research Center found that 34 percent of twelve- to seventeen-year-olds have experienced online bullying during their lifetime. Doctors point to bullying as arising from a number of causes: strained relationships with parents, low self-esteem, inconsistent discipline, and unsupportive peers. Sometimes bullies are victims of bullying themselves. Sometimes kids are modeling the behavior they see in their parents. And cyberbullying has gotten worse. It's because our comments are often anonymous. We can inflict cruelty without any consequences. We lose common courtesy because it's so easy to disregard other people. In a lot of cases, compassion and empathy completely disappear. And there are violent video games. What kind of influence does that have? Do our children really need to be counting the number of people they've killed? There are studies that claim video games don't have a negative impact on kids, but I question those studies. Violence in any form hardens kids. It teaches the exact opposite of kindness, and it can certainly promote bullying.

Something else I've learned in my decades of teaching: A sense of humor develops at a late age. Teenagers often don't understand what's funny and what's cruel. We used to do an April Fools' edition of the school newspaper, but I realized over the years that I couldn't trust my high school students to get the tone right. They thought making fun of someone's speech impediment was okay. I taught them that it wasn't. It was too hard to monitor, and so we stopped this tradition. They learn with time, but issues with humor can lead to cruelty in the adolescent years.

At its core, bullying is a breakdown in kindness that exposes uncomfortable truths about human nature. We seem to target those who stick out. Some of the kids who are bullied lack skills — academically or socially. Kids who are awkward in any way are especially vulnerable. They look funny, say the wrong things, and struggle to interact with their peers, and the other kids pick up on it. The term *schadenfreude* comes to mind, the act of taking delight in someone else's misery or suffering. It's sad, but it's part of human behavior.

Standing out in a good way can be a problem too. I had a student who won a statewide physics award and refused to tell the other students because she was worried that they would make fun of her or be jealous. It's envy, and as researchers have proven, envy is often the starting point of schadenfreude. You become jealous of someone else's success, and then you wait to pounce when they fail. Parents and schools should teach kids about these innate human tendencies. We might not be able to change our fundamental nature, but having conscious awareness could revolutionize how we treat each other.

Of course, even if all kids are aware, bullying will still happen. When it does, I do everything I can to stop it. If I see any type of negative behavior in my classroom, I start by giving a speech — forever the English teacher telling a story. Basically, I'll talk about a kid who was bullied and how it affected him for the rest of his life. I innovate every time, tailoring these speeches to what this particular class needs to hear. Kids don't think about the far-reaching implications of their behavior toward others in high school, but once I start talking about it, they stop and listen. Most important, the kids see me modeling acceptance on a daily basis. I don't care where you're from: China, Africa, or East Palo Alto. You belong in my class and your opinion matters. The only time the kids see forceful behavior from me is when I'm defending everyone's right to be there and be included.

I'm very careful not to single out the victim during these speeches. That kid doesn't need any more stress. Often I'll talk to him after class. I'll say, "Let's talk about what happened today in class. Is there something I can do to help you?" He'll usually respond, "I am not sure." And then I say, "Let's talk about it. I have seen this before, and I can help you." That usually works.

I'll also talk to the bully, again, after class. Bullies need kindness too. Their behavior is usually because they have been bullied or because they enjoy seeing someone suffer. They learned this behavior from someone else. What these kids need is someone who can understand where they're coming from, and why they act the way they do. They also need to know how hurtful bullying can be, how it can cause long-lasting psychological damage. Do they really want to be responsible for destroying another kid's life?

If your child is being bullied, this is the time to step in. Kids are too young and too vulnerable to handle vicious bullying on their own. Pursue every avenue you can. This is really tough, and there's no simple solution, but here are a few ideas. Talk to the school administrators and the teacher. All schools are actively working against bullying, but in spite of these programs, it still happens. Sometimes you won't get a positive response from the school, so you should try again. This is your opportunity to learn how to be a pest, to make enough noise so that the situation will be addressed. Be sure to talk to your child about why bullying happens, how it can affect people, that sometimes kids are mean and don't understand what they're doing. He needs to know that he's not alone, that many people experience bullying, and that he has the strength to stand up to it. Sometimes communicating with the parents of the bully can be helpful, as long as they're open to stepping in. You can also talk to your child's friends and their parents as a way of bolstering his circle of support. Above all, make sure your child knows he can come to you for guidance.

What's even worse than being bullied? Being excluded. One survey of more than ten thousand Australian students found that "social exclusion had a strong association with adolescents' psychological distress and low emotional well-being."[22] My students struggle with this all the time. Oliver Weisberg, one of my students back in the 1990s, was a great kid, but he found it hard to be accepted as a freshman. He'd transferred from another high school, and during his first year he wrote a reflection on being a freshman and how it felt to be excluded. He titled it "The Pain of Being Nobody." He wrote about how difficult it was to be the new kid in the class, how other kids would purposely invite someone to their house while Oliver was listening and not invite him. Or they would describe their fun weekend with friends and make sure Oliver overheard. I remember it so many years later because his essay was written from the heart, and it was true not just for Oliver but for all kids. Being excluded is one of the worst feelings there is. That's why excommunication is the harshest punishment in most religions, and why isolation is the worst form of punishment in prisons. Abandonment is one of the greatest fears kids face. Exclusion triggers it.

Watching isolated kids reminds me of how profoundly we need kindness and community. One of my main defenses against exclusion is to make sure that I do community-building exercises at the beginning of the school year. I want all kids to be included; it is one big family. Another exercise I started doing years ago in my freshman classes was to have them write on three-by-five cards the names of three other students they wanted to be in their group. I read all the cards and search for the kids whose names don't show up on any cards, and I purposely make sure these kids are put in a group and that the kids all get along. I also talk in class on a regular basis about inclusion no matter the ethnic background, their intellectual capabilities, or their looks. I talk about how diverse friendships are what makes life exciting, and I make sure they know that they don't want to be responsible for making anyone's life miserable or, even worse yet, ending it.

This spring I got a thank-you note from a student that said, "You're not just a teacher, you care about us as people." It's true. I care a lot. I care about what they eat, their emotional health, their plans for the future. I'm seen as a friend by my students. I know that many teachers don't think it is appropriate to be seen as a friend. Schools of education still recommend that teachers keep their distance, especially in today's world, where teachers are afraid to be too friendly.

I'm thankful that some schools are rethinking that philosophy. Kindness is about the world, not just our own personal happiness. It is about everyone's happiness. It is hard to be happy when others are suffering. What I do is simple: I show my students as much kindness as possible and hope they reflect it back to the world. A nice perk is that it always comes back to me. Dominic, the student who was placed in my class accidentally but more than earned his spot, is a great reminder of this. His mother has given me flowers every year since he graduated. She's never forgotten how my class turned her son around. Many teachers have stories like this. These are the memories that keep us teaching. There is nothing as gratifying as helping a kid succeed through kindness. You can change a life forever.

9

Teach Your Child to Give a Damn

JUST AFTER JANET WAS BORN in 1970 and we had moved into our new house on the Stanford campus, I went to the Palo Alto Library to check out a book. I was told that the libraries were for Palo Alto residents only. Stanford is not part of Palo Alto; it is an unincorporated area of Santa Clara County. They advised me to use the Santa Clara County Library instead, which was a few miles away. I was shocked, because kids from the Stanford faculty area went to the Palo Alto public schools. I thought, *This is really unfair to Stanford children. They have unequal access to important facilities.* I was angry and my mind went into action. What could I do to change this policy? With two kids in tow, I went to Palo Alto city council meetings as well as Stanford campus meetings and argued my point. I think having my kids with me helped. It was an easy battle to resolve, because fortunately everyone agreed. I got the impression they had all been worried about it even before I showed up, and I realized that some changes are easier to make than we think. In this case, all I had to do was notice the problem and communicate it to the people in charge. Today, all students in the Palo Alto schools, regardless of where they live, have access to the Palo Alto libraries, a wonderful resource.

When the girls were a little older, I took it upon myself to convince Stanford to build a neighborhood park. There were 160 families in our community, called Frenchman's Hill. We needed a place for the kids to congregate and for families to get to know each other. That's what parks are for, so why didn't we have one? I think they just forgot about it. I started agitating, wrote letters, made appointments, met with people, and got a petition signed by many parents. The Faculty Staff Housing Committee and the Land and Building Development Committee finally agreed to the park — if *I* designed it. Wow, I was thrilled. That was the fun part. I remember looking through mail-order catalogues of playground equipment and designing the best park possible. The Esther Wojcicki Playground was a huge success. The climbing equipment looked like a beautiful castle: Kids would crawl into a hole at the bottom and climb up inside of it, peeking out from little windows along the way. We installed high-quality swings and rocking horses, and a slide that was built into the side of the hill, a major attraction.

In 1975, because of a dire need for babysitters in the new faculty area of the Stanford campus, I started a babysitting co-op to solve the sitter scarcity. We had a rotating secretary every month, and all you needed to do was make a call, schedule another parent to come over and take care of your kids, and then return the favor when you were available. The babysitting co-op built a wonderful sense of community, and it also allowed so many parents to take a little time for themselves. I'm proud to say it lasted for over a decade. A few years later, in 1980, I oversaw a massive upgrade of the SCRA (Stanford Campus Recreation Association) swimming pool. I organized the re-piping and re-plastering of the pool, relocation of some of the play structures, and upgrading of the clubhouse.

I was always looking for what could be improved, where a helping hand was needed. I thought it was my duty to contribute and make our community better. I still feel that way. If everyone just sits around and talks, nothing gets done. I was always a doer. All of this influenced my daughters, not because I lectured to them about the importance of serving the community or even because I wanted to serve as a model — but just because I cared. I tried to show them through my actions what they could achieve. This attitude is important to leading a good life, but I didn't realize at the time the profound impact it has on children's well-being, which has been confirmed by a number of interesting studies. Teenagers who volunteer with younger children experience both decreased negative moods and decreased cardiovascular risk, according to a study published in the *Journal of the American Medical Association*.[23] A 2016 study from India found that teenagers who performed volunteer work were significantly less likely to engage in illegal behaviors and also had fewer convictions and arrests between the ages of twenty-four and thirty-four.[24] Classrooms that emphasize social and emotional skills and help kids function as a community result in disadvantaged students outperforming state averages on standardized tests.[25] We also know the opposite is true. Failing to build relationships and serve a greater community can impact both physical and mental health. Researchers have argued that loneliness is a bigger public health risk than obesity. One study found that participants with stronger connections to other people had a 50 percent greater chance of living longer.[26] Feeling like we belong can be a matter of life or death.

But how many of us think about this when it comes to parenting? How many of us take up causes and show our kids, through our own behavior, how to fight for our communities? How many children feel empowered to take on the biggest challenges of our time and find a way to contribute? Are we really showing our kids how to serve others, or are we teaching them how to escape into their own lives?

It's sad to say, but I've noticed more and more kids completely focused on *themselves*. Where *they* want to go to college, vacations *they* want to take, things *they* want to buy. Sometimes it feels like we're training a nation and a world of narcissists, and I don't think it's a stretch to say that helicopter parenting has played a big role in this. Kids are growing up feeling like they're the center of the universe. They're chauffeured by their parents, put into competitive activities that teach them being number one is the most important thing, and they're made to believe that if they're not perfect, if they don't achieve at all times, they'll be failures in life. No wonder kids are more self-centered (and anxious) than ever before.

As young adults, they're not only lacking grit and independence; they're wholly unprepared to take on causes that could make the world a better place. Instead they focus on money, because that, they think, will make them happy and fulfilled. It's the American idea: Get rich, then do nothing. Sit on a beach. Go out for an expensive dinner. Go to Las Vegas. But these kinds of pursuits turn people into narcissists and thrill addicts. There seems to be a number of them here in Silicon Valley, people who worry about themselves before anyone else. They don't prioritize the good of the community, they don't fight for social causes, and they aren't pursuing a life of meaning and purpose. As a result, they often end up isolated and depressed. I've met lots of unhappy millionaires and even some unhappy billionaires.

A lot of them probably started out as directionless kids. When talking with my friend Ken Taylor, former chair of philosophy at Stanford, he reflected on how confused students seem to be when it comes to living a good life. Taylor told me he can see kids' priorities just in the majors they choose. According to Taylor, 37 percent of all declared majors at Stanford, some 1,000 students, are computer science majors. Why? "Because if you get a degree from Stanford in computer science," he says, "you can step into the valley as a twenty-two-year-old starting at a hundred K per year, while believing that one hundred K a year is just a start, it's nothing." For some students this is the right choice because computer science really is their passion, but Taylor told me that other students in the program need to take the introductory course, CS 107, three times before they pass. Because computer science isn't their passion, or because their talents and skills are better suited to another field. Taylor says one of his main roles as a professor, especially when teaching freshmen, is to be subversive, to free students from the influence of their parents, who have in many cases modeled the idea that a well-lived life is "all about acquisition and status."

No wonder kids are confused. It's because their parents and teachers are confused too. The whole adult world needs to be aware of this. Why do you think that here in the States we have an epidemic of opioid addiction and depression and suicide? We don't seem to have the right information about how to live well, how to take care of ourselves and others. We don't seem to understand the point. We're chasing money and possessions. Not service, not purpose. If we have a purpose at all, it's to make *ourselves* happy. But if there's one thing I know, it's this: You're happiest — as well as most beneficial to society — when you are doing things to help others.

Bill Damon, the director of the Stanford Center on Adolescence and author of *The Path to Purpose,* thinks about this problem a lot. Damon is an expert in teaching kids the most important life skills. Here's what he has to say about self-centeredness and purpose: "Especially in these days of intense focus on individual performance and status, a real risk in the development of today's young is self-absorption. For the sake of both their mental health and their character development, all young people need to hear the message 'It's not about you' every now and then. Finding a purpose that contributes to the world beyond the self is a premier way of tuning in to that message." Thinking beyond the self—that's the key. How many of our kids are doing that?

When I visited Damon at Stanford, he told me about a formal dialogue he'd had with the Dalai Lama in Vancouver, in which he'd asked what parents can do to help their children find meaning in their lives. The Dalai Lama gave two recommendations: 1) Give your child a vivid sense of how empty and non-gratifying a life without purpose is. If you have nothing to believe in, you don't attach yourself to anything, you don't develop a purpose and follow it. You aren't serving others. Even though hedonism is fun for a little while, it gets old fast, and you get bitter. 2) You also must vividly portray the joy of living a meaningful life. Whether it's through stories, theater, religion, or modeling purposeful behavior yourself, we have to teach our kids what meaning looks like. And it doesn't look like a new Mercedes and a vacation home on Cape Cod. Meaning is connection, relationships, contribution, and service. That's what our children should understand about a life well lived.

But here's the thing: It goes way beyond your personal achievements. It's so much deeper than the meaning *you* derive from helping and serving other people, and how happy *you* become. When we talk about serving the community, creating social activism, and fighting for change, what we're really talking about is improving our culture and society at large. After all, isn't that the point of having children? To move the culture forward? To make us all more humane, more compassionate, more connected? And to bring us together to tackle the daunting problems we face as a species, such as combatting global warming, sharing access to clean water, aiding refugees, and confronting disease and nuclear war? If we're not working together, we'll falter. We may not even survive. That's how important this is. That's how vital these lessons are for children. You may be wondering whether all this is in the domain of parenting. It absolutely is. *It starts with the family.* Then your family connects to another family, to the larger community, and in the end to the whole world. Kids are instrumental when it comes to solving the challenges that await us, many of which we can't even predict. So I say, for the sake of us all, let's prepare our children in the best way possible.

BUILDING A SENSE OF SERVICE

For me, a commitment to social activism was inevitable given what I experienced as a child. After the death of my brother, and then seeing my other brother, Lee, struggle with dyslexia in an era when dyslexic children were classified as mentally challenged, I felt called to protect the underdog. My whole family was the underdog, uninformed and disempowered. We didn't know how to protect ourselves, and I never wanted that to happen to any other family. I also grew up in the shadow of my family's long history of persecution. My parents fled Russia and the Ukraine, narrowly escaping the pogroms. We lost so many people on both my mother's and father's side. When I visited Auschwitz, I learned that dozens of other women named Esther Hochman (my maiden name) had died in the Holocaust. For some reason, I had been spared. But I always knew that I could have been one of those other girls who didn't make it out alive.

And then there was my family's own activism. My father was an early member of the Sierra Club. My uncle was the head of the United Jewish Appeal in the eastern U.S., and both of my grandfathers were rabbis and community leaders. My cousin Rabbi Benzion Laskin was the first Lubavitch rabbi recently honored for his work in New York City with the Chamah organization, an international Jewish nonprofit that provides educational programs and humanitarian aid. One cousin on my mother's side owns a group of after-hours clinics in Portland, Oregon; another cousin on my mother's side, Tad Taube, is a philanthropist who donated millions to Stanford and UC Berkeley as well as the Polin Museum in Warsaw. I also have a relative who was the UN ambassador from Argentina. We all embrace the Jewish concept of *tikkun olam*, which means "repairing the world." We're here to make things better, in any way we can. For me, that meant taking up journalism and political science during the height of Berkeley's free speech movement. Studying political structures and writing about injustice became my way of making a difference. On Stan's side, his father, Franciszek Wojcicki, was one of the founders of the modern state of Poland after the war; his mother, Janina, was head of the Slavic division of the Library of Congress, and Stan himself spent his life trying to understand how the universe came to be and finding ways to explain it to all of us.

Your family may have similar stories and a natural impulse to serve. You might know exactly how I felt as a college student convinced I could change the world. But what if you don't? What if you were told to focus on personal success and don't really know where to start? Well, I have good news: It's not that hard. The main thing you need is the right attitude — toward yourself and your children. You can start small. Volunteer for one hour in your community. Go to a city council meeting. Research an issue that affects your neighborhood. At the very least, you can vote. While you're at it, you can teach your child about the importance of participating in a democracy. Once you have service in mind, you'll see opportunities everywhere. Everywhere there's a problem to be solved, someone or some group to support and champion. It really is a way of being in the world, and when it comes to our kids, it pays to shape this perspective as early as possible.

And I do mean early. Recently I observed my granddaughter Ava's preschool "graduation." At her preschool, all ages are given bird names. Ava was leaving the "Sparrows" to join the "Robins." The ceremony began with the Sparrows congratulating each other on a fantastic year together. There were twenty-five kids taking turns speaking in support of each other, with no interruption by the teachers. One little girl walked up to my granddaughter and said, "I love you, Ava, and I'm so proud of you." I couldn't believe it! Then the Robins officially welcomed each new student. It was so positive and supportive. At the end, Ava walked through a symbolic tunnel of Robins, who high-fived her and cheered her on. The caring, dedicated teachers, two men and two women, clearly had a great relationship with the kids. And they had built a powerful sense of community where every kid felt like she belonged. Imagine the foundation this was building, even in the youngest children. All preschoolers should have a feel-good experience like this where they can understand that they are part of a group. They will be supported by their peers, and together they are part of a larger goal: learning and growing up. Wouldn't you love to be a Sparrow or a Robin? I sure would. Perhaps your child can be. I am working with an amazing group of caring entrepreneurs who will be starting preschool centers called WeCare. Their goal is to help parents find preschool care by creating licensed homecare centers. This will open up more quality preschools, make it easier for parents to seek out help, and provide jobs for those who need them.

As kids grow up, parents should support them in finding outlets in their communities. All you have to do is look around. What problems need solutions? How could your children participate? They could care for the elderly, join environmental cleanups, or help at a soup kitchen, as some of my grandkids do. Here's a big one: Encourage your child to mentor another kid. Most students graduate from high school without having a single person as their champion. People might think this isn't true, but ask a group of teenagers in your neighborhood if they feel they have a champion at school, someone who believes in them and is looking out for them. If they do, they're lucky, because the majority of kids don't. Everyone — including a child — has something of value to offer to another person. I think this alone could change the world.

To be clear, I'm not talking about "community service" as some kind of punishment. I don't like that term and don't like it to be seen as a punishment, because it has such a negative connotation. Forced community service has marginal benefits. It might open kids' eyes to seeing how other people live, but they might also resist because they know they're being punished. I'm talking about kids enjoying helping others, and making it a rewarding activity to do with friends. I recommend scheduling one activity per week for kids that helps other people. Let them pick their cause, and let them join forces with friends and classmates. We want them to understand that contributing is fun and meaningful.

Another caveat: Please don't manipulate community outreach so you can pad your child's college résumé. Sure, it looks good on an application, but colleges are completely aware when kids only volunteer for the credit. That's one reason colleges have started doing interviews, because it's easy to sense whether kids have passion or not. You can tell if they really care or they only care about getting accepted. When we propose volunteering as a résumé builder, it sends kids the wrong message. It shows them that everything is for personal gain, which is exactly the idea we must fight against.

If you look around, you might be able to find a sense of social activism in unexpected places. Take summer camp. Sure, your kids could go to a tennis camp to perfect their game, but what if camps could instill important values of caring and service? One of the most effective groups for teaching social activism that I've seen in recent years is Camp Tawonga, located near Yosemite National Park in California. It has been in existence since 1923 . . . a long time, and for good reason. This camp is incredibly successful because their goal is to start kids out with, first, a positive self-image. Tawonga builds this through activities like arts and crafts, swimming, hiking, and soccer, as well as through responsibilities to the group, like serving dinner and cleaning up afterward. And they proceed to deeper lessons. They also show kids how to develop a "partnership with nature." Campers explore the beautiful area through overnight camping trips that teach how important it is to protect the environment. They're taught how to become advocates and return to their communities with a newfound respect and motivation to take care of their own surroundings. That's the point of the camp. Not perfecting some skill for personal benefit, but broadening horizons and learning what it means to be an engaged citizen of the world.

Here's another idea for families: Plan holiday rituals around helping others. Anything that helps all of you to think outside yourselves. Invite neighbors over for meals, provide gifts for kids who have none, donate time or money to homeless shelters, or support a foundation that works with the poor. If you go camping, invite the people in the next tent for a drink or to share your BBQ. My personal goal is to do more of this with my family in the coming years. We all donate to organizations through our foundations, and we give away clothing, furniture, and toys to local charities on a regular basis, but there's a lot more we can do. We still have too many possessions, and there are people who need them more than we do. Not all families are in this position of having plenty, but if you are, why not make giving an important part of holiday celebrations? Caring for the well-being of others rather than dwelling on the number of presents you give or get can be a powerful lesson.

All teachers want to support and empower others to make the world better, but most educators are forced into following an outdated curriculum. Instead of making kids memorize facts, we should as a community support a curriculum that will help them understand the "why" of what they're learning and how they might apply this to make the world a better place. I realized early on that it was important to talk to students directly about this, to put all of their high school classes in context. Palo Alto High School does this, and I am very proud to be part of that school; I also know hundreds of other schools are doing the same thing. We need to support all schools, all teachers in their efforts to provide a curriculum that explains "why" and gives students an opportunity to do a real-world project. The point is to serve others. I say that as often as possible. And I'm a living example. I have enough money to retire, but I'm still teaching and lecturing. Why? Because relationships and helping others are what matters to me, and they're what should matter to all of us. Not being number one, not getting rich, but making a difference. I'm not saying kids shouldn't have a goal of being comfortable in life. Of course that's important, but beyond a certain level, the real rewards come from service, from relationships, from knowing that you did something to improve another person's life.

Years ago I started giving what I called the "Power of One" speech, because so many of my students seemed defeated before they even started. They assumed that one person couldn't make a difference, so why even try? I'd tell them the exact opposite, that anyone can make a difference. One of the most powerful examples I could offer was the story of Varian Fry.

In the 1990s, the Holocaust survivor Walter Meyerhof, a professor of physics at Stanford, asked me to help him promote a book and create a movie to share Fry's incredible story. As World War II began, Fry, a young Harvard philosophy graduate, heard that hundreds of Jews were hiding in southern France and the French government would not issue them exit visas. It seemed like an impossible fight, but Fry traveled to Marseilles in 1940 with a plan to circumvent the Vichy government and forge visas for about a hundred Jews. When that plan succeeded, he kept going. He ended up staying for two years and rescuing between two and four thousand people, among them Walter Meyerhof and his famous father, Otto Meyerhof, who had won the Nobel Prize in Physiology and Medicine in 1922. Others rescued by Fry include Hannah Arendt, Marc Chagall, André Breton, and Marcel Duchamp. Here was a man completely committed to his cause. One day he was a student; the next, he was a one-man savior. What he achieved was nothing less than miraculous, and more students needed to know his story.

I helped create a study guide and traveled with Walter around the country, speaking at conferences about Fry and *Assignment: Rescue*, the book he published in 1968. We helped produce a film of the same title, which was narrated by Meryl Streep. I was the head of education for the Varian Fry Foundation for ten years and oversaw the distribution of the film to more than fifty thousand students. I can't tell you how much this incredible story influenced kids at Palo Alto High and across the country. Every year my students took this message very seriously. They came away with the conviction that they don't have to wait around for someone to give them permission. They can take action now.

Every child needs a passion for service, just as Varian Fry had. Families and schools can do a much better job of supporting kids in finding something they believe in, something to fight for. My colleague Marc Prensky wrote the book *Education to Better Their World*, in which he argues for allowing students to identify "problems that the kids themselves perceive in their own world, both locally and globally. School then becomes about finding and implementing solutions to those real-world problems in ways that fully apply the strengths and passions of each kid." It's so important to bring the world's problems into the classroom and into the home. Prensky continues, "The short-term positive result of this is a better world immediately. But the long-term result is far more powerful:

We produce a population of adult citizens who have been empowered, by their education, to actually create solutions to real-world problems." This is where education should be headed. Kids are so capable. Why not let them tackle the biggest, most complex problems?

Kiran Sethi, founder and director of the Riverside School in Ahmedabad, India, is now developing the largest gathering of children in the world at the Vatican in November 2019. Hundreds of middle school kids from more than one hundred countries will be hosted by the pope to work toward solutions for the UN's 17 Sustainable Development Goals for the World:

- No Poverty
- Zero Hunger
- Good Health and Well-Being
- Quality Education
- Gender Equality
- Clean Water and Sanitation
- Affordable and Clean Energy
- Decent Work and Economic Growth
- Industry, Innovation, and Infrastructure
- Reduced Inequality
- Sustainable Cities and Communities
- Responsible Consumption and Production
- Climate Action
- Life Below Water
- Life on Land
- Peace and Justice Strong Institutions
- Partnerships to Achieve the Goals

The objective is to realize these goals by 2030, and Sethi thinks kids are an important part of the solution. I agree. These issues should be part of every curriculum, every dinner table discussion. How are middle-schoolers going to solve worldwide poverty and hunger? I have no idea, but I can't wait to find out.

As your kids enter the professional world, help them see their work as connected to the greater good in some way, not just to profit margins, not just to their own pocketbook. Remind them that some of the best business ideas come from the wish to solve the world's problems. As Peter Diamandis of the X Prize and Singularity University says, "The world's biggest problems are the world's biggest business opportunities . . . You want to be a billionaire? Find a billion-person problem that you can make a dent in." Fantastic advice.

Having the right professional models makes a huge difference. Marc Benioff, the founder, chairperson, and CEO of Salesforce, is another progressive leader when it comes to how businesses can be a force for the greater good. He's famous for his "1-1-1" model of philanthropy, which requires that companies donate 1 percent of equity, 1 percent of product, and 1 percent of employee hours to the surrounding community. Benioff has talked about a broader shift in business toward a sense of service: "When I went to USC, it was all about maximizing value for shareholders. But we're moving into a world of stakeholders. It's not just about shareholders. Your employees are stakeholders — so are your customers, your partners, the communities that you're in, the homeless that are nearby, your public schools. A company like ours can't be successful in an unsuccessful economy or in an unsuccessful environment or where the school system doesn't work. We have to take responsibility for all of those things." He firmly believes that his company has a responsibility to the community and is capable of contributing in important ways. "Salesforce is the biggest tech company in San Francisco," he says. "We can unleash a power onto this city. All of these people can go into the public schools and volunteer, and they can work and make the city better. They can improve the state of the city, improve the state of the world. All I have to do is give them permission to do that." We want our kids to be leaders like Benioff, leaders who have a vision for how their companies move the culture forward and make all our lives better. You might think this idea is out of step with the corporate mind-set, but I see more and more CEOs moving in this direction, and hope that all kids will someday be part of this effort.

SERVICE IN ACTION

When kids have an awareness of the world around them and an interest in being of service, anything is possible. They find and champion their own causes. I've seen it thousands of times, and it's always incredible. The great advantage of teaching journalism for teens is that it gives them a voice and an audience, and they feel empowered to participate in a democracy and in the world. I tell them that news is a sophisticated warning, a way of informing people so they can have better lives. My students aren't just consumers: in my classroom they become participants with a duty to serve. They carry the burden of finding the truth and protecting the underdog, and I've found over the decades that they take the responsibility seriously.

Take Claire Liu, a recent student of mine who says she was "given the space and the agency to question the structures and norms so deeply ingrained in [her] surrounding environment, to look closer at things like class divides and racial tensions on [her] high school campus, to challenge ideas like dress code, to explore income inequality and the Bay Area housing crisis." After volunteering at a homeless center across from Palo Alto High School, Liu became interested in underserved communities. She had discovered an "interesting paradox between the local community and Silicon Valley. It was a wake-up call to the problems that existed in a community that always seemed comfortable and perfect."

In a SpotLight feature article for our newspaper, Liu wrote about the Buena Vista Mobile Home Park and how long-term residents, many of them minorities and working-class poor, were being relocated so the land could be used to develop upscale apartments for young tech workers. She interviewed many residents of Buena Vista to capture their stories, bringing along a friend who spoke Spanish and could serve as her interpreter. These people told her how they'd have to move far away from their current jobs because they couldn't afford to live anywhere in the vicinity. Children would have to leave their schools and friends. One resident contemplated going back to living in his truck. Liu also interviewed a local activist who spoke of the many problems with affordable housing in Silicon Valley. Liu cared deeply about this cause and kept searching for answers, for anything she could do to help. Her article ends with a question about the paradox of Silicon Valley. There's so much innovation and tolerance in our community, but none of it's being used to find solutions for people who struggle the most. Liu is now majoring in persuasive technology and political influence (a major that she designed herself) at Cornell University, where she continues to investigate, question, and search for justice. I can't wait to see what she contributes to the world.

Ben Hewlett, another of my former students, made headlines in

1996 for a groundbreaking discovery about our school board. It all started when Ben needed a story idea for the paper. I had picked up my mail from the office and was walking down the hall when Ben asked, "Woj, what should I do for a story for this edition?" I handed him the minutes from a recent board meeting and suggested they might contain something.

The next day Ben reported that they'd had a closed meeting for several hours before opening it at ten thirty p.m. and taking all of three minutes to pass several resolutions giving raises to the administrative staff. "Isn't that strange?" he said to me. "How could they pass three important resolutions in a few minutes if they hadn't been discussing them in private earlier?"

I agreed that it was strange. The associate superintendent had been promoted to deputy superintendent and given a nine-thousand-dollar raise during a year when the budget was so tight that the principals were teaching classes. "Deputy superintendent" was a new position that no one in the public had heard about. All very suspicious.

Ben was shy, and he wasn't sure he should "pry into the spending habits of the most powerful adults in the district." But I thought he should, that he must tell that story. As Ben remembers, "Without any hesitation, Woj said yes, it was a good idea — they were public servants, and if they had done something wrong, they needed to be held accountable."

This was exactly the kind of injustice I've dedicated my life to exposing, and I knew this would be a transformative experience for everyone on the school paper. I guess you could say I was pretty excited. James Franco was my student that same year, and he remembers my excitement vividly: "You should have seen the joyful/ mischievous flash in Woj's eyes as she pushed Ben and the student staff to get the story out . . . Ben Hewlett's story was not something that would be read by a teacher and then locked in a drawer; it was a story that engaged with the outside world."

It was wonderful to see Ben come out of his shell. "I had the luxury of soaking in every drop of excitement, apprehension, and righteous indignation that flowed from exposing what I came to see as violations of the public trust," he says. "I conducted interviews, and I reviewed and photocopied documents and slogged through late-night editing sessions with other students. And through it all, Woj was there, never so far away that I couldn't ask her for help, but never so close that I felt compelled to do so." It wasn't all easy. Ben and his colleagues were attending the board meetings, and at one point a board member said, "Why are you going to a boring meeting? Shouldn't you be doing your homework or hanging out with friends?" The insult only emboldened Ben.

Along with his fellow students, Ben discovered that all the administrators had credit cards that were not properly managed. In fact, some administrators had charges to Macy's and Lord & Taylor — for educational expenses? Not likely. The students investigated further and composed a dynamite article about overspending and administrative incompetence at the district level. The article came out in late May 1996, and there was an uproar. Everyone — students, parents, teachers — was watching the school board very closely. In June, the superintendent resigned. In August, the business manager resigned. The nine-thousand-dollar raise was reversed, and the administrative credit cards were canceled and never reestablished.

"It's a good feeling to have an impact on the community that you're in," says Hewlett. "I'm a very private person, so I did not welcome the personal attention, but it was nice to have the work recognized, and to have [the *Campanile*] recognized, too." As the teacher, I was very proud of Ben Hewlett, and proud of all the students who worked with him and did the research. They made an important contribution and showed us all that teenagers are much more capable than we think, that they can expose injustice and fight for causes that impact everyone. From then on, the community read the *Campanile* with renewed respect.

Students like Claire and Ben go out into the world and make their mark. But they never stop being someone's child. Don't forget that you're a model until the end of your life. How you live and what you do matters, even during retirement. Here's my problem with retirement: Most of us are retiring from a meaningful life, moving away from purpose, away from our communities. For Americans, retirement is usually a time to do whatever you want. You can get up late, eat whenever you like (and more than you should), and sit on the front porch for hours. Many people do exactly that. They travel a bit, watch a lot of TV. In time, this becomes boring and unfulfilling, and retired people often become isolated and depressed. No surprise there.

My suggestion is not to retire, ever. Instead, how about a mini-retirement rewiring of yourself as a volunteer or mentor? Focus on giving back and being involved. You always need some kind of purpose and some way to make a contribution, and this is such an important lesson for your adult children. For senior citizens in the United Kingdom, one such purpose came in the form of chickens.

That's right, chickens. A project called HenPower found that caring for chickens — a simple act — resulted in the elderly feeling less depressed and lonely and experiencing an increased sense of overall well-being. It makes sense to me, because that's what we all need: personal control, a sense of purpose, something to care for. Isn't this what we want to teach our grown children, who in many cases have children of their own?

Parenting is never just about children: it's about the adults they become. The citizens they become. The changes they fight for and the ideas they contribute. That's why we have to start instilling the TRICK values early on, and relearn them ourselves throughout our lives, as often as necessary. These simple values pave the way to success, producing radical results. Young children need someone to believe in them, and they need respect for who they are. Without that, they can't develop the independence that will be vital to their success as adults in a changing, unpredictable world. Throughout their education, all students need the same values. As it is, most of the schools that treat children with respect are private schools. Now the child is no longer in a prison — she's in a learning environment. But the other kids? They're out of luck. We shouldn't have to pay for respect. We can do better. Students need to master TRICK at home, and their teachers need to employ it at school. We *all* need to employ it in the workplace. I'm not saying that all schools must adopt TRICK — I'm saying all schools should have TRICK-like principles. We still need to have a typical curriculum to teach the basics, but within it, kids need some opportunity to feel respected and empowered, to work on projects that matter to them, to learn about the problems in their communities and the world. When they're given just a taste of this, they stop battling and fighting. They grow confident, and they commit themselves to important projects.

I can see business changing and embracing these values, and I know more will follow suit. Google was one of the first companies to treat employees like real people who needed to be cared for. Customers expect to be treated better by businesses now. Think about Amazon's return policy — so easy, lots of respect for the customer. Zappos gained market share in the same way: building trust with their customers and delivering on their promises. I hope all companies will take note. This is the future.

We face so many problems today — problems that require radical solutions — and more await us. We must stop thinking that what affects another country won't affect us. That's a huge mistake. We can't dismiss an inhumane policy or far-off war as a weather pattern that won't drift our way. We are all interconnected, and the biggest challenges we face will deeply affect us all. Climate change is the most urgent. Look at all the droughts and fires. More every year. One of the many pressures on Syria over a decade ago was a major drought that forced millions of people to leave their homes in search of food and water. And though Syria may seem far away, what happens in that country also happens to us. What about refugees, disease, and air and water pollution? We can't have millions of stateless people wandering the globe; it makes all our lives miserable.

We can't escape these problems, and we can't solve them on our own. We need to plan intelligently together, to think about ways that we as a planet can work toward collaborative solutions. We have to be unified. This is a plea for us to use TRICK in all our interactions — *all our interactions*. If our politicians won't embrace these values, our communities have to organize and make our voices heard; we have to model the use of these values ourselves. We want to move forward, not backward. We have to resist and fight for what is right, not resort to violence.

Because in the end, this is the meaning of our full lives: improving ourselves, each other, our communities, the planet. Parenting may start small, but it has profound implications. We all share the future, and the way we treat our children is the way they'll treat the world.

Conclusion

IT WAS A WINTER afternoon in New York when I met Stacey Bendet Eisner, a prominent fashion designer and the founder of Alice + Olivia clothing stores. We planned to talk about her life and work, and what it's like to train millennial employees. I'm always curious about how younger workers are faring, how their parenting and education prepares them — or doesn't — for managing adult life.

Stacey walked into the restaurant looking glamorous in her teal overcoat. With her was her seven-year-old daughter, Scarlet, who was wearing some very fashionable kids' clothes. *Well*, I thought to myself, *this is going to be a different kind of meeting*. I figured we would have to pay lots of attention to Scarlet.

We all sat down, and Scarlet whipped out her drawing pad and pen and proceeded to draw with a smile on her face. I was immediately impressed. Stacey started talking about the new generation of employees, and how many of them lack grit and empowerment. "It's tough to find employees with creative ideas," she said. "Their biggest fear is making a mistake. And it's hard to be creative if you're afraid." We both agreed that it almost always comes down to parenting — my favorite topic. We talked about trusting kids and giving them more independence and responsibility, and at least some control over their lives — how important those skills are to succeeding in school and in life. I told her about the time I let my grandkids do their own shopping at Target and how upset my daughter had been. Stacey loved the idea, but admitted that it seemed harder and harder to give kids even small freedoms. Our afternoon meeting lasted about an hour and a half, and during that time, little Scarlet said not a word. By the end she had a portfolio of beautiful drawings. There were colorful maze designs as well as pictures of what looked like ice cream cones. I was amazed at her ability to concentrate and told her so.

Recently, I heard from Stacey again. She told me how much she appreciated my advice, but more important, how much Scarlet loved my advice. I didn't think Scarlet was paying attention, but apparently she was. Turns out she heard every word I said. *Every word.* Now whenever she and her two sisters want to do something on their own, they say, "Esther would say it's okay." Even in the middle of New York City, they've been crossing the street on their own to buy Italian ices at a nearby restaurant. They've gained a lot of independence just over the course of a few months, and Stacey has watched them become more empowered, more confident, more capable.

This family is a great example of how minor changes can produce major results. I'm happy our conversation had such an impact, and honestly, I'm not surprised. I've never met a kid who disliked what I've said, who didn't want more respect and freedom, who didn't immediately take to my method. That's because it's natural: it works *with* kids, not *against* them. All children want to be recognized and respected. They want to help other people and have an impact. They're innately optimistic and idealistic — the most wonderful qualities in children. So why not nurture the best in them? Why not encourage them to become empowered and compassionate? It will improve their lives as children and as adults, as well as the lives of everyone around them. Any step toward the TRICK values is a step in the right direction. And you can start at any time. It's never too late to say to your child, "I believe in you." It's never too late to step back and let the world teach its own lessons.

I know this because I've lived it, and I've seen it work every time. As I write this conclusion, another school year is starting. This is the thirty-sixth year that I've watched a new group of sophomores and juniors enter my journalism classes. Like so many high-schoolers, they're worried about whether they can handle the class, what grades they're going to get, and if they'll make friends. They've heard about the media arts program and all its offerings, and they've been told that the teachers in the program are different—there are now six of us—but the students still don't know what to expect. Until the first day, when they see that the Advanced Journalism class is being taught by their peers. That catches them by surprise.

My fellow teachers and I give a lot of speeches throughout the year, but the first time we address the students, we tell them that this class is unique, that the purpose of our time together is to empower them and give them the opportunity to learn the most important skills for life: TRICK. These are just words in the beginning, and kids have heard a lot of words by the time they are in high school. The difference is that they actually see this happening and realize they are going to be in charge. Just like seven-year-old Scarlet, they are thrilled to be empowered, thrilled to have control and the ability to choose their own projects.

Over the next two years, my fellow teachers and I watch as they transform from timid sophomores to young adults with voices and agency. After Beginning Journalism, they get to pick which publication they want to write for. There are now ten publications and even more coming. My colleague Paul Kandell started a new Entrepreneurial Journalism class in the fall of 2018, in which kids can come up with their own ideas for publications, and just as with a startup incubator, they can apply for funding. No matter the publication they choose, they will write articles that influence our community. The paper, the *Campanile,* has a tradition of being an important voice in Palo Alto, and one of the greatest lessons for students is how to make their voices heard. That is also true for the other student publications at Paly: *Verde, C Magazine, Voice, InFocus, Agora,* and *Proof.* They will become writers and thinkers who impact their world.

Throughout this process, they form a community that lasts after they graduate from high school, a community they can rely on for support. As one of my former editors said, "It's like a big family." We always have a party during the school year's final production week. It's a send-off for the seniors and a celebration of the great work everyone has done together. We wish them the best and tell them to keep in touch. Most of them do.

My program works at Palo Alto High School, and it can work in all schools and all homes worldwide. Consider a school called Centro de Capacitación Integral (CCAI) in Monterrey, Mexico, which is supported by the Vicente Ferrara Foundation and directed by Marco Ferrara (Vicente's great-grandson). I first met Marco five years ago when I was giving a talk in Puebla, Mexico, at the Cuidad de las Ideas Festival. He loved what I said about empowering students and asked me to be a mentor and advisor to the school. I happily agreed.

The school is built on a former dump site called San Bernabe, and the students are adults who somehow missed out on their education and have no job skills. The focus is on real-world learning based on TRICK and the moonshot philosophy described in my first book. More than half a million people are living in extreme poverty just in the Monterrey area, and the goal is to help these people out of poverty and subsequently improve the country. In the eleven years since the program first started, they have educated fourteen thousand people and will educate over ten thousand more in 2019. Each one of the students is promised a job after the program, which can take from six months to three years. It isn't just a job, though; it's a lifestyle. They focus on the whole person: self-esteem, nutrition, ethics, finance, sports, and more. They understand that self-respect, belief in oneself, and kindness are the most important life skills. Their motto is *Give a man a fish and you feed him for a day. Teach a man to fish and you feed him for a lifetime.* CCAI is raising successful people of all ages and striving to make a difference despite the odds. The world needs more goals like this.

And then there's my former student Kristin Ostby de Barillas, president and CEO of Boys Hope Girls Hope in Guatemala. Kristin works with kids who have some of the worst experiences imaginable. But they, too, can succeed if given a supportive environment that emphasizes TRICK. As Kristin says, "Young people growing up in poverty gain grit and resilience by force. If they can find a community of people who care about them, who help them to become lifelong learners and develop key life skills, they become the motivated, persistent, creative, team-oriented leaders our society needs today. They have the character that young people growing up with privilege need to develop." The organization has educational and residential programs in Guatemala City, and is making a difference one child at a time.

Today in the United States there are more than 4,300 Boys & Girls Clubs serving kids in poverty. Even here in Palo Alto, we have families living in RVs on El Camino Real, unable to afford housing anywhere in the area. In every city in America, rich or poor, there are opportunities to serve others. Legendary baseball player Alex Rodriguez was helped by the Boys & Girls Clubs, and now he is giving back to the Boys & Girls Club of Miami. We all can find a way to be of service. We all need to support the kids in our communities, in schools, in organizations like the Boys & Girls Clubs, in programs like CCAI in Monterrey, Mexico, and in our lives. TRICK works for all ages, all stages of life. Everyone needs to be trusted and given respect for who they are. Everyone needs to be given freedom and taught how to work with others. Everyone needs to be shown kindness so they can reflect it back to the world.

Because that is the real meaning of raising successful people: shaping the next generation, teaching the skills we all need to make life better for everyone. And that is what Steve Jobs wanted for his oldest daughter, Lisa, when he put her in my program in the early 1990s (he even showed up to interview me in advance — glad I passed!). As he famously said, "The people who are crazy enough to think that they can change the world are the ones who do." Perhaps he saw me as "crazy enough," and by the way, so do my own kids. Well, I feel "crazy enough," but I need many more crazies to join me in using TRICK regularly to give our children the power to change the world. TRICK only seems "crazy" to a system that is truly flawed and destroys the creativity, ambition, and dreams of students. Parents always want what is best for their children but so often what is seen as "loving" or "supportive" parenting is actually stifling the child's innate capacity to learn and grow. We are the crazy ones who will change the world by truly trusting and respecting our children enough for them to develop independence, to collaborate, and to be kind. This is what the future needs from them. This is what the future needs from us.

This book is part of a movement to change the culture of education and to help support the first educators: parents. Parents and teachers are always asking how they can help young people succeed. Well, here is the answer: rediscovering and teaching the core values in all of us and, by the way, in all religions — TRICK *with love*. That has been the core of every religion — including Judaism, Christianity, Islam — throughout history. Let's remember that. I hope you will share this book with other parents, educators, grandparents, therapists, coaches, caregivers — anyone who is responsible for the minds and hearts of young people.

Success begins with our kids and us. Let's all believe we are "crazy enough" to change our world together, and we will.

Acknowledgments

This book came about by accident. I wasn't thinking about writing a book until I had so many people asking me how I raised my daughters. They wanted to know the techniques and tricks I used. I considered it, but that was all I did — until one day when I met my amazing literary agent, Doug Abrams, founder of Idea Architects, at a book reading. It was through his vision and guidance that the book became a reality. I have numerous people to thank and acknowledge, people who helped me in many ways along this path. The first is Doug Abrams for helping me bring this book to you today. I couldn't have done it without his wisdom and guidance. Alongside Doug is my editorial assistant, Amy Schleunes, who was there for me day and night to challenge my ideas, help me clarify my thoughts, and make sure my writing actually made sense! Also, I would like to thank writer Katherine Vaz, who was a third pair of learned eyes, giving me invaluable suggestions and guidance that made a huge difference. Bruce Nichols, my editor, understood the book's vision from day one and has been a great collaborator all along.

On a more personal level, I would like to thank my husband, Stan, who tolerated and supported me when I was holed up for days, even weeks and months, on a bright red beanbag chair with a computer on my lap, writing this book. While he did wonder aloud, "What happened to my wife?" he did the shopping, made me dinner, and accepted my new reclusive lifestyle with grace. The same thank-you and appreciation go to my daughters, Susan, Janet, and Anne, my son-in-law, Dennis, and my nine grandchildren, who complained about my absence from family events ("Where is Nana?") but supported me when I explained what I was doing. "It is taking you such a long time, Nana," they lamented. Time moves more slowly when you are a kid. My children, being somewhat less tolerant, consistently reminded me of how many family activities I was missing, but nevertheless, they encouraged and supported me when they realized it was really going to happen.

This book would not have been possible without the support of hundreds of former *Campanile* students who sent in stories and memories of being in my class dating back to 1984, when I first started. I couldn't include most of them because of word constraints by my publisher, but I so appreciate getting all of those stories. I would particularly like to thank the editors in chief of the *Campanile*, who over the years have helped me shape the program and given me so many ideas about what could be better. It was their ideas that helped make the program what it is today. Some of the students are included here in alphabetical order, and I am sorry if I left out your name. Every student is important to me and you all know who you are: Karina Alexanyan, Lisa Brennan-Jobs, Aaron Cohen, Ben Crosson, Gady Epstein, James Franco, Ben Hewlett, Maya Kandell, Forest Key, Chris Lewis, Jennifer Linden, Claire Liu, Aidan Maese-Czeropski, Bilal Mahmood, Andrew Miller, Kristin Ostby, Lauren Ruth, Tomer Schwartz, Jonah Steinhart, Sammy Vasquez, Michael Wang, Oliver Weisberg, Andrew Wong, Brian Wong, and Kaija Xiao.

A large part of this book is devoted to the journalism program that I founded and the pedagogy that I developed at Palo Alto High and expanded through the years starting in 1998. Much of my success with the expansion of the journalism program is the result of a concerted devotion by my colleague, Paul Kandell, without whom I never could have built the program we have today. He took over *Verde*, a newsmagazine, in 2000, and *Voice*, an online publication, in 2002 and supported my efforts as I continued to add publications to the program to accommodate the interests of hundreds of students. He has provided me with interesting ideas and great conversations about using journalism as a way to empower students in the twenty-first century. The program now encompasses eight magazines as well as television, radio, and video production, and I am indebted to everyone who has contributed to the *Campanile* (www.thecampanile.org), *Verde* (https://verdemagazine.com), *C* Magazine (https://issuu.com/c_magazine), *Viking* (https://vikingsportsmag.com), *In Focus* (https://www.infocusnews.tv), *Voice* (https://palyvoice.com), *Proof* (https://issuu.com/proofpaly), *Madrono* (https://palymadrono.com), KPLY Radio (https://www.palyradio.com), *Agora* (https://issuu.com/palyagora), *Veritas Science*, and *Veritas Travel* (no websites for the last two — yet!). There are five other media teachers, all of whom have been incredibly supportive: Rod Satterthwaite, Brian Wilson, Paul Hoeprich, Brett Griffith, and Margo Wixsom. I am blessed to have such an exceptional group of colleagues.

I would also like to thank all those who took the time to be interviewed, some of whom talked with me informally on a regular basis. There are so many people who have helped me shape the ideas in this book. I tried to include all of them but I may have missed some. Forgive me if I inadvertently left you out:

Karina Alexanyan, MediaX Stanford

Stacey Bendet Eisner, CEO of Alice + Olivia

Marc Benioff, CEO of Salesforce

Gary Bolles, eParachute.com

Danah Boyd, President of Data & Society

Andrea Ceccherini,
   President of L'Osservatorio Permanente Giovani

Freedom Cheteni, President of InventXR LLC.

Ulrik Christensen, CEO of Area9

Shelby Coffey, Vice Chair of Newseum

Jessica Colvin, Director at TUHSD Wellness

Bill Damon, Professor of Education, Stanford University

Linda Darling-Hammond, Professor Emeritus of Education,
   Stanford University

Carol Dweck, Professor of Psychology, Stanford University

Charles Fadel, Professor of Education, Harvard University

Marco Ferrara, President of Vicente Ferrara Foundation

Cristin Frodella, Head of Marketing, Google Education

Ellen Galinsky, Bezos Family Foundation

Khurram Jamil, President of Strategic Initiatives, Area9

Heidi Kleinmaus, Partner, Charrette, LLC

Julie Lythcott-Haims, Author, Former Dean of Admissions,
   Stanford University

Ed Madison, Professor of Communications,
   University of Oregon

Barbara McCormack, Vice President of Education at Newseum

Dr. Max McGee, former superintendent of Palo Alto Unified Schools

Milbrey McLaughlin, Professor Emeritus of Education, Stanford University

Maye Musk, Mother of Elon Musk, Supermodel, Nutritionist

Dr. Janesta Noland, Pediatrician

David Nordfors, Co-Founder of i4j Summit

Esther Perel, Author, Psychotherapist

Marc Prensky, President of Global Future Education Foundation

Todd Rose, Professor of Education, Harvard University

Dan Russell, Google Search Quality & User Happiness

Sheryl Sandberg, COO of Facebook

Bror Saxberg, Vice President of Learning Science, Chan Zuckerberg Initiative

Michael Shearn, Compound Money, LP

Jamie Simon, Executive Director of Camp Tawonga

Peter Stein, CEO of Reunion

Jim Stigler, Professor of Psychology, UCLA

Linda Stone, Writer, Speaker, Consultant

Ken Taylor, Professor of Philosophy, Stanford University

Jay Thorwaldson, Former Editor of *Palo Alto Weekly*

Tony Wagner, Professor of Education, Harvard University

Ann Webb, Compound Money, LP

Veronica Webb, Supermodel, Speaker, Actress

Lina Williamson, Director of Entrepreneurship & Innovation, Brigham and Women's Hospital

Eddy Zhong, Co-Founder and CEO at Leangap

I want to give special acknowledgment to former principal of Palo Alto High Kim Diorio and my former student Dr. Karina Alexanyan, with whom I talked at length about my ideas for innovation in education and about student engagement and success. They are involved my new nonprofit GlobalMoonshots.org, the foundation I have set up to promote TRICK worldwide.

It has been an intense experience writing this book over the past year and a half. I am grateful to all those who supported me in my passion to spread TRICK to everyone around the world, especially to parents, families, and teachers.

Notes

1   "Mental Health Information: Statistics: Any Anxiety Disorder," National
    Institute of Mental Health website, last updated November 2017 (https://
    www.nimh.nih.gov/health/statistics/prevalence/any-anxiety-disorder
    -among-children.shtml, accessed October 22, 2018); "Major Depression,"
    National Institute of Mental Health website, last updated November 2017
    (https://www.nimh.nih.gov/health/statistics/major-depression.shtml,
    accessed October 22, 2018); Claudia S. Lopes et al., "ERICA: Preva-
    lence of Common Mental Disorders in Brazilian Adolescents," *Revista
    de Saúde Pública* 50, no. 1 (2016): 14s (https://www.ncbi.nlm.nih.gov/
    pmc/articles/PMC4767030, accessed October 22, 2018); Sibnath Deb
    et al., "Academic Stress, Parental Pressure, Anxiety and Mental Health
    Among Indian High School Students," *International Journal of Psychol-
    ogy and Behavioral Science* 5, no. 1 (2015): 26–34 (http://article.sapub.
    org/10.5923.j.ijpbs.20150501.04.html, accessed October 22, 2018); "Men-
    tal Disorders Among Children and Adolescents in Norway," Norwegian
    Institute of Public Health website, last updated October 14, 2016 (https://
    www.fhi.no/en/op/hin/groups/mental-health-children-adolescents, ac-
    cessed October 22, 2018).

2   L. Alan Sroufe et al., "Conceptualizing the Role of Early Experience:
    Lessons from the Minnesota Longitudinal Study," *Developmental Review*
    30, no. 1 (2010): 36–51 (https://www.ncbi.nlm.nih.gov/pmc/articles/
    PMC2857405, accessed October 22, 2018).

3   J. A. Simpson et al., "Attachment and the Experience and Expression of
    Emotions in Romantic Relationships: A Developmental Perspective,"
    Journal of Personality and Social Psychology 92, no. 2 (2007): 355–67

(https://www.ncbi.nlm.nih.gov/pubmed/17279854, accessed October 22, 2018).

4 Isaac Chotiner, "Is the World Actually Getting . . . Better?" *Slate,* February 20, 2018 (https://slate.com/news-and-politics/2018/02/steven-pinker-argues-the-world-is-a-safer-healthier-place-in-his-new-book-enlightenment-now.html, accessed October 22, 2018).

5 Ian M. Paul et al., "Mother-Infant Room-Sharing and Sleep Outcomes in the INSIGHT Study," *Pediatrics* 140, no. 1 (2017): e20170122 (http://pediatrics.aappublications.org/content/early/2017/06/01/peds.2017-0122, accessed October 22, 2018).

6 Jean M. Twenge et al., "Increases in Depressive Symptoms, Suicide-Related Outcomes, and Suicide Rates Among U.S. Adolescents After 2010 and Links to Increased New Media Screen Time," *Clinical Psychological Science* 6, no. 1 (2017): 3–17 (http://journals.sagepub.com/doi/abs/10.1177/2167702617723376?journalCode=cpxa, accessed October 22, 2018).

7 Ryan J. Dwyer et al., "Smartphone Use Undermines Enjoyment of Face-to-Face Social Interactions," *Journal of Experimental Social Psychology* 78 (2018): 233–39 (https://www.sciencedirect.com/science/article/pii/S0022103117301737#!, accessed October 22, 2018).

8 Lingxin Hao and Han Soo Woo, "Distinct Trajectories in the Transition to Adulthood: Are Children of Immigrants Advantaged?" *Child Development* 83, no. 5 (2012): 1623–39 (https://www.ncbi.nlm.nih.gov/pmc/articles/PMC4479264, accessed October 22, 2018).

9 Walter Mischel et al., "Delay of Gratification in Children," *Science* 244, no. 4907 (1989): 933–38 (https://www.ncbi.nlm.nih.gov/pubmed/2658056, accessed October 22, 2018); Dr. Tanya R. Schlam et al., "Preschoolers' Delay of Gratification Predicts Their Body Mass 30 Years Later," *Journal of Pediatrics* 162, no. 1 (2013): 90–93 (https://www.ncbi.nlm.nih.gov/pmc/articles/PMC3504645, accessed October 22, 2018); Ozlem Ayduk et al., "Regulating the Interpersonal Self: Strategic Self-Regulation for Coping with Rejection Sensitivity," *Journal of Personality and Social Psychology* 79, no. 5 (2000): 776–92 (http://psycnet.apa.org/doiLanding?doi=10.1037%2F0022-3514.79.5.776, accessed October 22, 2018).

10 Diana Baumrind, "Current Patterns of Parental Authority," *Developmental Psychology* 4, no. 1 (1971): 1–103 (http://psycnet.apa.org/doiLanding?doi=10.1037%2Fh0030372, accessed October 22, 2018).

11   Diana Baumrind, "The Influence of Parenting Style on Adolescent Competence and Substance Use," *Journal of Early Adolescence* 11, no. 1 (1991): 56–95 (http://journals.sagepub.com/doi/abs/10.1177/0272431691111004, accessed October 22, 2018).

12   Robert Hepach et al., "The Fulfillment of Others' Needs Elevates Children's Body Posture," *Developmental Psychology* 53, no. 1 (2017): 100–113 (http://psycnet.apa.org/record/2016-61509-005, accessed October 22, 2018).

13   Michael Tomasello and Katharina Hamann, "Collaboration in Young Children," *Quarterly Journal of Experimental Psychology* 65, no. 1 (2011): 1–12 (https://www.ncbi.nlm.nih.gov/pubmed/22171893, accessed October 22, 2018).

14   Marcy Burstein and Golda S. Ginsburg, "The Effect of Parental Modeling of Anxious Behaviors and Cognitions in School-Aged Children: An Experimental Pilot Study," *Behavior Research and Therapy* 48, no. 6 (2010): 506–15 (https://www.ncbi.nlm.nih.gov/pmc/articles/PMC2871979, accessed October 22, 2018).

15   Sarah Myruski et al., "Digital Disruption? Maternal Mobile Device Use Is Related to Infant Social-Emotional Functioning," *Developmental Science* 21, no. 4 (2018): e12610 (https://www.ncbi.nlm.nih.gov/pubmed/28944600, accessed October 22, 2018).

16   "Kids Competing with Mobile Phones for Parents' Attention," AVG Technologies website, last updated June 24, 2015 (https://now.avg.com/digital-diaries-kids-competing-with-mobile-phones-for-parents-attention, accessed October 22, 2018).

17   Brian D. Doss, "The Effect of the Transition to Parenthood on Relationship Quality: An Eight-Year Prospective Study," *Journal of Personality and Social Psychology* 96, no. 3 (2009): 601–19 (https://www.ncbi.nlm.nih.gov/pmc/articles/PMC2702669, accessed October 22, 2018).

18   Jane Anderson, "The Impact of Family Structure on the Health of Children: Effects of Divorce," *Linacre Quarterly* 81, no. 4 (2014): 378–87 (https://www.ncbi.nlm.nih.gov/pmc/articles/PMC4240051, accessed October 22, 2018).

19   Sara H. Konrath et al., "Changes in Dispositional Empathy in American College Students Over Time: A Meta-Analysis," *Personality and Social Psychology Review* 15, no. 2 (2010): 180–98 (http://journals.sagepub.com/doi/abs/10.1177/1088868310377395, accessed October 22, 2018).

20   Charlotte vanOyen Witvliet et al., "Gratitude Predicts Hope and Happiness: A Two-Study Assessment of Traits and States," *Journal of Positive Psychology*, January 15, 2018 (https://www.tandfonline.com/doi/abs/10.1080/17439760.2018.1424924?journalCode=rpos20, accessed October 22, 2018).

21   Jeffrey J. Froh et al., "Counting Blessings in Early Adolescents: An Experimental Study of Gratitude and Subjective Well-Being," *Journal of School Psychology* 46, no. 2 (2008): 213–33 (https://www.ncbi.nlm.nih.gov/pubmed/19083358, accessed October 22, 2018).

22   Hannah J. Thomas et al., "Association of Different Forms of Bullying Victimisation with Adolescents' Psychological Distress and Reduced Emotional Wellbeing," *Australian & New Zealand Journal of Psychiatry* 50, no. 4 (2015): 371–79 (http://journals.sagepub.com/doi/10.1177/0004867415600076, accessed October 22, 2018).

23   Hannah M. C. Schreier et al., "Effect of Volunteering on Risk Factors for Cardiovascular Disease in Adolescents," *JAMA Pediatrics* 167, no. 4 (2013): 327–32 (https://jamanetwork.com/journals/jamapediatrics/fullarticle/1655500, accessed October 22, 2018).

24   Shabbar I. Ranapurwala et al., "Volunteering in Adolescence and Youth Adulthood Crime Involvement: A Longitudinal Analysis From the Add Health Study," *Injury Epidemiology* 3, no. 26 (2016). (https://www.ncbi.nlm.nih.gov/pmc/articles/PMC5116440, accessed October 22, 2018).

25   "Setting School Culture with Social and Emotional Learning Routines," KQED News website, last updated January 16, 2018 (http://ww2.kqed.org/mindshift/2018/01/16/setting-school-culture-with-social-and-emotional-learning-routines, accessed October 22, 2018).

26   Julianne Holt-Lunstad et al., "Social Relationships and Mortality Risk: A Meta-Analytic Review," *PLoS Medicine* 7, no. 7 (2010): e1000316 (http://journals.plos.org/plosmedicine/article?id=10.1371/journal.pmed.1000316, accessed October 22, 2018).

Index